3

Continued on next page

CLARENDON LAW SERIES

CIVIL LIBERTIES

CONOR GEARTY

Professor of Human Rights Law and
Director, Centre for the Study of Human Rights, LSE

OXFORD
UNIVERSITY PRESS

OXFORD
UNIVERSITY PRESS

Great Clarendon Street, Oxford OX2 6DP

Oxford University Press is a department of the University of Oxford.
It furthers the University's objective of excellence in research, scholarship,
and education by publishing worldwide in

Oxford New York

Auckland Cape Town Dar es Salaam Hong Kong Karachi
Kuala Lumpur Madrid Melbourne Mexico City Nairobi
New Delhi Shanghai Taipei Toronto

With offices in

Argentina Austria Brazil Chile Czech Republic France Greece
Guatemala Hungary Italy Japan Poland Portugal Singapore
South Korea Switzerland Thailand Turkey Ukraine Vietnam

Oxford is a registered trade mark of Oxford University Press
in the UK and in certain other countries

Published in the United States
by Oxford University Press Inc., New York

British Library Cataloguing in Publication Data

Data available

Library of Congress Cataloging in Publication Data

Gearty, C. A.
Civil liberties / Conor Gearty.
    p. cm. — (Clarendon law series)
Includes bibliographical references and index.
ISBN 978-0-19-928300-2 (alk. paper)
ISBN 978-0-19-923616-9 (alk. paper)
 1. Civil rights.   2. Human rights.   I. Title.
K3240.G43 2007
342.08'5—dc22   2007026126

Typeset by Newgen Imaging Systems (P) Ltd, Chennai, India
Printed in Great Britain
on acid-free paper by
Biddles Ltd, King's Lynn

ISBN 978-0-19-923616-9 (Hbk)
ISBN 978-0-19-928300-2 (Pbk)

1 3 5 7 9 10 8 6 4 2

For Diane, with love

Preface

This book offers an account of civil liberties law that is designed to complement standard texts and as such is aimed at helping students who are wrestling with undergraduate or graduate courses in civil liberties and/or human rights law. It is also intended to appeal to a wider audience, drawn from students in disciplines other than law and from among the wider public as well, in other words all those who are interested in getting to grips with a subject of great contemporary importance but of no little complexity. Hardly a day goes by without a report of what is often described as an 'attack' or an 'assault' on our 'traditional' civil liberties, but what these liberties are, how absolute they happen to be, and how these latest attacks differ from the many that have occurred in the past are very rarely if ever discussed. This book sets out to deal with these issues, offering a theoretical and historical as well as a legal account of the subject. As will be obvious right from page one, I have a particular view of what a study of civil liberties properly entails—I see the subject as especially concerned with political freedom and it is this perspective that gives the book its frame of reference, its intellectual compass with which to steer through what might otherwise be an unmanageable thicket of statutes, regulations, judicial decisions and executive practices. My hope is that I am able, through writing this book, to contribute to what I think of as the important task of putting civil liberties law and practice on a firmer theoretical footing than it currently enjoys, thereby enabling the subject more confidently to define—and thence to defend—what I see as its core values. It follows that the book is not only an exegesis of the relevant law but also an argument in favour of prioritizing a particular approach to the subject.

This book has been written while I have been Rausing Director of the Centre for the Study of Human Rights at the London School of Economics and Political Science (LSE) and I am delighted once again to acknowledge my good fortune in being able to work in such an enjoyable, stimulating, and supportive environment, and in particular with the Manager of the Centre, Zoe Gillard, and her team. My interest in civil liberties began at University College Dublin where I was the lucky recipient of the inspirational teaching of Fr Fergal O'Connor. In Cambridge I benefited from the accumulated wisdom and scholarly insights of Paul O'Higgins and David Williams, completing my PhD (on environmental law, of all things) under the latter's careful guidance. It has been in writing about the subject with my colleague at Cambridge and subsequently at King's College London, Keith Ewing, that I really began to come to terms with its historical and ideological dimensions: I will be eternally indebted to Keith Ewing for the enormous assistance I have gained from watching him work, reading what he has had to say, and writing with him. Other former King's colleagues who have helped me with their comments and conversations on civil liberties over the years have included Robert Blackburn, Aileen McColgan, and (for his robust testing of my intellectual assumptions) John Phillips. At LSE I have benefited from a hugely stimulating intellectual environment not only at the Centre but also in the law and sociology departments. It is invidious to name names among so many, but I would like specifically to thank Carol Harlow, Francesca Klug, Joe Jacob, Martin Loughlin, and Tom Poole for the very particular help and guidance I have had from them. Colleagues at Matrix Chambers have been a consistent support as well, especially Murray Hunt (now with the Joint Committee on Human Rights), Rabinder Singh, Danny Friedman, Raza Hussain, and David Wolfe—being around such consummate practitioners has helped me to see how lawyers can contribute positively to a culture of civil liberties. Thanks go as well to Reuben Hasson, Zdenek Kavan, Gerard Quinn, Peter Leyland, and Adam Tomkins. From the world of politics and civil society I have learnt a great deal of direct relevance to this book from Matt Cavanagh, Shami Chakrabarti, Tom Lyne, Kevin McNamara, the late Mo Mowlam, and Nigel Warner. Lastly, I would like once again to thank Oxford University Press for being the usual very supportive publisher that I have come to know and trust. Particular thanks go to Melanie Jackson, who has been in charge of me at the Press and who has been tremendously supportive throughout—even when the Hamlyn lectures seduced me away from my desk for almost all of 2006. I miss hugely, as so many of us do I am sure, the immense presence of Peter Birks. I was his assistant for a few years when he was in charge of the Society of Public Teachers of Law (as the Society of Legal Scholars was then called) and got to know him a bit and admire him a very great deal. I am so sorry he is not here to read this book.

Contents

Table of Cases

Table of Legislation

UK Legislation

Part I

Introduction: General Principles

I

Renewing Civil Liberties

This book has a particular perspective on the law and practice of civil liberties. It sees the subject as inextricably bound up with representative government. On this account, civil liberties is another name for the political freedoms that we must have available to us all if it is to be true to say of us that we live in a society that adheres to the principle of representative, or democratic, government. It follows that the subject as developed here is concerned with the right to vote, which as I shall argue presently (and perhaps, at first glance, surprisingly) is the core civil liberty, and also with those other basic freedoms—life, liberty, thought, expression, assembly, and association—that help give full meaning to that right. The prohibition on politically motivated ill-treatment (at its most extreme, torture and other inhuman and degrading treatment) is also within the book's remit. These are the freedoms which are essential to the proper functioning of our contemporary political community; they are the oil without which our democratic engine would grind to a halt. An alternative way of describing this book, therefore, would be to say that it is about the law and practice of political freedom.

The book is not neutral about its subject: civil liberties are not just another branch of law, or discourse, or system to be delineated and explained; the standing of civil liberties as a series of vital prerequisites for political freedom inevitably make the chapters that follow partisan on their behalf, applauding as well as describing, and criticizing gaps in their protection when these are encountered. The book is primarily about civil liberties in the UK but it is not content to allow itself to be entirely restricted to British shores. It follows governmental power where it takes it, and in the modern era that requires brief trips abroad, to Brussels, Strasbourg and—further afield—to Washington, New York and to whatever other seats of international power impact on British society and law. While it is true that the nation state has surprised many with its durability, the fact remains that questions of democratic representation and of civil liberties arise in these places as well as in the (for the British lawyer) more familiar worlds of Westminster and the Royal Courts of Justice.

The approach to civil liberties taken here might be thought to be narrow—but a deliberate preference is being made to promote the interests of clarity over the claims of breadth. Few branches of legal knowledge are as perplexing in their scope, uncertain in their reach, or downright confusing in their application as that of civil liberties. The precision of the book's remit derives from a desire to impose order on potential chaos. The tensions in the subject go far beyond the usual stresses and strains of a phrase that has been popping in and out of the case law and the political and legal literature for generations; they go to its very core, pulling it not only in different but very often also in apparently opposite directions. Is the subject about protecting the citizen from the state or about enabling him or her to participate in government? Many of the textbooks suggest one or the other of these approaches; sometimes they manage to propose both at the same time. Or is it concerned, as practitioner guides have often assumed, with controls on police power: law suits for assault, false imprisonment and the like, access to a solicitor when in custody, and to a jury when on trial for a crime? But if this is what it is about, where do these first two meanings fit: is the rallying cry to be 'criminal justice', 'individual liberty' or 'democracy', or some variation of all three? And what of the relationship between civil liberties and human rights? Does not the latter term stand in relation to the former as lively offspring to aged and befuddled parent, and if so has the time now come for euthanasia, with the result that this book should be an extended obituary notice rather than an aspiring-to-be-contemporary legal text?

All of these versions of civil liberties—including that which now calls it a branch of human rights—have their own justifications embedded in our law, our history, and our political practice. They are incapable of complete reconciliation; to forge a common meaning from such disparate ascriptions would be to choose vacuity in the name of unity. The point can be made by way of a couple of extreme assertions. A subject cannot be simultaneously about *both* facilitating representative government *and* insulating individuals entirely from the reach of that government, about empowering and disempowering the people (or the state) at one and the same time. Nor can it sensibly expect easily to move from discussion of high political principle into the application of paragraph this of police code that on some technical issue of post-arrest, pre-charge police power. A subject that tries to do all these things achieves none of them, and deserves the decline into conceptual redundancy that is sure to follow. Of course, good arguments can be made that, thought through properly, a fair measure of individual liberty is essential to democratic governance, and that democratic freedom depends on exactly the sort of empowerment that flows from the enjoyment (by each member of the community) of a highly individual kind of personal liberty. It is equally obvious that the concretization in the law of various general democratic insights necessarily requires a plunge into the particular. While appreciating these various blurrings on the edges of its argument, this book seeks through its deliberate focus on the political to give fresh life to the subject.

Slimmed down and rid of the burden of extraneous demands from other fields (radical libertarianism; controls on police powers; due process; jury trial; criminal justice; etc), the study of civil liberties can be restored to where our democratic culture suggests it can be very well located: right at the centre of our public law, at the intersection between law and democratic politics, giving life to the latter and an ethical focus to the former. And positioned thus, it can connect effectively with its voracious progeny human rights, drawing for support from that term's remit insofar as it flows with the grain of civil liberties while sifting out the less community-oriented entitlements that have sometimes led the idea of human rights into an ambiguous relationship with democratic politics. I start this work on human rights in Chapter 2 and it then runs as a theme throughout the book. There is a daunting generality to the idea of human rights which the connection with democratic politics via the complementary ideas of civil liberties and civil and political rights can go a long way towards reducing into a more manageable intellectual form. However, this does require us boldly to say of important elements of human rights law that, vital though they are, they do not fit within a book on civil liberties, or at least such a book constructed in the way that this one is. The most obvious of these is the role of that law in protecting the foreigner from abuse outside the jurisdiction:[1] to be beyond our community is not to be beyond our moral responsibility (especially if it is us who have put the person there) but it is to engage issues other than those of our domestic political freedom, the topic of this book.

Human rights law, at least in its Strasbourg manifestation,[2] also supplies a substantive content to the idea of democracy, locating its meaning not only in the designing of a mechanism for producing a representative government but also in requiring of that legislative assembly that it reflect in its actions 'the demands of that pluralism, tolerance and broadmindedness without which there is no "democratic society" '.[3] True to its procedural foundations, this book resists the temptation to expand its version of

---

[1] The line of cases begun by *Soering v United Kingdom* (1989) 11 EHRR 439.
[2] A leading example being *Lingens v Austria* (1986) 8 EHRR 407.
[3] Ibid, para [41] (footnote omitted).

democracy to the point where it would turn itself into a report on the ethical content of the laws that Parliament produces: this would be to provide a commentary on the driving as well as oil for the engine. Of course I do not say that assessing laws from this ethical perspective is not important, it is just that it is something that another field—human rights law—can more confidently do. A further self-imposed limitation is suggested by this quotation from the Strasbourg authorities: the book takes the 'society' that makes up 'democratic society' to be that of the UK across which the laws of the elected Parliament at Westminster range. Inevitably, there are issues about the unity of this society, and about its fragmentation into different national, ethnic, religious, and even cultural identities. The currency of contemporary discussions about multi-culturalism and how this fits within the concept of a democratic society are not the less important for being judged to be outside the scope of this book. Here I understand the 'political' to be the range of conduct engaged in by those who seek power or to influence the exercise of power in our democratic polity. Critical assessment of the nature of that polity and how it might be reformed to improve its democratic credentials belong to an important—but different—discussion.

Perhaps I ought, at this juncture, to repeat that this book is certainly not intended to imply by some kind of strategy of suggestive omission that the established system of democratic rule in the UK is beyond reproach or that the broader issues with which human rights law is also concerned are unimportant—far from it. It is equally clear that it would be wrong to deny that versions of civil liberties different from the one chosen here, those based on individual freedom or on the dictates of criminal justice, for example, do not have an important role to play in law's contemporary story, or that properly controlled and explained they, too, can be brought under the umbrella of civil liberties, differently defined. It is just that these are not part of this segment of that long narrative. The view taken in this book, that civil liberties as we understand them best today are the living manifestation on the ground of our state's commitment to the principle of representative government, certainly reflects a core societal value, but it is also clear that there are other values as well—such as the principle of fairness in the administration of the state, and the freedom of every person to thrive as best he or she can—and that these have in the past and can still today be described as part of the world of 'civil liberties'. However, it is these other values that are more clearly reflected in the versions of civil liberties that I am *not* pursuing in this book. The vital importance our legal and political culture accords to safeguards on the abuse of police power, for example, clearly flows from our belief in procedural fairness and is reflected in our extensive administrative law, of which both human rights legislation and more specific provisions on the police form a part. As we shall see in the next chapter, the concept of individual freedom (to secure human flourishing) is also a significant value, one which has long under-pinned much of what remains valuable about the UK's culture of toler-ance. The rallying cry of 'live and let live' is certainly part of the political version of the civil liberties story I am telling in this book, a good thing in itself which effective democratic government both encourages and facili-tates—but it must never on the view of the subject embraced here develop a life of its own, be permitted to collapse into 'everyman (and women) for him (and her) self '. The full fleshing out of these versions of our subject, reflecting other values that make us the successful society that we largely are, is better found in other, more appropriate works of specialization, whether they are called by the name of 'civil liberties' or by some other appellation.

It is the origin of civil liberties in a variety of our overlapping core values that gives the subject the uncertainty which it has been the first task of this book to tackle: it is almost as though the idea has too rich an intellectual heritage, and has too many claims imposed on it by the better parts of our past. Identifying the essential meaning of civil liberties is like embarking on an archaeological dig knowing that the 'truth' can never be found because it has never really existed, that the best that can be uncovered are the different layers of meanings put down by past generations, each com-pelling in its own time perhaps, but at the same time leaving residues of apparent incoherence to bewilder later generations. In the dig that follows in the next chapter, the narrative has two goals in its sights: to explain where certain ideas come from for which the law and practice of civil lib-erties in the form developed here should, as has already been suggested, have no further use, and to identify those layers of meaning to be found in the past to which we need now to pay especial attention if our subject is to thrive in the way that this book argues it should. With this ground cleared, the next task is to move from theory to practice and to show how the model of civil liberties to which this book commits itself has evolved over time, which institutions have been vigilant on their behalf, which negligent, and how the subject has ebbed and flowed under the pressure of events. Chapter 3 tells this story of civil liberties but also introduces the counter-narrative of national security, one that is as old as democracy itself, and which has over time placed huge strains on our commitment to political freedom and our attitude to the rights to be accorded both to those within and those outside our community. The chapter ends with information from the British Social Attitudes Survey of 2005, which allows us to con-sider contemporary attitudes to civil liberties and how these have been affected by the anxiety induced by the current national security scare, the growing fear about subversive violence and how this has given impetus to state action against terrorism.

In Part Two, which makes up the bulk of the book, the focus shifts to the substance of civil liberties protection, looking both at how the rights and freedoms essential to the democratic health of the nation are secured in Britain today, and also at how the national security concern identified in Chapter 3 impacts on those rights. In Chapter 4, I address what, right at the start of the book (and it will be remembered with modest trepidation), I declared to be the primary civil liberty of them all, the right to vote; in so doing, I critically assess how much our current system of government is now in need of a change so as to achieve afresh the equality of voter-power that is the essence of the democratic system of government. The point is an important one in a book like this because so much civil libertarian protest takes place quite separately from the parliamentary process, drawing angry strength from the belief of many of those involved that Parliament as a democratic chamber has been irredeemably corrupted by power and wealth. Many of the flashpoints in the law and practice of civil liberties, engaging the rights to life, liberty, due process, expression, assembly, and association (dealt with in turn in Chapters 5, 6, 7 and 8, respectively) take place on these margins of our parliamentary democracy, with protestors justifying themselves by saying they have no option other than aggressive public protest and the government and the mainstream politicians replying by asserting (or thinking even if they do not say) that our democratic system has now made such extra-parliamentary action—at least in any kind of extreme form—unnecessary. This mismatch of perspectives explains many of the tensions in our subject today, the anxiety about terrorism, direct action and intimidatory protest in one quarter, the belief in the impotence of Parliament and the failure of our democratic system in the other. The law and practice of civil liberties has to stay a consistent and principled course between these two opposing views.

In the single chapter making up Part Three, the book goes beyond the nation state to test from a civil libertarian perspective the validity of the laws and practices of those entities beyond our shores that exercise governmental and governmental-style power over us. In the final, concluding chapter, however, the book confirms its over-arching purpose as being somewhat closer to home: to set down a theoretical understanding of civil liberties which gives the subject a better chance of performing the role for which it is best suited, namely the provision of the legal framework within which Britain's system of representative democracy can operate most effectively. There can be little doubt that recent large-scale trends in world affairs, from the end of the Cold War, through globalization to our current concerns with environmental degradation and international terrorism, have put many traditional ideas and values under severe strain. Not the least of the societal assumptions to have been subjected to critical appraisal recently has been our belief in the value of civil liberties. Our commitment to political freedom, indeed on some accounts to representative democracy itself, has seemed at best jaded and 'old hat', at worst positively unhelpful to our efforts to address current problems. Properly focused, the law and practice of civil liberties can assist once again in the renewal of our democratic political culture, as important a task now as it has ever been in the past.

2

Theoretical Foundations

In this chapter I explore further the two main versions of civil liberties to which I alluded in Chapter 1, describing the intellectual origins of each and explaining how they have come to gain such a strong hold on our subject despite their manifest differences.[1] First, I analyse the connection with individual liberty and then counterpoint this with a version of our subject more in line with the democratic thinking that is at the core of this book. The role of the Human Rights Act 1998 as a (partial) guarantor of civil liberties and as the promoter of certain human rights values is then considered, with the Act's especial strength being (as we shall see presently) its capacity to confront and to some extent resolve the potential majoritarian crisis that is inherent in all democratic systems that promote and/or depend on a strong sense of community.

LIBERTY AS FREEDOM

One very important theme in the history of the idea of civil liberties sees the subject as concerned first and foremost with individual freedom. By freedom here is meant primarily the proposition that people should be able to go about their business without being subject to unnecessary constraints, particularly of the kind imposed by government and executive power. 'Unnecessary' is an important word: there are many different views as to the degree of intrusion into liberty that should be permitted. But the general thrust of this approach is to be presumptively antagonistic to anything that interferes with what individuals want to do. We can see immediately that this version of civil liberties takes its believers down an individualistic, anti-government route. Its advocates are the kinds of people who these days can be found assuming that identity cards, CCTV surveillance[2] and the like are assuredly wrong simply because their inherent

---

[1] The criminal justice model offers a practitioner-based approach which is not considered further here.

[2] 'Drivers challenge spy camera law', *The Observer*, 24 September 2006. (Two drivers argued that speed cameras breached their Article 6 due process rights under the European Convention on Human Rights.)

intrusiveness means that they 'invade' or 'erode' our civil liberties.[3] Their parents might have been just as opposed in their day to compulsory crash helmets on motor bikes and obligatory seat belts in cars. Such enthusiasts for civil liberties can be persuaded to accept a restriction to freedom where harm to others is a consequence of doing nothing, so smoking bans in public places and harsh drink-driving laws do not always incur their wrath. But they have real difficulty in imagining how general (as opposed to individual) harm can justify restrictions on freedom, and they are constitutionally mistrustful of government assertions that this might be the case.[4]

To the modern eye, this might look like a Conservative position to adopt, and it is perfectly true that the people who feel at home in that Party are the sorts of people who can become passionate about the iniquities of the 'nanny-state' or who argue fervently at dinner parties that 'an Englishman's home is his castle' (and therefore, it is implied, a place that is rightly impenetrable to all—including the King's forces).[5] But the power of this strand to civil liberties thinking lies in its being more deeply entrenched in our thought processes than any merely partisan political idea could ever aspire to be. Its origins are more Whig/Liberal than Tory, lying as it does at the very core of the English constitutional battles of the seventeenth century. It was this version of liberty that provided the intellectual rationale for the upheavals that then occurred and which produced the framework of English (subsequently British) government that has subsisted more or less ever since.[6]

Writing in the middle of the seventeenth century, the influential political philosopher Thomas Hobbes declared that 'liberty or freedom signifieth (properly) the absence of opposition'. He was famous for the horrible state of strife into which he believed men were born, where liberty abounded to counter-productive effect:

Because the condition of man . . . is a condition of war of every one against every one; in which case everyone is governed by his own reason and there is nothing he can make use of that may not be a help unto him in preserving his life against his

---

[3] And DNA databases as well: see 'Suspect Nation', *Guardian*, 28 October 2006.
[4] A further example is the recently emerged 'Backlash' group which opposes government proposals to criminalize the possession of certain kinds of violent pornography as an infringement of liberty: see *Guardian*, 31 August 2006.
[5] Sir K Joseph, *Freedom under Law* (London: Conservative Political Centre, 1976). Cf Q Hogg, *New Charter* (London: Conservative Political Centre, 1969).
[6] See CA Gearty, 'The United Kingdom', in CA Gearty (ed), *European Civil Liberties and the European Convention on Human Rights: A Comparative Survey* (The Hague: Martinus Nijhoff Publishers, 1997), ch 2. A very valuable sourcebook is RL Schuyler and CC Weston, *Cardinal Documents in British History* (Princeton, NJ: Princeton University Press, 1961).

enemies; it followeth that in such a condition every man has the right to every thing; even to one another's body.[7]

A generation later, John Locke, thought that 'Liberty, 'tis plain, consists in a power to do or not to do; to do or forbear doing as we will. This cannot be denied.' Thus it was clear to Locke that:

> [m]an being born, as has been proved, with a Title to perfect Freedom, and an uncontrolled enjoyment of all the Rights and Privileges of the Law of Nature, equally with any other Man or Number of Men in the World, hath by Nature a Power . . . to preserve his Property, that is his Life, Liberty and Estate, against the injuries and Attempts of other Men.[8]

Although they were very different in many important ways, both Hobbes and Locke saw 'our freedom [as] a natural possession, a property of ourselves'.[9] In the context of the disputes then ongoing between a (partly) representative Parliament and an entirely unrepresentative Crown, the way Locke in particular worked through the implications of this idea fitted well with the revolutionary atmosphere of the times. His view that the Englishman's basic freedoms were inherent in him meant that to the extent that they had been handed over to government they had been merely lent for limited ends. It followed from this that the executive power was in an important way contingent: it could be seized back if the terms of the deal were no longer being honoured by the executive branch or Royal personage party to it. That there had been no such agreement in any real sense and that this was all the highest of high theory mattered little when it happened to coincide with political and military interests. In 1688, the last of the Stuart kings, James II, found his throne declared 'vacant' by Parliament because, among other iniquities, he had 'endeavoured to subvert the constitution of his kingdom by breaking the original contract between the king and people'.[10] Locke came to be identified with this 'glorious revolution'; vindicated on the ground in this way, his ideas were rewarded by being able gradually to deepen their hold on people's minds.

The notion of free individuals roaming at will beyond politics, doing whatever they want to their heart's desire whenever they want to do it, and giving up only a very little freedom to government, and even then very

---

[7] Cited in J. Mahoney, *The Challenge of Human Rights. Origin, Development and Significance* (Oxford: Blackwell Publishing, 2007), p 12.

[8] Ibid, pp 19–20.

[9] Q Skinner, 'The Paradoxes of Political Liberty', in D Miller (ed), *Liberty* (Oxford: Oxford University Press, 1991), p 183, at p 200.

[10] See SB Chrimes, *English Constitutional History* (3rd edn) (Oxford: Oxford University Press, 1965), p 162.

reluctantly and on the strictest terms (protect me; guard my property; keep order; enforce contracts), probably sounded far-fetched even in the seventeenth century and it certainly seems ludicrous to our modern, historically oriented ears, alive to the need to connect theory to practice.[11] But if it is a lunacy then it is an enduring one, and like many peculiar ideas that nevertheless have survived, indeed thrived, from generation to generation, it has had the good fortune to have had a sequence of powerful supporters whose interests have been served by advocacy of it—in the history of ideas such advocates have often been more influential than the thoughtful readers who are merely convinced of the truth of a proposition. First, of course, there were those who threw the king out and needed to explain to themselves and others why they did it. In the nineteenth century, writers such as Albert Venn Dicey made much of the unwritten British constitution's commitment to negative liberty, the freedom to do that which no law prevents—clear echoes here of John Locke.[12]

When democracy and socialism began to seem to threaten the status quo at the end of the nineteenth century and the first half of the twentieth, the notion of pre-parliamentary basic liberty returned to centre stage as a convenient intellectual shield for those who were anxious that their belief in parliamentary sovereignty (on a restricted, propertied franchise) should not now be transformed into an engine for radical egalitarianism: prepolitical rights or freedoms (with regard to property and the making of contracts, for example) were a good way of marking off territory into which this potentially socialist Leviathan should definitely not be allowed to go.[13] Just when democracy seemed to have secured the upper hand, along came the Cold War and a fresh set of reasons presented themselves for celebrating negative liberty. Many Western writers and almost all its political leaders found the old-style Anglo-American model of innate individual freedom altogether more appealing than the Stalinist and Maoist versions of communist 'freedom' that were its main ideological rivals at the time.[14]

A chief spokesperson for negative liberty during this period was Isaiah Berlin. He used the platform of his inaugural lecture as Chichele Professor of Social and Political Theory in the University of Oxford in 1958 to set out

[11] See, further, CA Gearty, *Can Human Rights Survive?* (Cambridge: Cambridge University Press, 2006), ch 3.
[12] AV Dicey, *Lectures Introductory to a Study of the Law of the Constitution* (2nd edn) (London: Macmillan, 1885).
[13] Ibid. For the similar story in America where, however, a bill of rights was available see JW Ely Jr, *The Guardian of Every Other Right. A Constitutional History of Property Rights* (2nd edn) (New York, NY: Oxford University Press, 1998).
[14] Karl Popper, for example: see K Popper, *The Open Society and its Enemies* (London: Routledge, 2002 (one-volume edition)).

his ideas on the subject. Of course there are a wide range of thinkers who could be invoked at this stage, of perhaps more substance and greater durability than Berlin,[15] or with a clearer commitment to the perspective on liberty with which I am about to associate him.[16] But as an Oxford don and a highly successful public intellectual before the term came into vogue,[17] Berlin is a useful emblem of a position that is embedded in the British intellectual tradition. Berlin was a refugee from continental Europe who had first-hand experience of the capacity of ideological fervour to make people truly miserable. This made him very hostile to those mainly continental philosophers who had been able to persuade themselves that they had found the answer to what it takes to achieve true freedom, and whose view was that it was right, indeed essential, for their discoveries to be brought (forcibly if needs be) before the people—even if they did not appreciate the message being presented to them, or had not the remotest desire to act on what it seemed to dictate. Berlin had in mind targets such as Rousseau who had famously written that 'anyone [who] refuses to obey the general will will be compelled to do so by the whole body; which means nothing else than that he will be forced to be free', and the latter part of Berlin's inaugural address, afterwards published as an extended essay, was a powerful attack on the dangers of the 'rationalist argument' which 'with its assumption of the single true solution, [had] led by steps which, if not logically valid, are historically and psychologically intelligible, from an ethical doctrine of individual responsibility and individual self-perfection to an authoritarian state obedient to the directives of an elite of Platonic guardians'.[18]

An effective lecturer will deploy a counterpoint to drive his or her critique home, a comparator against which the idea being attacked can be found wanting, and Berlin found his in the modest excellence of the Hobbes/Locke tradition whereby '[p]olitical liberty' was 'simply the area within which a man can act unobstructed by others . . . You lack political liberty or freedom only if you are prevented from attaining a goal by human beings.'[19] 'By being free in this sense' Berlin meant 'not being interfered with by others. The wider the area of non-interference the

---

[15] Hayek, for example: see, in particular, F Hayek, *The Constitution of Liberty* (London: Routledge and Kegan Paul, 1960) and the same author's *Law, Legislation and Liberty* (London: Routledge and Kegan Paul, 1982).

[16] See S Veitch, *Moral Conflict and Legal Reasoning* (Oxford: Hart Publishing, 1999).

[17] See J Gray, *Berlin* (London: Fontana Press, 1995).

[18] I Berlin, 'Two Concepts of Liberty', in D Miller (ed), *Liberty* (Oxford: Oxford University Press, 1991), pp 33–57.

[19] Ibid, p 34.

wider my freedom':[20] this was 'what the classical English political philosophers meant when they used this word'.[21] It was 'assumed by these thinkers that the area of men's free action must be limited by law'[22] but the point was that the law was to be always (to use an appropriately English metaphor) on the back foot: no Rousseaun cover drives but rather the occasional tentative trickle to cover point. Freedom occupied a narrower space than was often assumed and was all the better for it: 'You lack political liberty or freedom only if you are prevented from attaining a goal by human beings. Mere incapacity to obtain a goal is not a lack of political freedom.'[23] So if 'a man is too poor to afford something on which there is no legal ban—a loaf of bread, a journey around the world, recourse to the law courts—he is as little free to have it as he would be if it were forbidden him by law',[24] but this does not mean that he lacks *political* freedom. 'It is only because I believe that my inability to get a given thing is due to the fact that other human beings have made arrangements whereby I am, whereas others are not, prevented from having enough money with which to pay for it, that I think myself a victim of coercion or slavery.'[25] But this was a point of view which was far from being universally true; it depended 'on a particular social and economic theory about the causes of my poverty or weakness'[26] and only worked as my 'being deprived of freedom'[27] if this theory was accepted. Needless to say Berlin did not accept it.

Here we have the anti-redistributive tendency in this approach to liberty laid bare for all to see: government is an unpalatable necessity and certainly has no business interfering with any of our freedoms merely on behalf of those of us who happen to have been born unluckier/poorer than the rest. To be fair to Berlin, he was not entirely certain that economic obstacles were altogether irrelevant to freedom, much less so than FA Hayek, for example, for whom the concept was much more clearly and narrowly focused on the absence of deliberate interference by other people.[28] But Berlin's attack on continental philosophy combined with his celebration of the traditional English canon and his assurance that Marxist-style observations about inequality and exploitation flowed from what was merely 'a particular social and economic theory', made his contribution highly influential in the decades that followed. Its appeal to both liberal and conservative thinkers and practitioners has given it the durability to survive sometimes scathing academic criticism, and whether he has indirectly influenced them or not, his view of liberty is one that is

---

[20] Ibid, p 35.   [21] Ibid, quoting from Hobbes.
[22] Ibid, p 36.   [23] Ibid, p 34 (notes omitted).   [24] Ibid, pp 34–5.   [25] Ibid, p 35.
[26] Ibid.   [27] Ibid.   [28] See works cited at n 15 above.

shared by many in Britain today. But in keeping with 'the liberal credo, "the less we have of politics . . . the more liberty we will enjoy," '[29] Berlin's approach has next to nothing to say about democracy; indeed, he admits his version of freedom 'is not, at any rate logically, connected with democracy or self-government'.[30] Liberty in his sense is 'principally concerned with the area of control, not with its source'.[31] Berlin expanded on this point in the following way:

Self-government may, on the whole, provide a better guarantee of the preservation of civil liberties than other regimes, and has been defended as such by libertarians. But there is no necessary connection between individual liberty and democratic rule. The answer to the question 'Who governs me?' is logically distinct from the question 'How far does government interfere with me?' It is in this difference that the great contrast between the two concepts of negative and positive liberty, in the end, consists.[32]

It is rare that the disconnection between liberty and democracy is made quite so clear as this, reducing an apparently indissoluble bond into a merely possible connection. If true, it would render the underlying approach of this book misconceived and its whole thrust misguided.

CIVIL LIBERTIES, FREEDOM, AND THE COMMUNITY

There are other pathways, however, and one in particular that makes better sense of the remit that this book sets for its subject. It is important at this juncture to recognize that if I insist there is more to liberty than the right to be left alone, it does not follow from this that I must therefore accept Berlin's rather caricatured version of positive liberty with its (to his mind) inexorable drift to totalitarianism. Of course, Berlin is something of a straw man and I am looking only at one of his essays in isolation, not to analyse him but in order to make general points about the history of our subject. Risking caricature in the pursuit of clarity, it might be said by way of response to Berlin that the whole world of ideas cannot be reduced to a choice between the wise English and the wild Europeans. There is a quite separate strand to civil liberties thinking which sees political liberty as intimately connected with freedom and which regards the practice of a full political life as being the true route to freedom—but which determinedly and clearly does not feel it has to embrace tyranny as the inevitable result of

---

[29] H Arendt, 'Freedom and Politics', in A Hunold (ed), *Freedom and Serfdom. An Anthology of Western Thought* (Dordrecht: D Reidel Publishing Co, 1961), p 191, at p 192.
[30] Berlin, n 18 above, p 42.   [31] Ibid, p 41.   [32] Ibid, p 42.

making this commitment. This is a layer of meaning to our subject which is even earlier than the contract-based fictions promoted by Hobbes, Locke, and (in its modern form) Berlin. The key to recognizing it lies in taking more care over words than this book has up to now.

The topic we are concerned with is not *liberty* as such or *freedom* as such but rather that bundle of freedoms that together we class as *civil liberties*. Berlin uses the last of these terms in the passage quoted above without acknowledging that it might in some way alter the nature of his argument, veer the discussion in a different direction, away from liberty and freedom—but this is exactly what it does. These various freedoms we call civil liberties are not another way of speaking of one single capacity for freedom that we each separately have; they are plural not singular. Nor can they be accurately described as the various freedoms that inhere in our persons as autonomous beings; rather they are our *civil* liberties, in other words they are those of our freedoms which are necessarily tied up with our engagement with persons outside ourselves. This takes us inevitably into community, and into a radically different view of the person, together with an altogether different perspective on freedom, from which a fresh and (it is argued here) altogether more convincing approach to civil liberties can be seen to emerge.

The roots of this different narrative lie in what Quentin Skinner has called in his Tanner lectures on human values 'the classical republican tradition' of Greece, Rome, and (later) Renaissance Italy.[33] As with the negative view of liberty I have been discussing, the classical story starts with the big picture concepts. According to Skinner, 'the discussion of political liberty was generally embedded in an analysis of what it means to speak of living in a "free state"'.[34] From the Greek thinkers, later supplemented by adaptive intellectual Catholics of whom Thomas Aquinas was pre-eminent, emerged the idea that humans are moral beings, that they are inevitably social, and that they have a purpose. On this account, freedom was not at all about dodging bullets and shooting back in some theoretical land of lawless nature while plotting to give up power to a potentially order-enforcing and (you hoped) benign Leviathian. The action of seeking to realize one's purpose in life is an inevitably social one and it is to the extent that one is realizing this purpose that one can be said to be flourishing—and 'flourishing' in this way, thriving, growing, leading a 'full life', is what constitutes freedom on this account.

[33] Also of great value is JGA Pocock, *The Machiavellian Moment: Florentine Political Thought and the Atlantic Republican Tradition* (Princeton, NJ: Princeton University Press, 1975).
[34] Skinner, n 9 above, p 193.

This approach to freedom and liberty firmly embeds both these large terms in society, making our mixing with others part of our freedom rather than a (necessary) subversion of it. But it does suggest that there are certain ends that have to be pursued if we are to be properly free: shades here of the Rousseaun approach that so excited the animosity of Isaiah Berlin. Certainly, from both the Christian and later Enlightenment perspectives, we are rightly to be viewed as moral agents committed to certain normative ends. It follows that, just as with those who committed themselves to negative liberty above everything else, the kind of political system that actually pertains mattered less on this account than whether it created the conditions for the actualization of human freedom: 'the form of association we shall need to maintain will of course be just that form in which our freedom to be our true selves is capable of being realized as completely as possible'.[35] So we could have a benevolent dictator or a pope or a king—legitimacy depends not on the authority of the people but on the validity of the moral purpose expressed by the ruler for his or her people, and on his or her skill at fostering such a sense of purpose among those subject to this kind of executive power.

If this is what freedom (and therefore, as we shall see presently, the subject of civil liberties) is about, then once again we would be forced to admit that there is no necessary connection between our subject and democratic governance. But two things have happened since the hey-day of the classical tradition. First, we have become far more sceptical of uniform moral purpose. Berlin was right about this—too many lives have been lost to fuel the absolute moral certainty of twentieth-century leaders for us to be other than suspicious of unequivocal right answers that happen to be in the hands of those whose control of the army, the police, and the prisons gives them the power to seek to realize, or more accurately impose, their goals. The problem with 'human flourishing' is that what it involves can all too easily lie in the eye of the beholder, the 'human' concerned is too often the leader at the expense of the led. This insight has led to a lessening of commitment to the pursuit of particular and allegedly objectively moral ends. Crudely put, we no longer, as an intellectual community, trust rulers in this way anymore.

Second, and related to this first point, in the second half of the twentieth century by way of reaction both to the horrors of war and to important philosophical work in the area of linguistics and philosophy,[36] there has

---

[35] Skinner, n 9 above, p 190.
[36] See GEM Anscombe (ed), *Wittgenstein's Philosophical Investigations* (3rd edn) (Oxford: Blackwell, 2001).

emerged an even deeper but strongly held conviction that finds the classical approach anathema. On this view, it is quite right that we should not have certainty as to our goals on this earth (or anywhere), precisely because in fact there is no such certainty; in other words, there is no particular kind of life or mode of living that is or should be demanded of us at all or which, even if there is, is capable of being put into words. It should not be searched for because it cannot be found or at least cannot be articulated. As Margaret McDonald put it 'Men do not share a fixed nature, nor, therefore, are there any ends which they must necessarily pursue in fulfilment of such nature.'[37] Some leading proponents of this view go so far that they are thought of as post-philosophers[38] and while this description is not to the taste of all, there can be no doubt that doubt, uncertainty, and agnosticism about truth have become key themes of our 'post-modern' times.

I appear to be entering deep philosophical waters at this point, but the civil libertarian implication can be put in the form of a simple question: if freedom is more than the right to be left alone, and yet there is no compulsory outcome or specific kind of moral living that equals freedom, how are we to determine what we should be doing, both as individuals and as members of a community? This is where the republican tradition makes its contribution to the classical perspective, tackling this core point about the content of a moral life and introducing what in the context of the argument in this book can be called a civil liberties solution to the dilemma. The layers of meaning from which the version of civil liberties being deployed in this book has emerged are venerable indeed, too detailed to go too deeply into here. Among the key contributors are Livy, Sallust, and Cicero from the Roman age, and Machiavelli, Harrington, Milton, and Montesquieu from Renaissance and post-Renaissance times. The large insight supplied by this thread to the story is that free states will be places 'far from all external servitude' that are 'able to govern themselves according to their own will'.[39] The important point is that the community should be self-governing and managed by reference to laws freely chosen by its members. The link between communal and individual freedom is made particularly clear by Machiavelli: it is only 'in lands and provinces which live as free states' that individual citizens can hope 'to live without fear that their patrimony will be taken away from them, knowing not merely that

---

[37] M MacDonald, 'Natural Rights', in J Waldron (ed), *Theories of Rights* (Oxford: Oxford University Press, 1984), p 21, at p 30.
[38] R Rorty, *Contingency, Irony, and Solidarity* (Cambridge: Cambridge University Press, 1989).
[39] Skinner, n 9 above, p 195.

they are born as free citizens and not as slaves, but that they can hope to rise by their abilities to become leaders of their communities'.[40] What is interesting here is that freedom is not about achieving certain substantive outcomes as such, it is about being able to govern yourself. Of course, there was a moral dimension to all of this, a commitment to virtue that was necessary to make the idea work. But what is significant for present purposes is that for the first time we are catching sight of an emphasis on methods of governance as a key attribute of freedom: Machiavelli writes about any citizen being free to become leader as being part and parcel of what it means to be free. In this way engagement in governance becomes part of the responsibility of citizenry, a way of maintaining freedom, since, as Hannah Arendt put it, '[t]he state is not a work of art, because, if for no other reason, its existence never becomes independent of the actions of the men who created it'.[41]

And what of the goals of the proponents of such a free society, the outcomes to which they should (if we are to follow the classical position) be devoted? This is how Skinner put it in his Tanner lectures:

They emphasise that different classes of people will always have varying dispositions, and will in consequence value their liberty as the means to attain varying ends. As Machiavelli explains, some people place a high value on the pursuit of honour, glory and power: 'they will want their liberty in order to be able to dominate others'. But other people merely want to be left alone to their own devices, free to pursue their own family and professional lives; 'they want liberty in order to be able to live in security'. To be free, in short, is simply to be unconstrained from pursuing whatever goals we may happen to set ourselves.[42]

This is not just an anticipation of the negative liberty of Hobbes and Locke: freedom does not exist in advance of society but is realized through participation in community. The kind of place in which this kind of freedom can be best assured will be somewhere in which the government is genuinely reflective of the will of the people. It follows that there will be an emphasis on civic spirit and this will involve a commitment to protection of the state but will also insist on the importance of (to use a phrase made famous by a distinguished American constitutional theorist centuries later) 'keeping open the channels of political change',[43] on making sure that the state remains truly self-governing and does not collapse into factionalism, oligarchy, or dictatorship. For the same reason, there will be a

---

[40] The quote is in Skinner, n 9 above, p 195.
[41] Arendt, n 29 above, p 197.   [42] Skinner, n 9 above, p 196 (footnotes omitted).
[43] JH Ely, *Democracy and Distrust. A Theory of Judicial Review* (Cambridge, MA: Harvard University Press, 1980).

commitment to political accountability and to law, the latter being both negative in impact—coercing us to be truly committed citizens—but also positive—creating liberty by giving practical expression to the community's judgments about the ends that it has decided it is essential (for now) to pursue and to which private preferences must defer; as Machiavelli remarked, while it 'is hunger and poverty that make men industrious . . . it is the laws that make them good'.[44]

It might be true that as Hannah Arendt put it the notion 'that the meaning of politics is freedom' stands in contradiction to 'modern social theories',[45] but that is not a reason in itself for turning back or reaching out for some confusing compromise with different narratives. The republican tradition that has been crudely outlined above was certainly not 'democratic' in the modern (or perhaps even in any) sense—the self-governors were transparently never the whole of society—but that is not to say that it does not fit very well with the democratic approach to government which took hold in the nineteenth century and which, with the end of the Cold War, has become the key political movement of our global age. Viewed from this historical distance and with the needs of the contemporary present in our minds, we can applaud this approach for having made it possible for us squarely to face the two points highlighted above, about the mistrust of leaders and our post-modern uncertainty about the attainability of objective truth. Of course, the republican tradition required loyalty to leadership and also perhaps belief in their virtue but the important breakthrough was that this was required to be sustained by active participation, the sort of engaged citizenship that fits well with our current idea of what a properly functioning democratic system should look like. The contemporary relevance of this is further reinforced by our continued (and, to many, surprising) emphasis on the nation state as the ideal unit of governance. Contrary to the expectations of many, globalization has not brought in its wake any spectacularly sharp movement towards international or even regional governance; even after 11 September 2001, the movement has been as firmly in the national as it has been in the global direction.[46]

The republican tradition dovetails with the brand of the law and practice of civil liberties being developed here in two other ways. First, it

---

[44] Skinner, n 9 above, p 199. It is clear that this version of civil liberties does depend on society being homogenous to the extent that it requires from all those who belong to it a commitment to a concept of freedom that involves the flourishing of all members of society in a self-governing community of equals.

[45] Arendt, n 29 above, p 200.

[46] T Poole, 'Harnessing the Power of the Past? Lord Hoffmann and the *Belmarsh Detainees Case*' (2005) 32 *Journal of Law and Society* 534.

depends on a sense of moral confidence about it having established the
(objectively) right approach to the challenge of government,[47] in exactly
the same kind of way that democratic participation and civil liberties protection are today regarded as essential even in a society that has a very
relaxed view about the ethical content of the laws that such a system
produces. As was said in Chapter 1, this is a book that is not neutral about
its subject-matter. Second, the emphasis of the republican tradition on
community engagement usefully reminds us of what is entailed in self-
government. The commitment to 'keeping open the challenges of political change' imposes various duties on the state: the right to participate in
the formation of the government (by voting); the right of the electors to sufficient information in order to be able to make the right decision about
whom to support; the freedom to think for oneself; to communicate one's
thoughts; to assemble with others in order to do so; and to associate formally
with similar-minded persons in order better to push one's point of view. As
Chapter 1 has already made clear, these are the rights and freedoms that
make up the civil liberties that are the subject-matter of this book. Freed
from its dependence on speculation as to the pre-political rights of man, and
therefore emancipated from an over-dependence on Locke and his intellectual successors, it is possible to appreciate afresh quite how contemporary
this reading of civil liberties is, and how important.

CONFRONTING THE MAJORITARIAN DILEMMA: CIVIL LIBERTIES AND THE HUMAN RIGHTS ACT 1998

A nagging doubt remains, an echo from Berlin's lecture. I have already, a
paragraph or two back, made a point (albeit tucked away in a footnote)
about how this version of civil liberties depends on a view of our society as
relatively homogenous in outlook, at least as far as the requirement to
respect political freedom is concerned. A question that can hardly be
avoided here is the following: supposing the self-governing society of
active citizens I have been applauding wants to impose particular values
that concern things apart from political freedom—religious belief, for
example, or the necessity to live life in a conventional way? The republican
version discussed here does not on its face eliminate the risk of majoritarian excess, of what today might be recognized as the oppression of minorities or as attacks on the 'human rights' of particular individuals. One of

---

[47] See P Pettit, *Republicanism: A Theory of Freedom and Government* (Oxford: Clarendon
Press, 1997).

the bloody lessons of the twentieth century is that there is bound to be more than a glimmer of Rousseau even in the state organized on perfect democratic principles.

It was precisely for this reason that the idea of human rights took hold so strongly after the Second World War, as an antidote to this potentially deadly majoritarian virus. One answer to this problem would be to stress quite how all-encompassing is the concept of individual freedom on the republican/community account. We could say that what makes each of us free is not only our belonging to our society as such but also the fact that this society to which we belong is one that is rooted in the mutual celebration of different cultures and traditions. Seen like this, respect for difference becomes part of our sense of individual freedom and not something in opposition to it, with attacking minorities becoming therefore an attack on our own sense of freedom as individuals, a kind of self-mutilation. But perhaps this is to ask the idea of freedom to do too much civilizing work; we must be careful not to snap the already stretched band of republican freedom by pushing it into too remote a circle of belonging simply because of the moral benefits that we think we can spot from doing so.

Is there a fallback position? The temptation would be to revive a stronger sense of human rights—something above politics—in order to be able to meet the point.[48] But it is no good turning to that branch of government that might at first glance seem able to rise to this occasion, the judicial: the civil libertarian contradicts himself or herself if he or she relies on the judges to protect some broad concept of human rights which is outside the political process I have just been describing, for this is to commit the liberal error of assuming there to be truths outside politics to which all politics must be subject. The lively debate about whether the UK needed a judicially enforceable bill of rights which took place during the 1990s was largely focused on the key question of whether rights were to continue to be constituted by Parliament as the elected representatives of the people (the republican approach) or were instead thenceforth to be the responsibility of a non-representative judiciary (the liberal perspective). Indeed, some judges and other scholars, following the implications of the latter approach to its logical conclusion, argued that the judges already had the power to enforce such rights, whether or not Parliament legislated on the matter.[49]

In the end, as is well known, Parliament came up with the shrewdly drafted Human Rights Act 1998, which entered into force on 2 October 2000.

[48] See Gearty, n 11 above, ch 3.

[49] See, for an authoritative treatment, M Hunt, *Using Human Rights Law in English Courts* (Oxford: Hart Publishing, 1997).

I say 'shrewdly drafted' and this reveals my preferences. For here we have a measure which I would say reconciles the demands of a republican constitution[50] with the sensibility that is inherent in the term 'human rights', a sensibility that involves not just political rights but also a commitment to such values as equality of respect and human dignity. These are concepts which when concretized in law can function as bulwarks against the oppression of vulnerable outsiders, ethnic minorities, and others. The effect of the crafty balancing trick pulled off by the 1998 Act is to guarantee (so far as any paper assurances can be said to guarantee anything at all) the protection of these potentially exposed persons and groups within a community that remains nevertheless for constitutional purposes both homogenous and organized on the republican principle of self-government. The Human Rights Act 1998 plays a large part in the chapters that follow, and its involvement is usually (but as we shall see not always) benign, shoring up political freedom and asserting in a substantive way the rights of outsiders and vulnerable citizens alike. How has it managed to do this while remaining within politics?

Enacted in November 1998 but not coming into force until nearly 2 years later (October 2000), the Human Rights Act 1998 incorporated into UK law the majority of the rights and freedoms set out in the European Convention for the Protection of Human Rights and Fundamental Freedoms (European Convention on Human Rights), an agreement which had been signed up to by a previous Labour administration in 1950 and which had entered into force in 1953. The charter was initially only capable of being enforced by inter-state proceedings in a special regional court, the European Court of Human Rights in Strasbourg, although from 1966 successive UK governments had permitted individuals the right to take cases against them to this body, where it has been possible to argue that Convention rights have been infringed. This is the Strasbourg jurisdiction that became a common currency of legal discourse from the 1970s onwards, with the 1998 Act preserving the right of application to Strasbourg while at the same time opening up the Convention to judicial oversight at the domestic level as well. The result has been a boon in human rights law as the courts have become familiar with human rights arguments across a whole range of litigation subject areas.

The cases are many and the textbooks and commentaries lengthy and detailed. What is immediately apparent about the Convention is that its

---

[50] See JM Jacob, *The Republican Crown. Lawyers and the Making of the State in Twentieth Century Britain* (Aldershot: Dartmouth Publishing, 1995), and more recently A Tomkins, *Our Republican Constitution* (Oxford: Hart Publishing, 2005).

primary thrust is as a promoter and defender of what we have been calling here political rights in the republican sense of the term—'civil and political rights' in international law language but civil liberties as far as this book is concerned. The right to free elections (Article 3 of Protocol No 1) is supplemented by the guarantees of freedom of thought and conscience (Article 9), of expression (Article 10), of association (Article 11), and of assembly (Article 11). The protection against discriminatory treatment in the enjoyment of all Convention rights (Article 14) is also important in the civil libertarian context. The political dimension to these various provisions has been drawn out and amplified in the case law of the Strasbourg court and, since 2000, in the British courts as well.[51] In the chapters that follow many of these judicial decisions will be weaved into the narrative and this brand of human rights will be seen to be making an important contribution to the ongoing protection of civil liberties on which our freedom (in the republican sense) depends. To the extent that the Human Rights Act 1998 does all these things then it is a civil libertarian charter.

But the Human Rights Act 1998 goes beyond the political and confronts directly the risks in the majoritarianism inherent in the republican approach to government. With the exception of the right to vote, the remit of each of the rights detailed above extends past the political—the expression guaranteed by Article 10 might be commercial rather than political, the association guaranteed by Article 11 a grouping of like-minded hobbyists as well as the politically engaged, and so on. And a significant number of the rights set out in the Convention are aimed at the protection of the individual as such, without any explicit political or civil libertarian gloss. These include: the right to life (Article 2); the right not to be subjected to 'torture or to inhuman or degrading treatment or punishment' (Article 3); the right not to be 'held in slavery or servitude' or to be 'required to perform forced or compulsory labour' (Article 4); the right to liberty (Article 5); the right to respect for privacy (Article 8); the right to freedom of religion (Article 9); the right to marry (Article 12); the right to property (Article 1 of Protocol No 1); and the right to education (Article 2 of Protocol No 1). Some of these, such as Articles 3 and 4, are judged so fundamental that no derogation from them is ever permitted. Of course, many or all of these rights may incidentally benefit civil liberties and the political freedoms upon which democracy depends but they reach beyond this to extend their protective cover to the entirety of human kind within their jurisdictional reach.

---

[51] See generally CA Gearty, *Principles of Human Rights Adjudication* (Oxford: Oxford University Press, 2004).

This embraces the rights of minorities to the extent that each member of any such group is individually protected, with a kind of corporate protection resulting, fortified by the prohibition against discrimination in the enjoyment of these various rights set out in Article 14. Thus does the Human Rights Act 1998 roll together the two approaches to our subject, being both liberal (in its attitude to individuals) and republican (in its commitment to civil liberties). How can it achieve this without descending into incoherence?

The answer lies in remembering the origin of all of these rights. They are not human rights in an ethereal sense, brought to earth by some celestial messenger or rationalist supremo. Rather, and altogether more modestly, they make up Parliament's response in 1998 to the risk of oppression that, as we have seen and as that Parliament appreciated, is inherent in the republican form of government. The legislators consciously enacted a rod for their own back, a charter of rights to keep them and their successors on the straight and narrow. The Human Rights Act 1998 shows that the parliamentarians of that year (and more to the point those among them who were serving in government) knew that, to adapt a remark of Machiavelli's that I have already used, it is 'the laws that make them good'. The Parliament that was convened in 1997 has required of itself and future legislators that they be good in this sense. But, crucially, these are not human rights as I have been using the term earlier in this chapter: they emerge out of the parliamentary process rather than precede it; they are beneficial outcomes from the fray rather than moral absolutes hovering above it. This applies both to the political rights and to the more dignity-based provisions that are to be found in the measure.

It is therefore entirely unsurprising, inevitable indeed, that Parliament in 1998 should have reserved to itself (and its successor Parliaments) the right explicitly (or by necessary implication) to breach Convention rights if it (or its successors) chose to do so, and (even more dramatically) to repeal or alter the Human Rights Act 1998 itself if this was the desire of the legislature on some future day. As regards the first of these, the Act requires the judges to interpret legislation compatibly with the Convention rights '[s]o far as it is possible to do' (s 3) but it specifically prohibits them from striking down legislation, allowing instead the making of a 'declaration of incompatibility'. This quasi-remedy serves to indicate judicial distaste of this or that provision and it requires a governmental or legislative re-engagement with the matter which has led to the infringement of the right, but it carries no orthodox legal consequences whatsoever. Government and Parliament can as a matter of law ignore such declarations, and while this may be unlikely or even (over time) unthinkable, it is a vital safeguard for the continuing good health of Britain's 'republican' form of government (albeit one disguized as a constitutional monarchy): the people of the day can speak as they wish untrammelled by the judgements of their forbears as to the meaning of right and wrong. For the same reason the existence of the Human Rights Act 1998 itself is always up for grabs, capable at least potentially of being removed from the statute book, and indeed, as we shall see in Chapter 3, anxieties about terrorism and asylum have generated discussion to exactly this effect.

This precariousness applies also to the political rights set out in the Convention. Even from the point of view of pure theory, it is clear that civil liberties in the political rights sense need not be absolute in order to be effective. The language of human rights must not fool us into asserting an absolute position that is in fact untenable. These political rights are not freedoms that stand alone as worthy in themselves but are rather instrumental, their value being derived from the way in which they make democratic society possible. It follows that the freedoms can be restricted or even truncated where the interests of the democratic system itself demand. This can happen in two ways, one running with the grain of civil liberties, the other pushing against. First, the civil liberties of the powerful might need to be restricted so as to give everybody a fair chance of influencing political debate: this would explain why controlling campaign funding at election time is appropriate from the point of view of civil libertarian principle, for example, or why a right of reply to alleged media inaccuracies might rightly be imposed on a broadcaster. On the other hand, rather more negatively, the state may on occasion judge that the greater (democratic) good lies in the restriction of civil liberties, either because the nation is facing some terrible emergency or because the action being taken is thought to be necessary in the name of national security, public order, or some other overarching societal goal. Interestingly, the Human Rights Act 1998 has embedded these potential deviations from civil liberties into the law: Article 15 of the Convention (indirectly incorporated into UK law via s 14 of the Human Rights Act 1998) permits derogations from the political rights in the Convention '[i]n time of war or other public emergency threatening the life of the nation'. If this drastic action is not required, departures from the rights can still be permitted on a case-by-case basis where this is judged 'necessary in a democratic society'.

Needless to say, this is one of the most sensitive areas in all of contemporary civil liberties law. The interface between the macro-needs of democracy (survival of the state; the demands of the public interest; the pursuit of the common good) and the usual way of ensuring democratic health (via civil liberties/political rights) is often a tense place, riven with rival perceptions of what is required. The sorts of questions that arise include the following: Can the wealthy be restricted in what they can spend to achieve their political goals and if so to what extent? Should this or that political party be banned because of the subversive nature of its activities? Can we lock up these activists because we are concerned that they are attacking our (or some other state's) political structures? Can we prohibit political speech where its sole intention is to incite hatred? Even more fundamentally, when can we say that the state is under such attack that it has a right, even a duty, to give up some traditional civil liberties in order to survive? This being a key fault line in the otherwise often complementary relationship between democracy and civil liberties (in the political rights sense), it will come as no surprise to learn that we shall encounter the working through of many of these examples in real situations of legal conflict in the chapters that follow. As we shall see, the question often resolves itself into a matter not of substance but of jurisdiction: which organ of the state has the power to make these decisions, and what degree of oversight should the other branches of government assert over these determinations once they are made?

The Human Rights Act 1998 shows us that among the fundamental values that underpin the culture at the present moment are not only a determination to preserve civil liberties and political rights but also a commitment to human dignity and equality of respect for all. The qualifier 'at the present moment' is important here: everything can change and this applies as much to these values as to anything else; the past is littered with cast-off fundamental commitments that look merely quaint today. The comfort offered by the Human Rights Act 1998 to political activists but especially also to vulnerable groups in our society—ethnic minorities, foreigners, and other outsiders—is doubly qualified, by the uncertainty of its proper enforcement on the ground in a situation of public tension and by its inherent contingency.[52] The latter, in particular, is an inevitable consequence of its being seen for what it is, a part of politics rather than a message from another, more moral place, the child of civil liberties rather than its parent.

It follows that one can be totally committed to the ethical value of the Human Rights Act 1998, and willing to argue for its inherent worth and its indispensability to the success of our society, whilst at the same time accepting that the people through their representatives have the power to expunge this language from the law, and that this applies as much to the

---

[52] L Clements and PA Thomas (eds), *The Human Rights Act: A Success Story?* (Oxford: Blackwell Publishing, 2005).

civil liberties themselves as it does to the wider ideas of human rights that go beyond political freedom. So the limited answer we are left with when it comes to securing human rights (in the European Convention on Human Rights sense) in Britain is that the Human Rights Act 1998 has made their removal as a matter of law more difficult but not impossible, and of course the political atmosphere of the day might also have the effect of reducing its paper guarantees to a set of dead letters. The Human Rights Act 1998 is not the only dyke that we have erected against a potentially authoritarian tide: there is our strong societal commitment to diversity and pluralism and also (at a more institutional level) the operation of separation of powers (including for these purposes devolution) and of the rule of law (embracing in this context our obligation to adhere to international human rights law). With these various liberal and constitutional glosses on elective democracy we have sought to harness to good effect the qualities of the latter without allowing it to overflow into tyranny. This may appear unsatisfactory because it is a precarious situation in which to leave civil liberties. Can we not do more than work as hard as we can as citizens to make sure that our version of what is the best becomes (or remains) the community's common sense? There is no alternative to politics, and one of the chief advantages of the idea of civil liberties used as we use the term here is that, unlike the misleadingly absolute language of human rights, it makes this crystal clear.

3

Democratic Freedom and National Insecurity

In this chapter I take the theoretical insights into our subject that have just been laid out and deepen our understanding of them by weaving these ideas into the history of the practice of civil liberties in Britain. This examination of the rise of political freedom is necessarily set against a background of societal anxiety. There has never been a time in Britain when the utility of civil liberties has not been intensely disputed: there is no 'golden age' of freedom lurking somewhere in our distant past. Although the momentum is generally positive, the graph tracking the health of our subject has been up and down rather than always on the rise. The perennial concern, varying in intensity from time to time, has been about the kinds of radical change that a commitment to civil liberties might produce, either purposefully (more democracy; greater equality) or as a side-effect of the freedom upon which such a political perspective is naturally thought to insist (more anarchy). Asserting freedoms of thought, speech, assembly, and association so as ultimately to be able to achieve a state governed on a representative basis has inevitably involved clashes, both with those whose interests were certain to be adversely affected by the success of just such a project, and with those who have felt that too high a regard for civil liberties inevitably leaves the state vulnerable to attack. Conflict is therefore very much part of the civil liberties story, whether generated from within or threatening from without.

The normal civil liberties response to this, today as in the past, is to bemoan disorder and violence in all their various forms while at the same time deploring the state's attacks on civil liberties, and resisting all of the concessions that a particular situation might be said to demand. This is understandable: there is a natural desire in such protagonists to argue for ever-better protection of civil liberties, without regard to broad context or to the precise exigencies of the moment, and to see all departures from the Grail of political liberty as plunges towards a police state. But to remove civil liberties from the world in order to turn them into ahistorical truths that are detached from everyday life is to miss much that is of interest in our subject. It is also to damage it by parading a purity that is then rightly laughed at by those whose interests lie in undermining what is important as well as what is merely impossible. In fact, our subject can only be understood when it is embedded in the messy history from which it has over generations slowly but surely emerged. The tensions that such an enquiry throws up, being deep within the very structure of civil liberties as it is conceived of here, return frequently in different forms and shapes in the course of this book. In this chapter I turn first to this story of the emergence of our subject and how it has overcome the anxieties of the past. The next task is to assess the danger posed by the main contemporary challenge to political freedom, the so-called 'war' on 'terrorism' and on 'international terrorism'. I end with an overview of contemporary British attitudes to civil liberties, drawing on data from a comprehensive British Social Attitudes Survey conducted during the Summer of 2005, with extensive interviews having taken place both before and after the 7 July Al Qaida-related attacks on London that year. With this work done on the past, the present, and also (fortified by the data from our survey) with some guesses about the future, we will be ready to turn, in Part Two, to the substance of our civil liberties as we enjoy them today.

FORGING A DEMOCRATIC STATE: THE THREE PARADOXES OF CIVIL LIBERTIES

The subject of civil liberties as I am using that term is the product of the tensions that result from three paradoxes that lie at its heart. These relate to national security, to democracy, and to political violence, and I shall deal with each in turn. The first can be simply put: to be effective, civil liberties protection must provide a mechanism for its own failure. Or to put it another way, an absolutist civil liberties culture is not one in which civil liberties are unqualifiedly protected. The point here is not just the obvious one that every guarantee of the right to vote and to the freedoms of expression, assembly, association, and so on, necessarily have to contain exceptions on account of the fact that these concepts are simply too wide to be of use without further modification. This is of course true: even the entitlement to vote is predicated on a minimal level of mental capacity and, as the public law cliché puts it, no one has the right falsely to shout fire in a crowded cinema. But the point is deeper than this. Democratic freedom sometimes requires the truncation of these rights even in their political, civil libertarian manifestation.

It is not inherently contradictory for a democratic culture to prohibit certain kinds of political expression, whether in the form of speech, membership of an organization, or public protest. Most democratic states ban many substantive communications that could broadly be described as forms of political expression. How wide or narrow such censorious actions are depends on the history and politics of the state concerned and in particular on how fragile and/or vulnerable its institutions are to the sentiments being banned: the Germans are understandably more anxious about Nazis[1] than are the Americans,[2] the British keener to crack down on racially motivated hate speech[3] than other countries that do not share its colonial past and diverse population today. The European Convention on Human Rights contains a number of clues as to what is going on with these apparent subversions of our subject. Many of the key civil liberties set out in that document are capable of being overridden where this is for certain legitimate goals and is prescribed by law, but crucially this can be done only when it is also considered 'necessary in a democratic society'. Article 17 declares that 'Nothing in this Convention may be interpreted as implying for any State, group or person any right to engage in any activity or perform any act aimed at the destruction of any of the rights and freedoms set forth herein or at their limitation to a greater extent than is provided for in the Convention.' As mentioned in passing in Chapter 2, if things get really rough, this paradigmatic political rights charter permits states to derogate from their obligations under it in 'time of war or other public emergency threatening the life of the nation' (albeit only 'to the extent strictly required by the exigencies of the situation').[4]

Most democratic constitutions have clauses along similar lines. If they do not, the responsible authorities tend to imply them into the document (if they are judges[5]) or assert them (if they are elected leaders[6]). This should not surprise us or disturb us as a matter of principle. The test of a successful democratic culture is not its willingness to implode when faced with illiberal forces inclined to misconstrue the freedoms offered by such a society as invitations to destroy it. This is the case whether the threat comes from the Left, the Right, or from some pre-modern brand of politicized religion. The willingness of representative democracy to equip itself to fight against forces that would destroy it must entail an openness to the curtailment of civil liberties where this is judged essential to survival. Those

---

[1] *German Communist Party Case* (1957) 1 *Yearbook of the European Convention on Human Rights* 222; *Kosiek v Federal Republic of Germany* (1986) 9 EHRR 328.

[2] *Village of Skokie v National Socialist Party of America* 373 NE 2d 21 (1978); *Collin and National Socialist Party v Smith and the Skokie Village of Skokie* 578 F 2d 1197 (1978); cert denied: *Smith v Collin* 439 US 916 (1978).

[3] Incitement to racial hatred: see p 145 below.   [4] Article 15.

[5] *Dennis v United States* 341 US 494 (1951).

[6] There is a very good summary of the attitude of President Bush to such matters in D Cole, 'What Bush Wants to Hear', *New York Review of Books*, 17 November 2005.

who reject this premise as an unwarranted invitation to authoritarianism are likely to be closet libertarians rather than civil libertarians as this book understands that term. If there can be no serious argument against the need for such a democratic override button, however, there is great controversy over who should have the right to push it. The difficult question is not one of principle alone but of applied principle, of certainty moderated by practice.

The issues were simpler in the era before mass suffrage. Power was then in the hands of a sequence of elites whose invariable tendency was to confuse the threat they personally (or as a class) faced with a danger to the country as a whole. In such situations, the claims of national security were often a mere camouflage for the vested interests that lay behind them. In 1688, King James II no doubt thought he was putting England first even while Parliament put him to flight for, among other misdeeds, 'endeavour[ing] to subvert the constitution of his kingdom'.[7] Two generations later, the justly celebrated civil liberties case of *Entick v Carrington* established that the executive branch's version of state necessity did not necessarily accord with that of the law of the land.[8] The importance of this case lay in the way it established on behalf of the judges a claim to have a shared responsibility for the assessment of what kinds of abridgements of civil liberties were required in the name of national survival. Many of the advances in civil liberties in the eighteenth century were made in the courtroom, by brave judges, courageous counsel, and unintimidated juries.[9]

With the growth of the democratic movement at the end of that century and its revival after a period of repression inspired by anxiety about the possible contagiousness of the French revolution,[10] advocates of civil liberties found themselves facing the hostility not only of a propertied class used to parliamentary power but also their allies on the bench, now increasingly unsettled by the prospect of sharing power with the merchants and other beneficiaries of the industrial revolution. During the first half of the nineteenth century, the national interest was wheeled in to provide a rhetorical veneer for class partisanship, but once again it was unsuccessful.[11] Resistance to a widened franchise involved savage repression,

---

[7] See the opening remarks of the Bill of Rights, 1688.
[8] (1765) 19 St Tr 1030, 2 Wils KB 275.
[9] See, e.g., *Ashby v White* (1703) 2 Ld Raym. 938.
[10] EP Thompson, *The Making of the English Working Class* (London: Victor Gollanz, 1963).
[11] Note that nationalism was also an important ingredient in forcing social change: see the superb five-volume work by J Hutchinson and AD Smith (eds), *Nationalism. Critical Concepts in Political Science* (London: Routledge, 2000).

military attacks on protestors and, when the modest reform measure of 1832 came up for debate, warnings of imminent national doom in both Houses of Parliament.[12] The same cycle was then played out in the course of the late nineteenth and early twentieth century as a truly democratic culture secured its niche with the support of the socialist and trade union movements and via a strong commitment to a universal right to vote.

So much for the past, when resistance to the democratic goals of civil libertarians turned the assertion of even the basic freedoms of expression, assembly, and association into highly dangerous acts, potentially treasonable or seditious if the authorities chose to see things that way. But with the role of the monarch now purely titular and that of the courts very much secondary to the legislature, and with an elected Parliament to which the executive is accountable and upon which it depends for support, it might be thought that the issue of who determines what can be done in the name of national security would have fallen away. In fact, if anything, it has become more acute than ever. The democratic era has not delivered a blank cheque to the authorities. Far from it: this phase of history has been marked by huge conflicts over whether actions taken to control civil liberties have been truly in the national (as opposed to some factional) interest, and it has not been a conclusive answer to this simply to say that those making the decisions now belong to a government elected by the people. The issue, as it has played out during the twentieth and early twentieth-first centuries has been essentially one of trust.

At the very threshold of the democratic era, during the First World War, the authorities took a range of powers to control civil liberties.[13] This was done in order to protect the state at a time of great stress and both Parliament and the courts agreed with the measures taken, the first through enactment of the basic emergency laws and subsequent benign oversight of the executive rules that flowed from this legislative source, the second through decisions supportive of the executive branch when individuals adversely affected by the regulations sought to challenge in court the truncation of their freedom. The widening of the franchise to encompass the whole adult population took place in the decade following the end of the war, but at the same time, Parliament enacted a series of measures which effectively transformed into ordinary law many of the emergency restrictions on freedom that had been agreed during that conflict.[14] The rationale was no longer the war, of course, rather it was the threat to the

---

[12] E Pearce, *Reform! The Fight for the 1832 Reform Act* (London: Jonathan Cape, 2003).

[13] See KD Ewing and CA Gearty, *The Struggle for Civil Liberties. Political Freedom and the Rule of Law in Britain, 1914–1945* (Oxford: Oxford University Press, 2000), ch 2.

[14] Ibid, chs 3–6.

nation's survival posed by the success of the communist revolution in Russia, the commitment of the newly formed USSR to the export of that revolution, and the ready support shown for the realization of this aim in the British context by the newly formed Communist Party of Great Britain.

The history of civil liberties between the First and Second World Wars is one in which government ministers—now increasingly able to point to their own democratic legitimacy—first justified to Parliament and the public at large the enactment of illiberal legislation on the basis of this external and internal threat to national security, and then—for the same reason—stoutly defended the deployment of these laws against activists on the Left alone. One example of such partisanship—among many that could be chosen—was the support shown by the Home Secretary of the day Sir William Joynson-Hicks for sedition prosecutions brought in 1926 against members of the Communist Party: they had been engaged in 'the wrong kind of speech' and for that reason were rightly exposed to the law.[15] During the 1930s, the civil liberties disputes were more about the partisan way in which the authorities exercised their power to control speech rather than about the fact of such powers as a matter of principle. The question asked was not, 'Why do we have these laws?' so much as 'Why continue to attack the communists and the hunger marchers with the full majesty of the law while turning a benign constitutional eye on the true threat to Britain, the Mussolini-backed British Union of Fascists?'. This was why the Left-inclined civil libertarians of the period saw no contradiction between defending the right to protest of the hunger-marchers on the one hand while pressing for a national public order law and trying by force to break up fascist meetings on the other. The difference was over which political speech to curb, not whether as a matter of principle such controls should exist at all.

After the only moderately illiberal hiatus of the Second World War,[16] the Cold War that dominated politics for the following four decades provided a fresh set of justifications for a range of national security laws, all of which impacted adversely on the political freedom of those on the Left. Pointing to a now full-blooded democratic mandate, and relying on information that it was often impossible for security reasons to place in the public domain, ministers of successive governments were able to oversee

---

[15] Ibid, p 139.

[16] Comparative to the first and to what might have happened: for full accounts see N Stammers, *Civil Liberties in Britain during the 2nd World War: A Political Study* (London: Croom Helm, 1983) and AWB Simpson, *In the Highest Degree Odious. Detention without Trial in Wartime Britain* (Oxford: Clarendon Press, 1992).

a wide variety of serious truncations of civil liberties: the bringing of espi-
onage charges against campaigners for nuclear disarmament,[17] the use of
public order legislation to take action to prevent protest against the
Vietnam War,[18] the deployment of US nuclear weapons in Britain[19] and to
curb the expression of dissent on many other issues,[20] and the prosecution
of journalists, military personnel, and civil servants for disclosure of information in breach of the ludicrously draconian s 2 of the Official Secrets Act
1911, including (by way of illustration) prosecutions brought against
Crispin Aubrey, John Berry, and Duncan Campbell for an interview Berry
gave about his work in government communications[21] and against Sarah
Tisdall for having leaked details of the government's strategy for taking
delivery of cruise missiles at RAF Greenham Common.[22] Ministerial
judgments about the needs of national security were during this period
taken largely at face value. There was general public acceptance that some
dilution of civil liberties protection (or at least the protection accorded to
Left-wing radicals) was a price worth paying to keep intact the state's
overall commitment to democratic freedom. Members of the senior judiciary were invariably equally supportive when such matters came before
them. The case law of the Cold War period is littered with dicta closely
identifying the interests of the state with the interests of the government
of the day[23] and explicitly deferring to ministerial judgement on what
national security requires, even in situations where such judgement calls had
devastating effects on individual civil liberties.[24] Nor was the Strasbourg
bench frequently to be found developing a different, more civil libertarian
perspective on these issues.[25]

   This community of interest, so evident during the Cold War now seems
a long time ago. Even then it is true there were occasions when government could not get its own way. The journalist Jonathan Aitken was
acquitted of offences under the Official Secrets Act, arising out of his
coverage of Britain's complicity in the Nigerian civil war, when the judge
presiding at his trial told the jury that the section under which charges had

---

[17] *Chandler v Director of Public Prosecutions* [1964] AC 763.
[18] *Williams v Director of Public Prosecutions* [1968] *Crim Law Rev* 563.
[19] *Kent v Metropolitan Police Commissioner* (1981) *The Times*, 15 May.
[20] D Williams, *Keeping the Peace. The Police and Public Order* (London: Hutchinson, 1967).
[21] See *Attorney-General v Leveller Magazine Ltd* [1979] AC 440.
[22] See KD Ewing and CA Gearty, *Freedom under Thatcher. Civil Liberties in Modern Britain*
(Oxford: Oxford University Press, 1990), pp 139–43.
[23] *Council of Civil Service Unions v Minister for the Civil Service* [1985] AC 374.
[24] *R (Hosenball) v Secretary of State for Home Affairs* [1977] 1 WLR 766; *R (Soblen) v
Secretary of State for Home Affairs* [1963] 1 QB 829.
[25] *Glasenapp v Federal Republic of Germany* (1986) 9 EHRR 25; *German Communist Party
Case*, n 1 above; *Council of Civil Service Unions v United Kingdom* (1987) 10 EHRR 269.

been brought would be better off being 'pensioned off'.[26] The jury in Clive Ponting's prosecution, for having revealed details of the truth behind the sinking of the General Belgrano (in the course of the Falklands War), was similarly robust, this time defying a strenuously pro-prosecution summing up by the trial judge before returning verdicts of not guilty.[27] But in the immediate post-Cold War period of the 1990s, these exceptions to judicial deference became, if not the rule, then much more frequent than in the past. The judges may have been reacting to the derision heaped upon their colleagues in the late Thatcher years for the stoutness with which they supported her administration's hounding of the press for having reported some of the allegations contained in that late 1980s best seller, *Spycatcher* (by the former security service employee Peter Wright).[28] Or it may have been the disastrous series of miscarriage of justice cases that awoke a new sense of responsibility in the judiciary. A factor too might well have been the kind of people who were getting a chance on the bench, less class-bound and innately conservative than their ermine predecessors.[29] It is also likely that the lightening of international tension after 1989 gave the judges the perception of a freer rein than in the past with which to scrutinize and hold accountable executive action in the national security area.

An important factor in the surge of judicial assertiveness post-1989 has surely also been the collapse in the trust normally accorded government in the arena of national security. Here the Arms-for-Iraq inquiry, chaired by the distinguished judge (now Lord) Richard Scott,[30] and the debacle over the false basis for the invasion of Iraq in 2003 have played pivotal parts. Despite the indulgent report into the latter (in the context of an inquiry into the death of the government scientist David Kelly) by the law lord, Brian Hutton, the effect of the 'fiasco over Iraqi weapons of mass destruction'[31] in particular would seem to have been to undermine trust in

---

[26] 'The 1911 Act achieves its sixtieth birthday on 22 August this year. This case, if it does nothing more, may well alert those who govern us at least to consider, if they have the time, whether or not section 2 of this Act has reached retirement age and should be pensioned off': Caulfield J, as quoted by Jonathan Aitken in his book of the case, *Officially Secret* (London: Weidenfeld and Nicolson, 1971), p 198.

[27] *R v Ponting* [1985] *Crim Law Rev* 318.   [28] See pp 128–30 below.

[29] K Malleson, *The New Judiciary: The Effects of Expansion and Activism* (Aldershot: Ashgate, 1999); R Cornes and A Le Sueur, *The Future of the United Kingdom's Highest Courts* (London: Constitution Unit, University College, 2001).

[30] A Tomkins, *The Constitution After Scott: Government Unwrapped* (Oxford: Oxford University Press, 1998).

[31] *A v Secretary of State for the Home Department* [2004] UKHL 56, [2005] 2 AC 68, para [94] per Lord Hoffmann.

government in the eyes of many senior judges.[32] The problems this has caused for the executive branch in the context of the latest anxieties about national security, rooted in concerns about international terrorism post 11 September 2001, are matters we consider further below, when we turn specifically to the interaction between national security and anti-terrorism laws. It is in the context of such laws that the tensions generated by this first paradox of civil liberties protection are manifested in contemporary form, as a bitter dispute both within the branches of the state and between civil society and government, not as to whether to defend the state but as to who should have the power to say and do what is required, and with what levels of accountability.

If the first paradox of civil liberties is concerned with the subject's requirement to contain within itself the seeds of its own destruction, the second is likewise taken up with absorbing another contrary impulse within its deep structure. Understood in the sense in which I am using the term there, the historic purpose of civil liberties as the law and practice of political freedom has been to secure a representative system of government; in its classic form this is what all the protesting and speech-making and associating have been about. The achievement of this form of rule does not, however, bring an end to our subject or even a restriction of it to the legislative arena; rather the reverse in fact—one of the tests of the success of a democratic culture is its willingness to accept political expression which is not focused on the duly elected representatives of the community but which lies well outside the parliamentary mainstream. This continued appreciation of the need for popular protest in a country with plenty of formal democratic channels open to it is another of our subject's historical legacies which fortunately we have been unable to shake off. During the ongoing democratic revolution of the seventeenth through until the mid-twentieth century, civil liberties had to exist separately from the legislature because (albeit to a lesser and lesser extent as time went on) that body was not representative in a truly democratic sense.

So it was no answer to the arguments of civil libertarians to point out that as a result of the Bill of Rights Act 1688, parliamentarians had all the freedom that they needed in order to be able to legislate without pressure from the Crown or other external forces. To those who saw such men as not more than the representatives of a gendered, propertied elite, it mattered not a jot that they were free as long as the mass of people were not able to join in the process of electing them. As the franchise widened, so this

---

[32] See *Report of the Inquiry into the Circumstances Surrounding the Death of Dr David Kelly CMG* (London: The Stationery Office, 2004).

argument for extra-parliamentary action gradually became less easy to make, although it certainly retained its force through the nineteenth century, when the denial of the right to vote to working class men and to all women rather diminished the democratic substance behind the ostensibly radical electoral reform of those years. The suffragettes were one of the last civil libertarian movements in this country who were able to say with perfect clarity that the elected persons making decisions about their future were in no way their representatives, having achieved their positions on the basis of votes cast by one gender only.

If these democratic developments did not render our subject redundant, they did affect it in important ways. The universal franchise having been largely achieved by the late 1920s, civil libertarian energy found itself caught up in two new fields of battle. The first of these involved defending the substance as well as the form of democracy by ensuring that all political parties, even those of the extreme Right and radical Left, should be able to form, to organize, to build a supporters' base, and to campaign in elections with a view to securing support in Parliament. This was not an easy task—as we have seen in our discussion of the first paradox of civil liberties, democratic government felt there was no great inconsistency with civil libertarian principle in attacking parties that had designs on power in order (as the government saw it) to do away with democracy altogether. So the Communist Party of Great Britain has always found itself in need of civil libertarian solicitude, just as has the British Union of Fascists (and afterwards the British National Party) in the years since the enactment of the Public Order Act 1936, the latter Party sometimes very controversially on account of the inclination of civil libertarians historically to see the threat to democracy from the Right as greater than that from the Left. Today, this part of the civil libertarian argument is played out in discussions over the banning of Irish nationalist and Islamic parties devoted to campaigning for goals thought anathema to the democratically elected leadership of this country: I look at this issue in detail in Chapter 8.

The second arena of dispute in the democratic age has not been about winning power to change the system but about exercising the rights to freedoms of expression, assembly, and association in order to influence legislators in favour of particular points of view. This is where the fact that we are now, formally at any rate (on which more below), a state organized entirely on democratic principles, becomes highly relevant. Such governments have a new way of rebutting public protest, pointing not to the substantive error of the policy change that is sought but rather to the inadmissibility of the mode of bringing it to the legislators' attention.

The country is a democratic one, the relevant decision-maker tells the crowd: go and write to your MP, run for office, or seek to inform opinion in more orthodox/less invasive ways. This democratically rooted counter-attack on civil liberties was first in evidence during the general strike in 1926 and in the treatment of the mass protests of the National Unemployed Workers' Movement (NUWM) in the early 1930s. In both cases, government ministers often justified their actions—Draconian emergency regulation in the first instance, and refusal to meet hunger marchers' representatives with their petitions in the second—with a new authority based on their democratic legitimacy and the existence of alternative mechanisms for calling executive decision-making to account. More recent protests that have similarly been on the margins of political debate have been equally vulnerable to control on the basis that such forms of protest are unnecessary in today's free society: examples include anti-nuclear (CND) activism in the early 1980s, 'stop-the-city' protests, eco-demonstrations, and other forms of 'direct action'.[33]

Of course, the political leadership did not in the 1920s and 1930s, and does not today, regard the fact of an operative democratic system of government as a sufficient basis for the removal altogether of these wider political freedoms: the paradox lies precisely in the need to continue to allow those civil liberties that previous civil libertarian gains appear to have rendered redundant. The men and women who run Britain today recognize the need for civil liberties as a matter of principle, and concede the legitimacy of this or that particular public protest as a social fact, but neither acceptance means that they welcome the practice of public protest with open arms. These democratically elected officials cannot help but see themselves as the current winners in (to them) an impeccably fair electoral race and with a consequent monopoly of wisdom which public protestors are seeking by the short-cut of direct action to undermine. From time to time ministers are emboldened to take a tougher line with protest than might otherwise have been expected, with the negative energy evident on such occasions flowing out of an underlying sense of grievance about the need for public protest in general. The frustration of the Blair administration at the anti-war demonstration mounted over many years in Parliament Square by Brian Haw, leading (as we shall see in Chapter 7) to legislation specifically designed to restrict him, is one example;[34] the same Prime Minister's whipping up of national anger about a proposed Mayday

---

[33] See H Fenwick, *Civil Rights. New Labour, Freedom and the Human Rights Act* (Harlow: Longman, 2000).
[34] See p 141 below.

protest in central London on 1 May 2001 was another.[35] What we see in each case is a playing out of the tension between democracy and civil liberties that is in turn a direct result of this paradoxical necessity for continuing civil liberties protection in a country in which civil liberties appear to have achieved their goal. (The words 'appear to' are important here, for it can be plausibly argued that our paradox has yet to kick in with Britain not yet being a properly democratic country: this is, however, a discussion that is beyond the remit of this book, taking us into the realm of constitutional rather than civil liberties law.)

The third paradox can be more briefly stated than the first two, but its central relevance to contemporary discussions on political freedom will be immediately grasped and it falls to be more fully explored in the next section of this chapter. The subject of civil liberties presents itself as necessarily involving a rejection of political violence as a matter of principle but, in fact, it has in the past depended on this sort of violence, or the threat of it, for its success. This is not only a point about the way in which parliamentary government was established in England by means of a successful usurpation of power, backed by the force of arms, at the time of the Williamite revolution. It is a reference as well to the political ferment which had built up by the early 1830s and which made the Great Reform Act of 1832 in many ways a pre-emptive counter-revolutionary strike. It encompasses the politically inspired subversion of the Chartists and the famous willingness of the suffragettes to engage in subversive violence to achieve their ends. Just as the Parliament of the 'glorious revolution' spoke of the need for rights to secure the nation from the disorder of a failed royal despotism, so generations later the Universal Declaration of Human Rights in 1948 asserted in its preamble that it was 'essential, if man is not to be compelled to have recourse, as a last resort, to rebellion against tyranny and oppression, that human rights should be protected by the rule of law'.

The achievement of political freedom has depended on violence in most countries; indeed, Britain has a gentler record on this score than most states (as long as we leave aside the colonies and Northern Ireland). The legacy of such successful subversion is an ambiguous relationship with political violence: generally condemning it but being quick to ensure that those accused of it receive a fair trial; deploring criminal acts but being ready to accept and defend conduct which is well into the zone of the lawless, complaining about the abuse of police discretion rather than the undeniable fact that a law has been broken; agreeing that inflicting

---

[35] See *Evening Standard*, 30 April 2001 and 1 May 2001. See also N Hertz, 'A Bad Day for Democracy', *The Observer*, 6 May 2001.

injuries to persons is wrong but being a bit uncertain about property and
being more than willing to describe as merely robust 'direct action' what
others would call a criminal mob. This edge to our subject is what keeps it
honest, stops it becoming the handmaiden of power, servant rather than
challenger of the established (democratic) order. But it does leave civil liberties vulnerable to being tarred with the wrongs of others. It is in the
state's recent and growing preoccupation with terrorism that civil liberties have faced their greatest challenge in the democratic era, with all three
paradoxes combining to impose immense pressure on the subject. How
these pressures are resolved will determine the future of civil liberties
protection in Britain. They are played out in many of the chapters that
follow and dealt with in more general terms in the next section.

THE SUBVERSIVE POWER OF THE COUNTER-TERRORISM NARRATIVE

Britain's first anti-terrorism legislation in the democratic era was passed
in 1939, in response to the resurgence in Irish Republican Army (IRA)
activity which occurred in the period leading up to the Second World
War.[36] The Prevention of Violence (Temporary Provisions) Act 1939 was
hurriedly passed in the lead up to the summer recess of that year, on the
basis of vague assertions from the Home Secretary about the serious
nature of the threat posed to national security, claims that were long afterwards shown to be very misleading.[37] The Act gave the authorities wide
powers to prohibit from entering Britain, to expel or forcibly to register
persons suspected of involvement in the preparation or instigation of acts
of violence 'designed to influence public opinion or Government policy
with respect to Irish affairs'.[38] Powers of arrest and detention without
charge for up to seven days were likewise included in the Act.[39] The measure was not utilized for very long, with a combination of a decline in IRA
activity and the onset of the conflict with Germany meaning that Irish
republican violence was no longer at the forefront of public anxiety. But it
was a template that lay ready to hand when a much more serious outbreak
of such violence in the early 1970s, including attacks on military and civilian targets across Britain, made the case for new anti-terrorism legislation
appear irresistible.

---

[36] Northern Ireland has had its own counter-subversive laws since its inception in 1922: see
Struggle for Civil Liberties, n 13 above, ch 7.
[37] OG Lomas, 'The Executive and the Anti-Terrorist Legislation of 1939' [1980] *Public Law* 16.
[38] Prevention of Violence (Temporary Provisions) Act 1939, s 1(1).   [39] Ibid, s 4.

Democratic Freedom and National Insecurity

43

We can now see that the Prevention of Terrorism (Temporary Provisions) Act 1974 marks an important moment in the law and practice of civil liberties in Britain, the point when the language of terrorism is introduced into the country's domestic law for the first time. Thought by its sponsors to be 'Draconian'[40] and intended to be short-term in its operation, the Act repeated the expulsion and detention features of the 1939 Act and also included the proscription of the IRA, denying its members the right to operate as a political as well as a covertly criminal association. It seems almost incomprehensible today that the proposal for the banning of the IRA and contemplated seven-day detention should have attracted such controversy among parliamentarians and the general public in the late autumn of 1974. This was despite the grave nature of the systematic political violence of the time and the high levels of fear and anxiety that this had provoked. It may well be that historians will see the furore over the 1974 Act as one of the last gasps of a liberal culture that was already in severe decline, a death rattle from the already departed (in every sense) 1960s.

Certainly the legislation gathered momentum as time went on, growing in size and stature as its useful provisions became better known to the police and the security services, being frequently added to and then renewed with such regularity as to be effectively permanent, and enjoying the full support of the judiciary on those few occasions that its provisions or the exercise of power under one or other of its sections were challenged in court.[41] At the same time, as a result of various inquiries and reviews, the terrorism law took on more of the characteristics of the criminal law, with higher levels of due process and greater judicial engagement ameliorating (while not obliterating) the measure's essentially extra-legal character. This process of growth, inexorable embedment in the mainstream law and increased normalization reached its logical conclusion with enactment of the permanent Terrorism Act 2000. Since then, of course, we have had a plethora of further statutory interventions, linked to the perceived need for action in the aftermath of the 11 September 2001 and 7 July 2005 Al-Qaida-related attacks in the US and Britain, respectively.

The evidence of the threat posed by counter-terrorism to the law and practice of civil liberties is scattered across the chapters that follow. The alleged necessities of counter-terrorism have engaged the right to life and the prohibition of torture and inhuman or degrading treatment or

[40] The Home Secretary of the day Roy Jenkins: see 882 HC Debs 35 (25 November 1974). There is now an excellent study of the Act's passage through Parliament: see D Bonner 'Responding to Crisis: Legislating Against Terrorism' (2006) 122 *Law Quarterly Review* 602.

[41] See, generally, CA Gearty, 'Political Violence and Civil Liberties', in C McCrudden and G Chambers, *Individual Rights and the Law in Britain* (Oxford: Clarendon Press, 1994).

punishment. Its demands have also impacted severely on other basic freedoms, such as those of speech, assembly, and association. It would be
absurd to claim that civil liberties are dead or dying in Britain. But they are
certainly under severe attack from a variety of sources and chief amongst
these is this idea that the country is engaged in some kind of global 'war on
terror' or 'clash of civilizations'[42] which threatens the integrity of the
nation in such exceptional and unprecedented ways that exceptional and
unprecedented actions are needed to defend it, that (to quote the Prime
Minister who has driven so much of the reorientation in this area, Tony
Blair) 'the struggle which engages us . . . is a new type of war' which
'demands a different attitude to our own interests'.[43] Here we find our
first paradox of civil liberties being played out in a most brutal fashion,
with leading members of the government declaring that the extreme
levels of terrorist threat now faced by the state warrant—precisely in the
interests of preserving our freedom—unprecedented controls on our
civil liberties. The necessities of national security that are said to follow
are, however, strongly contested, with opponents disputing the executive's claims and deploring the illiberal consequences that are the result
of acceding to them.

Many of the clashes in this area flow from the very concept of terrorism.
It feeds the law and practice of counter-terrorism, a subject which—for all
the ministerial protestations of good faith—threatens to operate on civil
liberties in the way that a vicious virus does on the human immune system,
first undermining its defences, then destroying the subject's confidence in
its own health and purpose, and eventually reducing it to a shadow of its
former self, perhaps even killing it off altogether. Understanding what this
has to do with political freedom (rather than solely with general ideas of liberty and of human rights) requires us to examine closely the legal definition
of terrorism and then to assess how its breadth impacts negatively on the
health of our political culture. For the law and practice of counter-terrorism
are not concerned solely with narrow questions of serious criminal activity
in pursuit of a range of ideological objectives: terrorist atrocities are within
the remit of the practitioners of counter-terrorism of course, but so is
much else besides. This was the case even when the main focus of counter-
terrorism in the UK was the secessionist-inspired violence of the IRA. In
its final form the prevention of terrorism legislation passed to deal with
that violence defined 'terrorism' as 'the use of violence for political ends,
[including] any use of violence for the purpose of putting the public or any

---

[42] S Huntingon, 'The Clash of Civilizations' (1993) 72 *Foreign Affairs* 22.
[43] T Blair, speech on global terrorism, 5 March 2004.

section of the public in fear'.[44] This was quite a broad approach to the subject, one which required no special level of violence or intensity of fear and which extended even to discriminate assaults, the concept of 'a section of the public' being capable of being defined as narrowly or as broadly as the exigencies of the moment required.

At least the term required some violent dimension by definition, and with the Northern Ireland peace process beginning to produce changes in IRA behaviour from the mid-1990s it was questionable whether there was a need at that stage for any kind of terrorism law at all. Under pressure from the then Labour opposition, in December 1995, the Major administration announced an inquiry to 'consider the future need for specific counter-terrorism legislation in the United Kingdom if the cessation of terrorism connected with the affairs of Northern Ireland leads to a lasting peace'. The review was conducted by the law lord, Lord Lloyd of Berwick but his freedom of manoeuvre on the key point of principle was rather hamstrung by the demand, also in his terms of reference, that he 'take into account the continuing threat from other kinds of terrorism'. In the report that he quickly produced,[45] Lord Lloyd had no real option other than to accept the need for some form of counter-terrorism law. He considered that terrorism should be re-defined as 'the use of serious violence against persons or property, or the threat to use such violence, to intimidate or coerce a government, the public, or any section of the public, in order to promote political, social or ideological objectives'.[46] Violence was a vital requirement in this proposed definition.

The most interesting feature of Lloyd's review from the perspective of today was his insistence that the subject be viewed as part of rather than separate from the mainstream criminal law. The 'key'[47] to his proposal to government lay in the classification of certain offences as terrorist offences: these included ordinary crimes with a 'terrorist' dimension (murder, manslaughter, etc) and also various terrorist crimes which Lloyd was proposing should appear in the legislation he was recommending ('directing a terrorist organization', 'preparation of an act of terrorism', among others). The effect of this change would have been to have brought terrorism law within the criminal law, a criminal code expanded to deal with the terrorism threat certainly but with no extra dimension to it that needed to be

[44] Prevention of Terrorism (Temporary Provisions) Act 1989, s 20. Note that from 1984 'international terrorism' had also been within the remit of the Act: Prevention of Terrorism (Temporary Provisions) Act 1984, s 14(1).
[45] *Inquiry into Legislation Against Terrorism*, Cm 3420, October 1996.
[46] Ibid. See Annex E to his report for an outline of Lord Lloyd's proposals for new legislation.
[47] Ibid, report synopsis, para 36(7).

addressed outside the mainstream process. So with perfect consistency, Lord Lloyd also recommended that the special power of arrest on suspicion of 'terrorism', a kind of activity that was not a criminal offence as such, be removed and that the prohibition on the admissibility of intercept evidence be lifted.[48] Had his views been adopted, an important start would have been made in the taming of the subversive power of counter-terrorism by the harnessing of its voracious capacity for repression to the criminal law (with all the procedural and evidential disciplines that this would necessarily have entailed). Arrests and searches and so on would still have been possible but they would have been for specific offences under terrorism and other legislation rather than for the more nebulous concept of suspected terrorism.

The proposal was not, however, accepted. In a consultation paper issued in December 1998, the new Labour administration invited further comment on the suggestion but declared itself as still 'to be persuaded'[49] on the point. Its preferred option was to continue with the general police power of arrest on reasonable suspicion of terrorism, with the latter term now to be redefined as 'the use of serious violence against persons or property, or the threat to use such violence, to intimidate or coerce a government, the public or any section of the public for political, religious or ideological ends'.[50] The government was clear both that 'the new legislation should bite only on the use of serious violence[51] rather than violence alone and that the 'social' objective in Lloyd's proposal had taken things too far. But by adding that 'serious violence' should embrace 'serious disruption, for instance resulting from attacks on computer installations or public utilities',[52] the concept of 'violence' was seriously attenuated and the seeds of a greatly expanded counter-terrorism framework were quietly put in place. To make the proposed new laws even broader, following Lloyd on this point, the government accepted that for the first time terrorism law should cover not just Northern Ireland-based and international terrorism but domestic terrorism as well.[53]

The stage having been set in this way, the Terrorism Act 2000 proceeded to put the new regime in place—some 14 months before the attacks of 11 September 2001. History may judge this piece of legislation to have been as important a benchmark in the decline of civil liberties protection in Britain as its 1974 predecessor. The definition in the 2000 Act covers actual or threatened conduct involving either 'serious violence

[48] Inquiry into Legislation Against Terrorism, Cm 3420, October 1996, paras 36(9) and 36(14).
[49] *Legislation Against Terrorism, A Consultation Paper*, Cm 4178, 1998, para 7.16.
[50] Ibid, para 3.17.   [51] Ibid, para 3.15.   [52] Ibid, para 3.17.   [53] Ibid, para 3.13.

against the person' or 'serious damage to property' where, first, the design in either case is 'to influence the government or an international organization or to intimidate the public or a section of the public'[54] and, second, the purpose is to advance 'a political, religious or ideological cause'.[55] Had the definition stopped there terrorism law would have only a peripheral relationship with civil liberties, belonging more clearly to criminal than to public law. But it did not. Action was also to be regarded as terrorist if with the same intention of influence or intimidation identified above and with one or other of the same purposes it either 'endanger[ed] a person's life, other than that of the person committing the action, or 'creat[ed] a serious risk to the health or safety of the public or a section of the public'; or was 'designed seriously to interfere with or seriously to disrupt an electronic system'. Violence, much less serious violence was no longer an essential feature of the definition; it was now merely one of a number of alternate component parts. With these remarkable expansions of definition, terrorism law burst its original banks in the criminal law and overflowed in the direction of direct action, civil disobedience, and of political protest generally.

The risk to civil liberties lies not in empowering law enforcement agencies to deal with the kind of violent action that is planned by those who would engage in such criminal activity for political ends. The threat lies rather in the way in which the underlying perspective of those involved in counter-terrorism leads to their dealing with terrorism suspects in a way that is entirely different from the manner in which they treat their 'ordinary' criminal antagonists. This quasi-militaristic rather than police approach is corrosive of the entire political and legal culture that democratic and civil libertarian activists have worked so hard to create. As we shall see, the impact on aspects of the due process safeguards in our legal system has been very severe. There is a further risk as well, firmly rooted in the breadth of the definition of terrorism, of counter-terrorist action having a negative effect on political freedom which extends well beyond the actions and activities of those whom the public would recognize as terrorist according to an ordinary, popular understanding of the term. This 'chill factor' affects not only the freedom of those political activists who are brought within the definition of terrorism by the breadth of the term in the 2000 Act but also the rights of those on the margins of such groups who find their freedoms curtailed by an over-energetic reading of the law by cautious members of the police, the security or crown prosecution services. We will see examples of exactly such

---

[54] This design was not, however, required if firearms or explosives were involved: s 1(3).
[55] Terrorism Act 2000, s 1.

counter-terrorism-inspired negative effects on freedom throughout this book, many of them similar to those that occurred in relation to Irish nationalist sentiment in the 1970s and 1980s.

A further important impact of the deployment of the language of terrorism has been on the judicial branch. We saw earlier how the deference that marked the Cold War period has been replaced by a more sceptical engagement with official judgments as to what national security requires. This has been much less the case where terrorism law is concerned. Here, as we shall see, despite a few not insignificant exceptions (the Belmarsh detention case,[56] the torture decision,[57] and the early rulings on control orders[58]), the old regime of restraint has managed to survive. True, the executive perceives the judiciary to be less than supportive, but in taking this line its members may be drawing too many conclusions from just a few cases, or reacting adversely to the refusal of the senior judiciary to allow themselves to be consulted on future legislation in the field. In the chapters that follow we shall see plenty of evidence of the courts being very slow to challenge ministerial and police assumptions about what the exigencies of national security now require in this new era of alleged 'global terrorism'.[59] It is not the language of Cold War national security. But nor is it the untrammelled commitment to civil liberties that beckoned briefly in the 1990s.[60]

The three sections of this chapter are very closely linked. The health of our subject as I have defined it in this book depends on its being able effectively to manage the tensions that flow from its paradoxical need to provide exceptions to itself, its continued insistence on the legitimacy of extra-parliamentary opposition, and its determination—rooted in its violent history—not to regard all disturbances of public order as inherently wrong. The danger of the counter-terrorism discourse is that it leads to a collapse of all these tensions in the direction of security and away from civil liberties.[61] A tranquil state that is rooted in fear is not a free society. That the risks are real here and not the tactical shouts of alarmist civil libertarians is evident from the data on public attitudes to which I now turn.

---

[56] See n 31 above.

[57] *A v Secretary of State for the Home Department (No 2)* [2005] UKHL 71, [2005] 3 WLR 1249, [2006] 2 AC 221.   [58] See in particular pp 120–1 below.

[59] An important decision indicative of the change is *Secretary of State for the Home Department v Rehman* [2001] UKHL 47, [2003] 1 AC 153: see, in particular, Lord Hoffmann's 'postscript' at para [62].

[60] As tentatively suggested by me in the past: see CA Gearty, 'Civil Liberties and Human Rights'. in P Leyland and N Bamforth (eds), *Public Law in a Multi-Layered Constitution* (Oxford: Hart Publishing, 2003), ch 14.

[61] An especially disturbing decision is *R (Gillen) v Metropolitan Police Commissioner* [2006] UKHL 12, [2006] 4 All ER 1041.

CONTEMPORARY ATTITUDES TO
CIVIL LIBERTIES AND TERRORISM

Conducted during the summer of 2005, this survey amounted to the most comprehensive examination to date of British public attitudes to civil liberties and terrorism.[62] The analysis of the data that follows, inevitably highly selective from the large amount of material that the team accumulated, focuses on two main areas. The first illustrates and then seeks to explain the changes in attitudes to civil liberties that have occurred over the past 20 years. The second looks specifically at attitudes to civil liberties in the light of the threat of terrorism, and shows to what extent the public are willing to 'trade-off' various civil liberties to tackle the threat of terrorism. The results make challenging reading for all civil libertarians.

One of the most important issues looked at in the survey concerned which rights people believed to be important for the democratic health of the country. The question posed was:

There are different views about people's rights in a democratic society. On a scale of 1 to 7, where 1 is not at all important and 7 is very important, how important to democracy is it that **every** adult living in Britain has . . .

. . . the right to protest against government decisions they disagree with?

. . . the right **not** to be detained by the police for more than a week or so without being charged with a crime?

. . . the right to keep their life private from government?

. . . the right **not** to be exposed to offensive views in public?

. . . the right to a trial by jury if they are charged with a serious crime?

. . . the right to say whatever they think in public?

As shown in Table 3.1, on each of these there were very high proportions of people deeming them to be important. Indeed, for all of them, bar the right to say whatever they think in public, a majority of people think they are very important. Interestingly, the right of every adult to say whatever they think in public, which it can be assumed people saw as essentially an unqualified free speech right by another name, received lower levels of support than the right *not* to be exposed to offensive opinions. There was also, comparatively, low significance attached to the right not to be detained by police without charge—something that has been the subject

[62] M Johnson and CA Gearty, 'Civil Liberties and the Challenge of Terrorism'. in A Park, J Curtice, K Thomson, M Phillips, and M Johnson (eds), *British Social Attitudes. The 23rd Report* (London: Sage Publications, 2007), ch 7. This section draws heavily on that chapter. Thanks go to the Economic and Social Research Council, whose support made the survey possible.

Table 3.1 Proportions viewing different rights as important or not important to democracy

		Not important	Important
Trial by jury if charged with serious crime	%	1	88
Protest against government decisions	%	3	73
Keep life private from government	%	5	67
Not to be exposed to offensive views in public	%	8	64
Not to be detained by police for more than a week or so without being charged with a crime	%	10	56
Say whatever they think in public	%	10	47
Base: 1075			

Note: in this table 'not important' includes those who answered 1 or 2 on the scale, 'important' includes those who answered 6 or 7 on the scale.

of sustained debate in recent years and particularly in the first months of 2005—just before the survey interviews took place.

The results in the table show no real pattern, and it is not the case that the political freedoms are seen as more important than, say, criminal justice protections. Rather than there being an overarching structure, it seems that people take each one on its own merits. But, what is clear is that there is a very strong commitment among the public to each of them with much larger proportions thinking they are important than not.

So far so good from a general civil libertarian perspective—and, of course, these questions ranged beyond the remit of this book to cover a far wider range of civil liberties than I am concentrating on here. But to understand the findings properly it is important to know about the past. The nature of public attitudes to civil liberties is something of an under-studied area. In particular very little is known about *changes* in these public attitudes. A notable exception can be found in the twelfth *British Social Attitudes* report from 1995 (Table 3.2). Back then Brooke and Cape found that attitudes across a range of civil liberties were becoming less libertarian over time. To what extent has that trend continued during the course of the past 20 years? Focusing now on the remit of this book in particular—political freedom—the question asked was as follows:

There are many ways people or organizations can protest against a government action they strongly oppose. Please show which you think should be allowed and which should not be allowed by ticking a box on each line.

Organising public meetings to protest against the government

Organising protest marches and demonstrations

There were four response categories of 'definitely should be allowed', 'probably should be allowed', 'probably should not be allowed', and 'definitely

Table 3.2 Attitudes to the right to protest against the government, 1985–2005

		1985	1990	1994	1996	2005
% saying 'definitely should be allowed'						
Public protest meetings	%	59	62	48	54	51
Protest marches and demonstrations	%	36	39	30	31	39
Base		1530	1197	970	989	860

should not be allowed'. On public meetings, 84 per cent of people thought that it should definitely or probably be allowed, and on the latter 73 per cent felt that way—overwhelming support for the right to take such action. Whether or not this is a move away from civil libertarianism depends very much on one's point of reference. Compared to 1985, views now on protest meetings are less civil libertarian, but compared to 1994 they are no different. Views on protest marches are as civil libertarian as they were in 1985, but *more* civil libertarian than they were in 1994.[63]

An alternative, and perhaps better, test of support for political liberty is how people view the rights of extremists. If people value such freedom for its own sake, then they should also agree with them for people with views different to their own.[64] To the extent that it can be assumed most people do not want to overthrow the government by revolution, the following question, with the same answer categories as before, is an effective one for this purpose:

There are some people whose views are considered extreme by the majority. Consider people who want to overthrow the government by revolution. Do you think such people should be allowed to . . .

. . . hold public meetings to express their views?

. . . publish books expressing their views?

Perhaps unsurprisingly, and anticipating the survey's findings on terrorism, there is much less commitment to civil liberties where the rights of revolutionaries are concerned. On holding meetings, the majority (52 per cent) believe they should *not* be allowed; on publishing books, 44 per cent believe it should *not* be allowed. Indeed, a mere 16 and 15 per cent, respectively felt they definitely should be allowed. As Table 3.3 shows, the proportion now saying they definitely should be allowed is the lowest that

[63] One obvious explanation for the difference between this and the other civil liberties asked about might be the proliferation of protests that took place before and around the time this survey was conducted, against policies that many people have much sympathy with, such as the Iraq War and inaction on world poverty.

[64] See G Evans, 'In Search of Tolerance', in A Park, J Curtice, K Thomson, L Jarvis, and C Bromley (eds), *British Social Attitudes: the 19th Report* (London: Sage Publications, 2002).

Table 3.3 Attitudes to the rights of revolutionaries, 1985–2005

		1985	1990	1996	2005
% saying 'definitely should be allowed'					
Hold public meetings	%	27	21	18	16
Publish books	%	27	21	21	15
Base		1530	1197	989	860

has ever been seen in *British Social Attitudes* surveys, and is about two-thirds of the proportion who held that view in 1985. Interestingly, as before, the change in attitudes to public meetings occurred between the mid-1980s and the mid-1990s, but there has been no large change since. When it comes to publishing, similar declines occurred before and after the mid-1990s. Further, these differences over time are not accounted for by an increase in the proportion thinking that they *probably* should be allowed. The combined proportion of these two groups has fallen from 52 per cent in 1985 to 42 per cent now on holding public meetings and from 64 per cent in 1985 to 47 per cent now on publishing books.

It seems unlikely that the rate of ageing has been sufficiently fast to account for all of the observed changes in attitudes to civil liberties, and indeed other findings (not set out here) show that some of the age differences were minimal in any case. One other strong contender to explain the trends the survey detected could be the changes in the way political parties have discussed the matters, and the lead they have subsequently given to the population generally, and their followers more specifically. Certainly from about the early 1990s, when Labour began consciously to echo the then Conservative government's rhetorical perspective on law and order, there has been a shared approach to the subject which has been much less civil libertarian than in the past. Fewer civil libertarian interventions have come from leading mainstream political figures: rather the reverse in fact, with both parties seeking to outbid each other as far as anti-civil libertarian initiatives have been concerned. This has had an impact on political as well as other civil liberties. Table 3.4 shows how the views of party supporters have changed over the 20 years in question on the right to hold public meetings.

The change among Labour supporters is startling, with the proportion thinking that public meetings should definitely be allowed declining from 67 per cent back in 1985 to 45 per cent now. Indeed, there has been a 15 point decline since 1996, the year before Labour was elected to government. In contrast, and most surprisingly, Conservative supporters have become *more* inclined over this period to express support for this position, rising from

Table 3.4 Change over time in proportion of party supporters thinking that public meetings to protest against the government should definitely be allowed

Public meetings definitely should be allowed	Year								
	1985	Base	1990	Base	1996	Base	2005	Base	Difference 1985–2005
% All	59		62		54		51		−8
% Conservative supporters	50		50		48		59		+9
% Labour supporters	67		72		60		45		−22
% Liberal Democrat supporters	71		73		55		59		−12
% Not party supporter	36		55		41		42		+8

one in two in 1985 to just under three in five now. This shift in Conservative attitudes may, however, be related to the Party having been out of power for nearly 10 years when these attitudes were surveyed. Whether this is the case or not, the fact is that these changes mean that the difference between supporters of these two parties has completely reversed—in 1985 Labour supporters were 17 points more likely than Conservatives to hold this view, whereas now Conservative supporters are 14 points more likely than Labour supporters to take this position. Table 3.4 also shows that supporters of the Liberal Democrats have become less likely over the 20 years to support public meetings, whereas those with no party affiliation have become more likely to.

On freedom of expression for revolutionaries the proportions of supporters of all parties who think it should definitely be allowed have declined. However, the support among Labour sympathizers for the pro-civil liberties position has fallen by roughly twice as much as it has for Conservative supporters, on both of these questions. In 1985, 34 and 33 per cent of Labour supporters held the view that meeting and publishing, respectively should definitely be allowed; now these proportions are 17 and 21 per cent. The proportion of Conservative supporters with such views in 1985 was 19 and 21 per cent; respectively; now it is 12 and 14. Liberal Democrat supporters are now the most in favour of these rights, with 21 and 22 per cent thinking they should definitely be allowed. All of this is again suggestive of the important role of political parties' positions in determining their supporters' views.

Table 3.5 Views on civil liberties by views on the risk of terror attack

	People exaggerate risks of major terrorist attack	
	Agree %	Disagree %
% definitely allow public meetings to protest against government	54	51
% definitely allow protest marches	45	36
% definitely allow revolutionaries to hold public meetings	23	13
% definitely allow revolutionaries to publish books	22	12
Base	192	555

Apart from population ageing and party political change, a third possible cause for this discernible hardening of attitudes on civil liberties is the increased risk of terrorism and the belief that the threat needs to be countered by more draconian legislation. Unfortunately the survey's data can only partially answer this because people were not asked about their fears of terrorism in surveys prior to this, and therefore its relationship to views on civil liberties cannot be tracked over time. It is possible, however, to observe the relationship between fear of terrorism and views on civil liberties. In the survey those questioned were asked to say how much they agreed or disagreed with the following:

People exaggerate the risks of there being a major terrorist attack in Britain.

Overall, 22 per cent of people agree, 43 per cent disagree, and 20 per cent disagree strongly. As Table 3.5 illustrates, on each of the questions about civil liberties, those people who thought that the risks of a terrorist attack were exaggerated were more likely to take the more civil libertarian line on each of the issues. So, for example, 23 per cent of those who think the terrorist threat is exaggerated think revolutionaries should definitely be allowed to hold public meetings, compared to only 13 per cent of those who do not think the terrorist threat is exaggerated. (Of those people interviewed before 7 July, more agreed that people exaggerated the risk of a terrorist attack than disagreed—44 per cent compared to 39 per cent. In contrast 20 per cent of those interviewed after July 7 agreed with that proposition whilst 68 per cent disagreed.)

Here is a hint of the possible impact that fear of terrorism has on the public's commitment to civil liberties. In the context of this chapter the really interesting question is as to how much political freedom are people willing to concede once the issue of terrorism has been explicitly raised. In the survey, those questioned were asked a series of eight questions with the following set up:

A number of measures have been suggested as ways of tackling the threat of terrorism in Britain. Some people oppose these because they think they reduce people's freedom too much. Others think that the reduction in freedom is a price worth paying.

People were presented with four answer options to choose from:

Definitely unacceptable as it reduces people's freedom too much

Probably unacceptable as it reduces people's freedom too much

Probably a price worth paying to reduce the terrorist threat

Definitely a price worth paying to reduce the terrorist threat

Table 3.6 shows the wording for each of the measures and the balance of opinion on each. There are vast differences in the proportions viewing the various measures as a price worth paying or as unacceptable. However, only two of the eight measures have a clear majority who think they are unacceptable: torture and the suggestion to ban peaceful protests and demonstrations.[65] Two measures show a fairly even split among the public—banning free speech and denying a trial by jury to people charged with terrorist-related crimes. The four remaining measures have large majorities of people believing that they are a price worth paying, despite the quite fundamental change to the way of life in Britain that they would entail. The three measures that have the highest proportions believing them to be a price worth paying are for people merely *suspected* of involvement in terrorism.

For four of the questions the survey was able to observe the role that the mention of terrorism appeared to have on people's views. Earlier in this section I showed the survey's results with regard to attitudes to various civil liberties without mentioning terrorism, and also the perspective of those questioned on the importance for democracy of various rights. By comparing answers to the questions here that tap these issues with answers to the questions discussed earlier, the survey can be seen to provide suggestive evidence about the effect that presenting them as measures to counter terrorism has on attitudes. This shows that of those people who thought that protest marches against a government action should

---

[65] It is likely that these two are rejected for rather different reasons—torture would seem to be the ultimate infringement on a person's freedom and many would argue is useless in obtaining reliable information, whereas in contrast banning protests would seem to be rather tenuously linked to combating terrorism.

Table 3.6 Proportions viewing anti-terrorist measures as unacceptable or a price worth paying

	Unacceptable %	Price worth paying %
Torturing people held in British jails who are suspected of involvement in terrorism to get information from them, if this is the only way this information can be obtained.	76	22
Banning certain peaceful protests and demonstrations.	63	35
Denying the right to trial by jury to people charged with a terrorist-related crime.	50	45
Banning certain people from saying whatever they want in public.	46	52
Having compulsory identity cards for all adults.	26	71
Allowing the police to detain people for more than a week or so without charge if the police suspect them of involvement in terrorism.	20	79
Putting people suspected of involvement with terrorism under special rules, which would mean they could be electronically tagged, prevented from going to certain places, or prevented from leaving their homes at certain times.	18	80
Following people suspected of involvement with terrorism, tapping their phones, and opening their mail.	17	81

Base: 1058.

definitely be allowed, 20 per cent thought that banning certain peaceful protests and demonstrations to help tackle the threat of terrorism was probably a price worth paying. Similarly, of those who thought that the right to protest against government decisions was important for democracy, 31 per cent thought that banning protests was a price worth paying. Related to this, 43 per cent of those people who thought that it was important for democracy that every adult in Britain had the right to say whatever they think in public, also thought that banning certain people from saying whatever they want in public was a price worth paying to tackle the threat of terrorism. On being held without charge, of those who disagreed that the police should be allowed to question suspects for up to a week without access to a solicitor, 54 per cent felt that the police should be able to hold *terror* suspects for more than a week or so without charge.[66] It is also possible to compare views on trial by jury according to whether terrorism is mentioned. Of those people who thought that it was important for democracy that every adult had the right to a trial by jury, 44 per cent thought denying it to terror suspects was a price worth paying. It is clear that, for these four measures at least,[67] there is suggestive evidence that presenting retractions of certain civil liberties as a means to counter terrorism has the effect of increasing the proportion of people who are prepared to accept them. Related to this is the role fear and experience of terrorism has on attitudes to these trade-offs, where it might be expected that those with more fear would be more willing to think limiting freedom to be a price worth paying.

CONCLUSION

The question posed by the data generated by this survey is whether the progressive trend it reveals is now capable of being put in reverse. The survey findings show that there has been a marked decline in societal commitment to civil liberties in the course of the past 20 to 25 years, and that this is not capable of being explained away by age, party affiliation, or education.[68] The extent to which this decline has been influenced by a growing fear of terrorist attack is difficult to gauge accurately in the absence of figures from earlier surveys. But what can be said with confidence is that the general public is both generally less convinced about civil liberties than they were 25 to 30 years ago and reasonably willing these days to contemplate the giving up of freedom where this can be presented as necessary in order to defeat terrorism. The findings are clear that where a change can be presented as necessary in this way then public acceptability will be that much higher. It may be that this reflects the assumption of those surveyed that suspected terrorists (rather than suspected criminals) are always going to be other people and so it is not their own freedom that they are sacrificing but rather that of people who are already in some ways of doubtful ethical provenance. But the fact remains that the label

---

[66] Clearly, the two questions do ask about slightly different concepts—without access to a solicitor compared to without charge, so it may be that people assume the terror suspects have access to a solicitor, which is why they are more likely to view it as acceptable.

[67] For our findings on identity cards see 'Civil Liberties and the Challenge of Terrorism', n 62 above, Table 7.11 (note that an errata slip has been issued with regard to this table, indicating that the word 'agree' in the table should be 'disagree').

[68] The last of these is not dealt with here: see ibid, p 162.

'counter-terrorism' does carry this strongly exculpatory dimension, inoculating its contents from a civil libertarian attack that might otherwise be thought to be devastating.

The temptation this offers to political leaders is obvious. There have been many examples of pieces of legislation passed in the aftermath of a terrorist atrocity which have contained powers dealing with far more than the specific terrorist problem that has generated the perceived need for immediate legislative action. If they care about preserving Britain's civil libertarian culture, politicians of all parties need to be disciplined about their deployment of the counter-terrorism card in public debate: it is a trump certainly, but overplayed it has the potential completely to distort the whole game. There are lessons in the survey for the civil liberties groups as well. The arguments for the importance of human rights and civil liberties cannot be taken as read: they need to be articulated and then repeated. It is not any longer enough (if it ever were enough) merely to say that human rights law demands this or that our commitment to civil liberties requires that. The survey shows a general public that remains on the whole committed to civil liberties, albeit with less enthusiasm than in the past and with a greater susceptibility to be persuaded to dispense with them. It is as though society is in the process of forgetting why past generations thought these freedoms to be so very important. Like the secular grandchildren of devout church-going believers, they know they should care and want to for the sake of their own offspring but cannot for the life of them articulate why. Civil libertarians need to re-evangelize the British public if they want to turn the graph back in what they would say (and many would agree) would be the right direction. But politicians need also to be part of the more mature discussion of civil liberties and the threat of terrorism that Britain now requires if it is to come through its current anxieties with the graph of freedom continuing on its traditional upward trajectory.

Part II

The Substance of Civil Liberties Protection

4

The Right to Vote

The right to vote is the most important of all the civil liberties possessed by an individual in a representative democracy. It marks a temporary endpoint in the process of debate and discussion that is the hallmark of a free society, the moment at which the voter puts to use the information, feelings, and instincts that the fact of his or her situated humanity and which the exercise of other freedoms has allowed him or her to accumulate. The multiple exercise of the individual right to vote creates the assembly of law-makers whose collective will is thenceforth to determine right from wrong, justice from injustice, and the sensible from the irrational. The job of such an assembly is to sketch out the truth of the moment on a canvas with tools provided by the very people who are the subjects of the drawing. The effect of the exercise of an individual right to vote is not necessarily precisely to choose one's rulers (a preferred candidate and/or party can be defeated) but rather to participate in the process of electing a government that is, broadly speaking, representative of the people. It is hard to imagine a civil libertarian culture without the right to vote, just as it has always been obvious that the right to vote without the support of the other civil liberties is bound to be a sham. The two exist in a necessary symbiosis, operating together to produce a system of representative decision-making which is open-minded about the content of the choices that are made, the shape of the drawing on the community canvas, but fervently determined that whatever is put down there should be done by the right artists, be the result, to shake free of metaphor, of a proper, democratic process.

The emergence of this kind of civil libertarian culture in the UK took centuries of hard graft, determination and, quite frequently, a fair degree of bloodshed. The idea of a representative assembly has been around for centuries but that this 'house of commoners' should exercise full legislative authority in the country at large is still not entirely accepted. It is true that the Royal assent to proposed legislation has become unimportant because it is now routinely supplied, with the monarch of the moment being under a strong constitutional (although not strictly legal) duty to sign into law whatever is put before him or her, regardless of what the magisterial view of the measure might be. But the House of Lords has proved more resistant to democratic neutering, its reduction in power and status being even today a subject of ongoing debate and discussion. What is clear is that its co-equal status with the House of Commons is long gone; the crisis over Lloyd George's budget of 1909 (with the truncation of the House of Lords' powers that followed in the Parliament Act 1911) saw to that. But even after its conclusive victory over the Crown in 1689, the House of Commons itself has only gradually—and often against the will of many of the membership at any particular point in time—become truly representative. Highlights on the journey to democracy have included the Representation of the People Act 1832 ('the Great Reform Act'), and further, similarly focused pieces of legislation in 1867, 1918, and 1948. It was only in 1928 that women were permitted to vote on the same basis as men, and various entitlements to vote more than once because of one's business interests or status as a graduate were finally removed as late as 1948.

Of course, it could be argued that the House of Commons has secured power only almost immediately to lose it overseas—to the Council of Europe with its European Court of Human Rights, to the EU with its European Court of Justice, and to the forces of globalization with their powerful international organizations, their world trade courts, and the like. I confront the implications of these important post-national trends later in this book. But for now I need to make the technical but not unimportant point that the Parliament of the UK is as a matter of law still entirely sovereign over its part of the world; a decision to withdraw from any of Britain's various international commitments might be unthinkable from a political point of view but that is no reason for saying such a resolution could not legally be made. The concept of legislative supremacy is at the apex of civil liberties,[1] an exposition on it not required in a book like this perhaps but nevertheless as vital to the effectiveness of the right to vote as are the secondary civil liberties that lead up to the moment of political choice. The latter make the vote possible; the former makes it worth casting.

THE UNIVERSALITY OF THE RIGHT TO VOTE

As the version of civil liberties developed in this book demands, the right to vote is secured by law for everybody, or at least in the UK context all those who are registered in the register of parliamentary electors for any given constituency; who are not subject to any legal incapacity to vote (on which more in a moment); who are either Commonwealth citizens or

[1] See *R (Jackson) v Attorney-General* [2005] UKHL 56, [2006] 1 AC 262.

citizens of the Republic of Ireland; and who are on the date of the poll aged 18 years or over. As a result of recent changes, British citizens resident outside the UK may now vote—in the constituency in which they were last registered as an elector—for a period of 15 years after they leave. This last expansion was controversial when it was introduced but appears no longer to attract the partisan comment that surrounded it in its early days. It is clearly potentially destabilizing to have an election outcome determined by absentee voters; however, the matter is one of judgement for the elected authorities of the day and would not seem to engage any issue of direct, civil libertarian principle in the sense in which I have defined the term for the purposes of this book.

The same is true of the current lively discussions over the right age at which to allow young people to vote—the answer will be found within the realm of political judgement and will not flow from any supposed civil libertarian imperative. This is also the case with the question of precisely which voting system is adopted: as long as the outcome is broadly representative, civil liberties takes no view on the merits of this or that method of achieving the required outcome. Thus the European Commission of Human Rights was surely right to resist efforts to have the 'first-past-the-post' system used in British parliamentary elections declared a breach of human rights, in particular the obligation on states (in Article 3 of the First Protocol) 'to hold free elections at reasonable intervals by secret ballot, under conditions which will ensure the free expression of the opinion of the people in the choice of the legislature':[2] this is a matter of constitutional law rather than of civil libertarian (or human rights) principle.

The important question that does arise from a civil libertarian perspective relates to the nature of the incapacities that can lead to a disenfranchisement. This is a serious matter, as there has to be a strong presumption of involvement on the part of each of those with a *prima facie* right of participation. Most of the exceptions are non-contentious. Peers with seats in the House of Lords, individuals convicted of corrupt or illegal practices at elections and persons whose mental or physical incapacity means they cannot understand what they are doing are all denied the right to vote. So, too, are aliens, but with opportunities for naturalization in place those of such persons with strong associations with the country have the chance to join in the electoral process if they so desire. More problematic is the disenfranchisement of all convicted prisoners, with the blanket nature of this bar having been the subject of a successful challenge in the European Court of Human Rights in Strasbourg. At the end of the last paragraph,

---

[2] *The Liberal Party and Others v United Kingdom* (1980) 4 EHRR 106.

I quoted the text of Article 3 of the First Protocol, and true to its civil libertarian roots, the Strasbourg court has interpreted this guarantee as one that 'enshrines a characteristic of an effective political democracy', one so important that it extends not only to parliamentary but also to European elections.[3] In an early case on the Article, the first that it heard, the court was unequivocal that the right was 'of prime importance in the Convention system'.[4] Against the background of cases like these, the long-established rule against convicted-prisoner voting in British general elections was always likely to run into difficulty in Strasbourg.

'Civic death' has been a feature of the criminal process in England and Wales since the time of Edward III. In 2000, the Representation of the People Act relaxed the ban for remand prisoners and unconvicted mental patients while continuing it for all convicted prisoners. As subsequently explained to the Strasbourg court, the rationale behind maintaining the rule was both 'to prevent crime and punish offenders' and at the same time to enhance 'civil responsibility and respect for the rule of law "by depriving those who have seriously breached the basic rules of society of the right to have a say in the way such rules are made for the duration of their sentence" '.[5] The government was sufficiently confident of the legitimacy of the prohibition to make a statement of compatibility with the European Convention on Human Rights (under s 19 of the Human Rights Act 1998) when it first put before Parliament the Bill that was to become the 2000 Act. In *Hirst v The United Kingdom*,[6] the applicant was a long-serving prisoner who together with two other inmates had failed in his effort to persuade the UK courts that the prohibition was a breach of his Convention-guaranteed right to vote. Noting that practice varied across Europe, the Court of Appeal had stressed the need to 'afford some leeway to the legislator' and when the issue came before it had found the question of prisoner voting to be 'plainly a matter for Parliament not for the courts'.[7]

This has been a disappointing decision, at a number of levels. The British appeal judges had shown no real appreciation of the importance of this particular right to the working effectiveness of the UK parliamentary system and as a result they had failed to approach the matter with any kind of principled presumption in favour of the entitlement to vote. The way the court expressed its deference to the legislature by a finding of no-breach ignored the fact that that deference would have been inherent

---

[3] *Matthews v United Kingdom* (1999) 28 EHRR 361. The quote is at para [42].
[4] *Mathieu-Mohin and Clerfayt v Belgium* (1987) 10 EHRR 1, para [47].
[5] *Hirst v The United Kingdom* (2004) 38 EHRR 825, para [42].   [6] Ibid.
[7] *R (Hirst) v Secretary of State for the Home Department* [2002] EWHC 602 (Admin), [2002] 1 WLR 2929.

even in a ruling the other way: it was common ground that the best the prisoner applicants could have hoped for was a non-enforceable declaration of
incompatibility, leaving Parliament the last say whatever the outcome of
the case. Finally, and perhaps most disturbingly, the court's insensitivity to
the civil libertarian dimension to the case was matched, perhaps even
exceeded, by its lack of feel for quite how vulnerable the prisoner community is in a majoritarian system of government, especially one with strong
populist and authoritarian tendencies that make displays of liberal pro-
gressiveness towards disliked minorities highly risky, even for otherwise
sympathetically minded politicians. Here is a case in the English courts,
not the last that we will come across in this book, in which the centrality of
the democratic/civil libertarian issue at stake was not given the attention
it deserved, at least partly because of the confusion sown by the needless
breadth of our subject, the multiplicity of meanings that are accorded to it
(from most of which I have sought in Chapter 2 to shake free).

Fortunately for the coherence of the linkage between theory and practice, and as already anticipated, the European Court of Human Rights
took a more robust view when the matter came before it. The precise
objectives behind the ban were unpicked with particular rigour. Early
decisions by both the court and the now defunct European Commission
had already 'emphasized in a number of different contexts that the fact
that a convicted prisoner is deprived of his liberty does not mean that he
loses the protection of other fundamental rights in the Convention, even
though the enjoyment of those rights must inevitably be tempered by the
requirements of his situation'.[8] The 'loss of the right to vote play[ed]
no overt role in the sentencing process in criminal cases in the United
Kingdom'[9] and, furthermore, there was 'no clear, logical link between the
loss of vote and the imposition of a prison sentence, where no bar applies
to a person guilty of crimes which may be equally anti-social or "unciti-
zen-like" but whose crime is not met by such a consequence'.[10] In fact
there was 'much force' in the argument 'that removal of the vote in fact
runs counter to the rehabilitation of the offender as a law-abiding member
of the community and undermines the authority of the law as derived
from a legislature which the community as a whole votes into power'.[11]

Although like the English court of appeal, the Strasbourg court recognized that there was some need for a margin of appreciation in this area,
particularly in light of 'the divergences existing in the law and practice
within Contracting States',[12] it was nevertheless disinclined entirely to

[8] *Hirst*, n 5 above, para [44].   [9] Ibid, para [45].   [10] Ibid, para [46].   [11] Ibid.
[12] Ibid, para [40].

exempt the British law from the usual test of proportionality. Here was the main difference with their colleagues in London. The provision before it was one which:

strips of their Convention right to vote a large category of persons (over 70,000) in a manner which is indiscriminate. It imposes a blanket restriction on all convicted prisoners. It applies automatically to all such prisoners, irrespective of the length of their sentence and irrespective of the nature or gravity of their offence.[13]

Noting that there was 'no evidence that the legislature in the United Kingdom ha[d] ever sought to weigh the competing interests or to assess the proportionality of the ban as it affects convicted prisoners',[14] the court declared itself reluctant to 'permit restrictions on the right to vote which have not been the subject of considered debate in the legislature and which derive, essentially, from unquestioning and passive adherence to a historic tradition'.[15] As 'the indispensable foundation of a democratic system', it was clear that '[a]ny devaluation or weakening of [the right to vote] threaten[ed] to undermine that system' and that the right 'should not be lightly or casually removed'.[16] International law increasingly treated the right to vote as important,[17] there was a well-argued Canadian case in favour of the right,[18] and the UK had been too blithe in its assumption that the ban could remain in place.

Despite its unanimous ruling against the UK, it is important if dispiriting to note that it was clearly not the court's intention to say that the Convention mandated provision of the right to vote to all convicted prisoners. The case is more one of a 'super due process' sort, with the lack of careful thought and reflection at the legislative stage being what had really caught the court's critical eye. The judges were not inclined to 'speculate as to whether the applicant would still have been deprived of the vote even if a more limited restriction on the right of prisoners to vote had been imposed, which was such as to comply with the requirements of Article 3 of Protocol No 1'.[19] Following the judgment, handed down on 30 March 2004,[20] the UK government has now embarked on a period of consultation

---

[13] *Hirst*, n 5 above, para [49].   [14] Ibid, para [51].   [15] Ibid, para [41].   [16] Ibid.
[17] For example, International Covenant on Civil and Political Rights, Article 25, the European Prison Rules (1987, Recommendation R (87) 3 Council of Europe), and the Code of Good Practice in Electoral Matters adopted by the European Commission for Democracy through Law on 5–6 July 2002, to each of which the court drew attention at the start of its judgment in *Hirst*: see ibid, paras [22]–[24].
[18] *Sauvé v Attorney General of Canada (No 2)* [2002] 3 SCR 519, paras [25]–[27].
[19] *Hirst*, n 5 above, para [51].
[20] See further *Hirst v United Kingdom (No 2)* (2005) 42 EHRR 849. The Grand Chamber indicated that it desired to 'use this occasion to emphasise that the rights guaranteed under

as to what to do next.[21] From the civil libertarian perspective it is clear what should happen: prisoners should be given the vote, with only technical and administrative objections being valid reasons for departing from such a general rule. This is not only on account of the importance which our subject attaches to representative government but also because of its suspicion of using the removal of voting rights as a punishment. Just as no one should be an outlaw, we should strive also to ensure that no one can be turned into an uncitizen.[22] The huge numbers of incarcerated convicts in Britain—and the numbers have increased since the decision in *Hirst* was handed down—make the need for a political voice for such an unpopular group more essential than ever. MPs with large prisons in their constituencies can simply ignore the inmates at present, whereas were they a voting bloc there would be just a chance that an alternative voice to that of populist authoritarianism might be more frequently heard on the backbenches, for sensible electoral rather than idealist reasons. If a time comes when a slightly less all-embracing ban on prisoner-voting is enacted and upheld as compatible with the Convention, then it may well be that civil liberties principle and human rights law will have to agree to differ. Such divergences are inevitable, given the location of human rights in strict law administered by judges on the one hand and the firm grounding of civil liberties in constitutional principle and representative democracy on the other.

DEEPENING THE RIGHT TO VOTE

The importance of voting goes beyond the mere guarantee that those with the capacity to make a choice between candidates for election should be entitled to exercise the right. Its underlying value is as a mechanism for ensuring the election of a group of legislators who are truly representative of (or more accurately as representative as the prevailing electoral system allows) of the communities over which they are empowered to rule while at the same time being required to serve. This necessitates that the voting

---

Article 3 of Protocol No 1 are crucial to establishing and maintaining the foundations of an effective and meaningful democracy governed by the rule of law': para [58].

[21] Department of Constitutional Affairs, *Voting Rights of Convicted Prisoners Detained within the United Kingdom—the Government's Response to the Grand Chamber of the European Court of Human Rights Judgment in the case of Hirst v United Kingdom: A Consultation Paper* (CP 29/06, 14 December 2006).

[22] See *Smith v Scott (Electoral Registration Officer for the areas of Clackmannanshire, Falkirk and Stirling)* [2007] CISH 9, where the logic of the *Hirst* position is applied to Scottish elections.

decision itself be one that is taken by an elector who is acting freely and with as much information to hand as he or she desires before making his or her choice.[23] As regards the first of these, the removal of opportunities for coercion has come to be regarded as a key feature of modern democratic practice. It was for this reason that the introduction of the secret ballot was heralded (not uncontroversially at the time) as a key advance for the democratic movement, and as we have seen the European Convention on Human Rights now explicitly includes this entitlement in the bundles of obligations it imposes on states to secure an effective political democracy. The recent move in Britain towards postal and other forms of voting has been designed to counter trends in voter apathy, but there are inevitably likely to be continuing concerns about the degree to which the voter's choice can remain secret in this new, more voter-friendly era. Like the current valuable discussion of the extension of voting rights to 16-year-olds,[24] this is an issue not the less important for being peripheral to our subject.

Our second example of deepening the right to vote is directly relevant to civil liberties, engaging as it does such core issues as freedom of expression and the right of access to information. Achieving the 'free expression of the opinion of the people in the choice of legislature' has long been understood to go beyond provision of the right to vote in secret. The term 'free' in this phrase is an important one. It reminds us that the playing pitch of politics must be a level one, with no one point of view being able to claim a spurious dominance by the investment of disproportionate sums of money. Civil liberties need this support if the subject is not to be a sham one. The law on election campaigns is set out in the Representation of the People Act 1983, as amended by the 1985 Act of the same name and the Political Parties, Elections and Referendums Act 2000. The maximum expense which may be incurred by a candidate or his or her agent is presently £5,483 for a county or borough seat, plus a further 6.2p in a county constituency and 4.6p in a borough constituency for every entry in the electoral register. For a candidate in a by-election, the limit is £100,000. The 2000 Act also imposes, and this for the first time, limits on expenditure by political parties and others to promote the election of candidates; the limit for parties is £30,000 per constituency contested. A party engaged across the country in a general election can expect to be

---

[23] So election statements have been rightly held to attract qualified privilege: *Culnane v Morris and Naida* [2005] EWHC 2438 (QB).

[24] *Power to the People. The Final Report of the Power Report* (London: Power Inquiry; note this is 'The Centenary Project of the Joseph Rowntree Charitable Trust and the Joseph Rowntree Reform Trust', 2006).

allowed to spend about £20m to promote their party's electoral success. There are now also special controls on spending in election campaigns by third parties, groups drawn from business and the trades union or wedded to a single issue such as Europe or a return to hunting with dogs. Such associations are permitted without constraint to spend up to a certain (reasonably low) limit to promote their particular concerns in a way that benefits one party at the expense of another, but if they desire to do more than this then they need to register with the Electoral Commission, thereby attracting a degree of regulatory attention (and it is hoped accountability) for what they do.

Dry though the text generated by such facts and figures is, and rarely though they appear in a textbook of this sort, such matters are of vital civil libertarian concern. Of course, the priority is a vote that can be effectively cast in the sense of being physically possible and not subsequently rendered irrelevant by electoral abuse. With such a capacity for choice in place, the next demand—luxurious in earlier eras but essential today—is that each candidate offering himself or herself for election should have a fair chance of having their ideas heard, whatever means might be at their (or their friends' and supporters') disposal. Civil libertarians tend therefore to be in favour of laws that work to prevent monopolies in print and other media: they are invariably vigilant in the protection of that political pluralism without which democracy can quickly disintegrate into a choice between identical reflections of contemporary power. The mere existence of political parties—albeit clearly essential if the representative system is to produce effective as well as representative government—excites their concern, as tending to favour certain candidates to the exception of others. The purpose of constituency and national spending limits is to try to prevent such in-built advantage spinning out of control into a perpetual duopoly of established, party political power. It is also intended to stop the power of money in its tracks, to reduce the influence of wealth by truncating its capacity to promote political spokespersons to represent its interests, in other words to use its deep pocket to reproduce in a new form the 'pocket boroughs' of old, with capital now taking the place of nobility as the caller-of-shots behind the scenes.[25] There can be

---

[25] In an extreme case this can involve the making available of financial support only to candidates of a particular political party whose perspective on an issue or issues is shared by the donor, as reportedly happened with regard to Conservative parliamentary candidates before the 2005 election. That the issue of influence is not one for Right-wing parties alone is evident from the degree of influence over Labour that the trades union seek to assert on behalf of their members in return for their substantial financial support for the Party.

no greater issue for civil libertarians: what is the point of the freedoms of speech, association, assembly and the rest, indeed of the right to vote itself, if all that the process produces is a *carte blanche* for capital, with competing versions of corporate self-interest fighting it out in front of a general public increasingly estranged by the mismatch between its true wishes and those that it is subtly coerced into sanctioning at the ballot box? This is what can cause the disillusionment with the current system that has led to the direct action in flagrant violation of the law with which this book is concerned in its later chapters on due process and free speech.

The 2000 Act has made a start on a necessary democratic counter-revolution, and further laws are likely to emerge in due course, but for the civil libertarian it must be viewed only as a beginning, with far tighter controls being essential if the electoral playing field is to be rendered truly fair. Twenty million pounds does not cease to be a ridiculously large sum to be able to throw at an election campaign simply because such an amount is now legally sanctioned. It is not impossible that further movement in this progressive direction might excite the animosity of human rights law, and in particular provoke judicial rulings that such controls on expenditure amount to an illegitimate restriction on the capacity of rich persons (both natural and artificial) to speak through (paid) third parties. There is already one somewhat disturbing Strasbourg decision on the point, albeit involving a successful challenge to expenditure limits which were probably unduly low even by civil libertarian standards.[26] The horrors of what an extreme interpretation of free speech can do to democratic politics are evident to all those who have the background knowledge to trace the money-driven US system back to a handful of key decisions of the US Supreme Court in the 1970s which disembowelled tentative post-Watergate efforts at reform.[27] If reform really gets under way in Britain, and the rich are faced with a serious threat to their currently grossly disproportionate influence on the parliamentary process, civil libertarians must gird themselves to respond to the various allegations of, perhaps also even judicial rulings on, breaches of free speech and of freedom of political opinion that may follow. They should be more than happy to do this: a truly vibrant democracy will be worth the price of a few ignored declarations of incompatibility and the squeals of a handful of overly pedantic human rights lawyers.

---

[26] *Bowman v United Kingdom* (1998) 26 EHRR 1.
[27] An important one of which cases is *Buckley v Valeo* 424 US 1 (1976).

A RIGHT OF ACCESS TO TELEVISION?

British law has long prohibited political advertising on television and radio and this position has recently survived a strong legal challenge rooted in human rights.[28] In the words of Ousley J, the law was aimed at 'supporting the democratic process in a wide sense, supporting a fair framework for political and public debate and avoiding an undesirable advantage being obtained by those more able and willing to pay for advertisements in the most potent and pervasive media'.[29] The prohibition therefore 'achieve[d] a very important aim for a democracy'.[30] One area where human rights and civil liberties ought also to dovetail extremely well together is that of election party broadcasting, an important component of Britain's democratic system. The issues here are manifestly different from those engaged by political broadcasting in general. Certainly, the priority accorded free speech by human rights law would seem to point in the direction of a robust defence of the British practice of according political parties air-time on a fair basis in the period leading up to a general election. The first party election broadcasts on sound radio took place during the general election campaign of 1924 and the first televised broadcasts in 1951, with the current position being that this opportunity to speak directly to the electorate is offered to each of the major UK parties plus those of the smaller parties that field a sufficient number of candidates across the country. Yet it is here that we have seen one of the most disappointing decisions of all under the Human Rights Act 1998, a case in which the civil libertarian dimension to human rights (and, indeed, basic human rights law itself) would seem to have been completely forgotten.

The litigation arose out of the 2001 general election. The rule that applied was that a party could qualify for a broadcast if it put up 88 candidates in England, 12 in Scotland, six in Wales, and three in Northern Ireland. The anti-abortion ProLife Alliance put up enough candidates in Wales to qualify for a broadcast there, and duly submitted a tape to the broadcasting authorities. According to the Court of Appeal, it consisted mainly of 'prolonged and deeply disturbing images' of aborted foetuses: 'tiny limbs, bloodied and dismembered, a separated head, their human shape and form clearly recognizable'.[31] A different set of laws, rooted in

[28] *R (Animal Defenders International) v Secretary of State for Culture, Media and Sport* [2006] EWHC 3061 (Admin).
[29] Ibid, para [109].   [30] Ibid.
[31] *R (ProLife Alliance) v BBC* [2002] EWCA Civ 297, [2002] 3 WLR 1080, para [62] per Simon Brown LJ, and para [13] per Laws LJ.

traditional concerns about the use of these media for salacious purposes, obliged broadcasters not to transmit anything 'which offends against good taste or decency'[32] and it was on this basis that the terrestrial broadcasters refused to take the tape they were offered. An emergency application for permission to seek a judicial review having proved unavailing, the ProLife Alliance submitted two more versions of their broadcast but each was rejected on the same ground as before. Eventually, a soundtrack without any images was broadcast on 2 June, five days before polling day. The final results for Wales were later to show that the Party secured a mere 1,609 votes or 0.117% of the total votes cast in the Principality.[33]

It was against such a background of manifest electoral failure (which could in all probability not in any credible way be explained away by reference to the suppression of the pictorial election broadcast) that Britain's first leading case on the breadth of political freedom under the Human Rights Act 1998 was to emerge. The Alliance complained to the Court of Appeal about the way in which their political rights had been illegitimately truncated at a particularly important, election-oriented moment. Perhaps even to its own surprise, the group found a tribunal more than willing to listen. From the moment Laws LJ commenced his judgment, with his remark that '[t]his case is about the censorship of political speech',[34] it was obvious how the case was likely to go. The High Court judge had been 'profoundly mistaken'[35] to regard the matter as falling within the 'conventional jurisprudence' of judicial review.[36] Instead, the real question was whether the considerations of taste and offensiveness invoked by the broadcasters were a 'legal justification for the act of censorship' in which they had engaged.[37] Deference and margin of appreciation and the like were all very well in ordinary cases but here 'the court's constitutional responsibility [was] to protect political speech'.[38] His Lordship thought that considerations of taste and decency would only 'very rarely'[39] be an adequate ground for interfering with free political speech at an election time. Both Simon Brown and Jonathan Parker LJJ agreed; as Laws LJ put it (in his characteristically flamboyant way): 'the milieu [the court was] concerned with in this case, the cockpit of a general election, [was] inside the veins and arteries of the democratic process'.[40]

---

[32] Broadcasting Act 1990, s 6(1)(a); ITC Programme Code, section 1; BBC Royal Charter 1996, cl 5.1(d); BBC Producers' Guidelines, ch 6.
[33] See A Geddis, 'What Future for Political Advertising on the United Kingdom's Television Screens?' [2002] PL 615, p 618.
[34] See n 31 above, para [1].   [35] Ibid, para [44] per Laws LJ.   [36] Ibid, para [22].
[37] Ibid.   [38] Ibid, at para [37].   [39] Ibid, para [44] per Laws LJ.
[40] Ibid, para [37].

The House of Lords took an altogether more staid approach when the matter reached it.[41] Strongly influenced by an article in *Public Law* that had criticized Laws LJ and his colleagues for requiring too much of the broadcasters,[42] the majority agreed with its author that neither the BBC nor the commercial channels were 'empowered by their legal instructions to conduct the kind of full proportionality inquiry that the Court of Appeal required of them'.[43] The Court of Appeal had effectively rewritten the broadcasters' obligations to include an exception to the taste and decency requirement in the case of party election broadcasts, and this the court should not have done. The Alliance had been wrong to ask for the law on taste and decency to 'be disregarded or not taken seriously' yet this was effectively what the Court of Appeal had required.[44] The human rights dimension to the case had been overdone: there was 'no human right to use a television channel';[45] insofar as the right to freedom of expression in Article 10 applied, it was as a 'right not to have one's access to public media denied on discriminatory, arbitrary or unreasonable grounds'.[46] Insisting on taste and decency requirements was none of these things: 'there [was] no public interest in exempting [party election broadcasts] from the taste and decency requirements on the ground that their message requires them to broadcast offensive material. The Alliance had no human right to be invited to the party and it [was] not unreasonable for Parliament to provide that those invited should behave themselves.'[47] And '[o]nce one accepts that the broadcasters were entitled to apply generally accepted standards', it was not 'possible for a court to say that they were wrong'.[48]

With all respect, the approach taken here to human rights law is fundamentally misconceived. The Human Rights Act 1998 is designed to affect the way in which legislation, enacted before and after that measure, is interpreted by the courts: this is clear from s 3 with its well-known requirement that all statutes be interpreted 'so far as is possible' in a way that is compatible with Convention rights. Because everybody who relies on statute law to inform their behaviour is assumed to know this, they are expected to take it into account in exercising whatever rights, powers, or entitlements any law gives them, to understand in other words that the statute on which they rely may afterwards (if litigation results) be read differently so as to ensure Convention-compatibility. As far as public authorities are concerned, the point is driven further home by s 6(1) with its requirement

[41] [2004] UKHL 23, [2004] 1 AC 185.   [42] Geddes, n 33 above.
[43] Referring to Geddes, ibid, p 621.   [44] See n 41 above, para [52] per Lord Hoffmann.
[45] Ibid, para [57] per Lord Hoffmann.   [46] Ibid, para [58] per Lord Hoffmann.
[47] Ibid, para [73] per Lord Hoffmann.   [48] Ibid, para [79] per Lord Hoffmann.

that such bodies exercise whatever discretion they might have under this or that statute in a Convention-compatible way. The Royal prerogative is also subject to the Human Rights Act 1998, either analogously with statute or with a s 6(1) discretion, depending on the way it manifests itself in law. On this analysis the basic laws governing how both the BBC and the commercial broadcasters interpreted the 'good taste or decency' criterion should have been required to have been read, if at all possible, in a way that was consistent with Convention rights. This should then have lead to a discussion of whether the relevant provisions needed to be read down so as to accommodate the Convention's strong presumption—inspired by the civil libertarian pedigree of the document which we discussed in Chapter 2—for free political speech. This was not 'rewriting' the law, merely reworking it in an almost routine way to render it consistent with one of the Convention rights. The approach of Laws LJ and his colleagues in the Court of Appeal was right and that of the majority in the House of Lords was wrong. (The wrong turning may have been precipitated by the decision by the Alliance not to challenge the offensive material restriction on its face and to concentrate only on whether the broadcasters' discretion to refuse to transmit the material was lawful: this is like trying to win a debate by using arguments based on points you have already conceded to the opposition.)

Given that its analysis of the law was right, was the Court of Appeal also correct in its finding that Article 10 had been infringed by the way in which the broadcasters had conducted themselves in this particular case? Once again the conclusion must be that Laws LJ and his colleagues were altogether more connected with the underlying principles of human rights (and civil liberties) law than their more senior colleagues. In the Lords it was only the dissentient Lord Scott who showed any feel for the 'general election context of the Alliance's proposed programme'.[49] Of course, the proposed broadcast was likely to offend taste and decency. In some ways that was its point. The Alliance was clear that it felt it necessary that it be exempted from the taste and decency requirements. No doubt in the past those who opposed slavery or capital punishment or who promoted votes for women would also have offended taste and decency had they been offered this kind of opportunity to put their point of view to the general public. One of the central planks of the political process in a democracy is to make moral progress possible by, among other changes, a reworking of what is meant by taste and decency. Sometimes this effort at reconstruction works, sometimes it does not. Invariably, however, it falls foul of contemporary standards of right and wrong. Democracy celebrates

---

[49] n 41 above, para [97] per Lord Scott of Foscote.

such tension as—to recall Laws LJ's apt analogy—the life-blood of freedom. So it really is beside the point for Lord Hoffmann to say, for example, that 'abortion is not in this country a party political issue'[50] or that it was 'necessary to bring some degree of practicality and common sense' to the question before the court.[51] All these comments reflect is that the issue has yet to come alive, not that it should never do so. As one of the majority judges Lord Walker conceded, he could not 'regard the broadcasters . . . as having failed in their duties by not imposing the more stringent standards which might have been appropriate 50 or more years ago'.[52] To say as Lord Hoffmann does that the 'election *merely* gave [the Alliance] an opportunity to publicize its views in a way which would have been no more or less effective at any other time'[53] is to fail to appreciate how central elections are to the perpetual quarrel over truth that it is the duty of democracy to foster.

THE CIVIL LIBERTIES OF PARLIAMENTARIANS

Once the electorate has spoken and sent its representatives to Parliament, the subject of civil liberties can allow itself to take a back seat, the various privileges accorded parliamentarians (such as the freedom from arrest and the guarantee of free speech) being rightly the province of constitutional rather than civil liberties law. Two matters of civil liberties concern do arise, however, at earlier stages in the electoral process, before the democratic engine has been brought fully to life, relating to laws which seek to prevent certain persons from running for election in the first place, and then to parliamentary practices which seek to deny those duly entitled a chance to participate in the government of the nation. As far as the first of these is concerned, there is (from the civil libertarian perspective) a particularly iniquitous piece of legislation dating from Britain's quarrel with the Irish republican movement in the 1970s and 1980s. The Representation of the People Act 1981 states that 'A person found guilty of one or more offences (whether before or after the passing of this Act and whether in the United Kingdom or elsewhere), and sentenced or ordered to be imprisoned or detained indefinitely or for more than one year, should be disqualified for membership of the house of commons while detained anywhere in the British Islands or the Republic of Ireland in pursuance of the sentence or order or while unlawfully at large at a time when he would

---

[50] Ibid, para [68] per Lord Hoffmann. [51] Ibid, para [69] per Lord Hoffmann.
[52] Ibid, para [121] per Lord Walker of Gestingthorpe.
[53] Ibid, para [68] per Lord Hoffmann (emphasis added).

otherwise be so detained.' This nasty (and, note, retrospective) law was
Parliament's response to the IRA prison hunger-strikes which were to
lead to the death of 14 prisoners, and in particular to the fact that one of
their number, Bobby Sands, had been elected to the House of Commons
while on his protest and only shortly before his death. Of a piece with the
Hirst case, the legislation is further evidence of the UK's disturbing tendency to shove its prisoners out of civic sight. But it also offends civil libertarian principle by changing the rules so as to avoid ever being sent a
message—a proposed new version of truth—by the electors of a certain
constituency where those voters wish to deploy a prisoner-messenger as the
best person to convey it. Instead of designing clever ways of avoiding a
second Bobby Sands, the Parliament of 1981 might have been better advised
to wonder why it was that so many citizens were so alienated from its rule as
to vote for a dying 'terrorist-criminal' convict to join its membership.

The second civil liberties issue arises where duly elected representatives are met by procedural preliminaries which are easily negotiated by
others but which for reasons of principle and/or conscience they find
impossible to comply with. The cause célèbre is that of Charles Bradlaugh,
the Member for Northampton in the mid-nineteenth century whose
determination to represent his constituents without swearing the oath that
would compromise his atheism produced a mini constitutional crisis and
(eventually) new, more accommodating legislation. The problems that a
much later rebel, the MP for Mid-Ulster, Martin McGuinness, encountered lay not in the requirement for a belief in God but rather for commitment to the Sovereign. As the parliamentary bible Erskine May puts it with
characteristically magisterial terseness: '[b]y long custom, a Member who
had not taken the oath was entitled to all the privileges of other Members,
save salary'.[54] On 14 May 1997, however, Speaker Boothroyd ruled that, in
future, the services available to all other Members from the six Departments
of the House and beyond would not be open for use by Members who
had not taken their seats by swearing or by affirmation.[55] McGuinness
challenged this _ad hominem_ expansion of the traditional position in
Strasbourg, but his case did not get past the admissibility stage with the
court ruling there had been no breach of the right to freedom of expression or of the First Protocol provision on voting.[56] The situation persisted
until the House of Commons resolved on 18 December 2001 that, with
effect from 8 January 2002, Members who had 'chosen not to take their

[54] Erskine May, _Treatise on the Law, Privileges, Proceedings and Usage of Parliament_ (23rd
edn) (London: LexisNexis, 2004), p 286.
[55] Ibid.   [56] _McGuinness v United Kingdom_, 8 June 1999, application 39511/98.

seats' might use the facilities of the House and the service of its departments, and claim support for their costs as set out in the Resolution of 5 July 2001 relating to Members' allowances, insurance, etc and allowances for travel within the United Kingdom for Members, their families, and staff.'[57] This was a belated recognition that the electors are not to be deprived of all the services of their representative merely because of his or her refusal (accepted by those voting) not to commit to a prevailing status quo that was not integral to (and might in an earlier age have been thought subversive of) the democratic structure of the nation.

CONCLUSION

The right to vote comes first in the pantheon on political liberties because so much of our freedom depends on the capacity freely to exercise it. Of course, the right is exercised only from time to time, usually where the legislature is concerned no more than once every four to five years. But the fact of the vote casts its benign democratic shadow over all the politics that precedes it. The vote carries with it the ancillary freedoms of political expression, assembly, and association, making the case for their protection in unanswerable terms. At a more basic level, the vote enables the people to turn the government out of office, to act apparently arbitrarily, ungratefully or even (in the eyes of some) irrationally. Not only can an administration on its last legs like that of John Major's in 1997 be mercifully dispensed with but so also can one like Churchill's in 1945, the defeat of Hitler being no answer to democratic choice. During that Second World War as during the 1914–18 conflict, Parliament had been persuaded of the need to postpone general elections that would have been held had peacetime conditions prevailed. In neither case did war persist so long that a second set of elections had also to be postponed. The power of the members of the lower House to delay their date with the electorate was not controversial at the time, and it was certainly not argued that the courts had any power to strike down or overturn the enabling laws that were enacted.

It is not inevitable that this will always be the case, however. Neither the First nor the Second World Wars existed other than in bloody reality for the entire country. But the concept of war has become looser since then, with in particular (as we saw in Chapter 3) the notion of a long 'War on Terror' having come to be accepted by some elements in government. In the US, the White House perception that it is engaged in just such a

---

[57] *Treatise on the Law, Privileges, Proceedings and Usage of Parliament*, n 54 above, p 286 (footnotes omitted).

Civil Liberties

conflict has underpinned an attempt at a redefinition of the powers of the executive branch which can only tenuously be described as democratic[58] and which has already incurred the enmity of the judicial (and now increasingly also the legislative) branch.[59] Nothing like this has yet happened in the UK but the remarks on the topic of Tony Blair as Prime Minister often had a disturbing urgency to them.[60] If elections were to be postponed in Britain (whether on account of terrorism or for some other declared emergency), in an Act passed in the proper manner by Parliament and enjoying the Royal assent, what would be the position of the judiciary? The answer may vary depending on the length of the proposed delay—there is a large difference between a short deferral and an indefinite shelving amounting to a *de facto* abolition. One response, however, might be to assert that the courts have no role whatsoever in such a situation and that the theory of legislative supremacy requires that it is for the Parliament of the day and that Parliament alone to regulate the manner and form of its succession.

This takes us to the nub of the matter so far as civil liberties is concerned. If we accept that our subject is about the law and practice of political freedom and that the clearest expression of that freedom is the exclusive power of a representative assembly to enact (or authorize the enactment of) general laws, then what are we to do as civil libertarians if the Parliament of the moment uses its power quite lawfully to emasculate or to destroy the political freedom that created it (in its current shape) in the first place? The point is easier if there is a coup—here all bets are off and the judges should side with democratic authority (although they rarely do[61])—or if the courts are being invited to do no more than adjudicate on how current law applies to a disputed election—as was arguably the case in the famous *Bush v Gore* decision of December 2000.[62] Were the latter situation to arise in Britain, it seems clear that the courts would have the power to set aside an invalidly held election and order a fresh vote. This happened recently in Thailand where that country's Constitutional Court found sufficient irregularities in the April 2006 polls to lead it to annul the poll.[63] In the absence of a written constitution with broad principles to

---

[58] D Cole, 'What Bush Wants to Hear', *New York Review of Books*, 17 November 2005.
[59] *Rumsfield v Padilla* 542 US 426 (2004); *Rasul v Bush* 542 US 466 (2004).
[60] See T Blair, speech on global terrorism, 5 March 2004.
[61] For a remarkable exception see *Republic of Fiji v Prasad* [2001] 2 LRC 743. For a gripping account by one of the main legal players see G Williams, 'The Case that Stopped a Coup? The Rule of Law and Constitutionalism in Fiji' (2001) 1 *Oxford University Commonwealth Law Journal* 73. [62] 531 US 98 (2000).
[63] *The Nation* (Thailand English language newspaper), 9 May 2006. See also Turkey: 'Turkish court rules presidential vote invalid', *Guardian*, 2 May 2007.

which the judges can credibly refer, however, it is hard to see how the courts in the UK could do more than hold the executive and the legislature rigorously to account within the current law (via among other legal devices a declaration of incompatibility under the Human Rights Act). In the context of such a profound threat as the abolition of elections by legislative fiat, the protection of civil liberties becomes the non-delegable responsibility of every citizen.

5

The Prohibition on Torture and the Rights to Life and Security of the Person

Together with the prohibition on torture and on inhuman and degrading treatment, the rights to life, to liberty, to security of the person, and to procedural fairness form the very core of the law and politics of international human rights. They appear in the Universal Declaration on Human Rights, signed in 1948, and also in the International Covenant on Civil and Political Rights, agreed in 1966. The Convention on the Rights of the Child contains a version of these various rights, as do the regional human rights instruments that define the subject for the Americas and for Africa. The European Convention on Human Rights prohibits torture in absolute terms in Article 3, guarantees the right to life in Article 2, and the rights to liberty and security of the person in Article 5. Article 6 deals with the guarantee of fair proceedings. Many contemporary domestic constitutions include these rights within the human rights sections of their basic law. Their centrality to human rights is immediately obvious: as we have seen, the subject has its roots deep in the autonomy of the individual and these are the entitlements that make real the very personhood that is at the core of human identity. We need to live our lives and to enjoy our physical integrity if we are truly to flourish as individual persons.

As this book has already sought to show, the subject of civil liberties is neither identical with human rights nor clear even as to its own remit. Where do the various rights referred to in the first paragraph fit? The books that adopt a wide approach to civil liberties, of the sort that was considered and rejected in Chapter 1, find themselves discussing these freedoms in what are invariably very broad terms: the extent of the police powers that inhibit their exercise; the civil actions for assault and false imprisonment that provide a remedy against their abuse; the entitlement of prisoners to assert such basic entitlements notwithstanding their incarceration; the levels of judicial oversight of police discretion; and so on. Defined in these various general ways, our subject cannot help but drift across the whole of public law, into the realms of administrative law, criminal justice, and (at its furthest extremes) criminology and penology.

My concentration here is on the narrower remit of civil liberties as the law and practice of political freedom, and this leads us to take a different approach, one that is less general certainly but at the same time more focused than these other ways of looking at our subject.

The emphasis in this chapter, therefore, is not with these basic human rights in general terms. Rather it is with how critical these entitlements are to the creation and maintenance of that culture of political freedom on which an effective representative democracy must always depend. You cannot run a free society in a country where activists risk being shot, tortured, interned, or subjected to show trials on account of their political views, and this is regardless of how fair the periodic elections might be, how open the media is, or how uncontrolled the arena of public protest. There is not much point in having the freedoms of speech, association, or assembly if choosing to enjoy them gets you shot, tortured, or imprisoned. The right to vote is an empty guarantee when offered on such terms. These rights to life, liberty, and security of the person, and the ban on torture operate together as a set of building blocks without which an effective political democracy cannot be put into place. They are the platform upon which the rights to freedom of conscience, expression, assembly, and association depend for their effectiveness. It follows that it is not the rights in general terms with which the law of civil liberties as I construe it here is concerned; rather it is with how these freedoms are guaranteed in the political arena—or (more to the point perhaps) with how they are to be protected from being truncated in ways which inhibit the expression of political ideas or the citizen's engagement in political will-formation. I deal with liberty and due process in the next chapter; here, our concern is with the right to life and security of the person and the prohibition on torture. Of its very nature, this inquiry will often involve discussion of the discriminatory exercise of official discretion, with politically engaged persons alleging that they are being treated differently from and less well than others, solely on account of their political opinion. This is something that the many non-discrimination provisions in international human rights law (including Article 14 of the European Convention on Human Rights) are specifically designed to stop.

THE PROHIBITION ON TORTURE AND INHUMANE AND DEGRADING TREATMENT OR PUNISHMENT

In recent years the main issue with regard to torture has been the degree to which evidence allegedly obtained by such means may be used by the authorities within this country to engage in counter-terrorist activities, to investigate offences, to underpin the exercise of administrative or quasi-judicial discretion or to prosecute crime.[1] The matter is of the first importance and raises directly the general question of the extent to which civil liberties protection should be accorded to those within the jurisdiction whose political activism lies mainly or exclusively beyond these shores.[2] Within the UK there is a well-embedded intolerance of such misconduct which extends across the whole legal and political culture, incorporating civil liberties along the way. Admissions obtained as a result of such ill-treatment cannot be used in subsequent proceedings and also leave those responsible for them vulnerable to criminal and civil proceedings.[3] Under s 134(1) of the Criminal Justice Act 1988, any 'public official or person acting in an official capacity, whatever his nationality, commits the offence of torture if in the United Kingdom or elsewhere he intentionally inflicts severe pain or suffering on another in the performance or purported performance of his official duties'. Passed at the highpoint of late Thatcherism, with concern being expressed in many quarters at the time about the extent of the erosion of freedom then under way, we can see that this explicit outlawing of torture is no passing new Labour fad, with its roots lying deep not only in state practice but also in domestic (and as it happens international) law.[4]

As Chapter 3 will have led us to expect, however, the one exception to this has been in the field of counter-terrorism, where bad habits learned in the course of colonial rule were displayed in Northern Ireland in the early 1970s, to disastrous effect. Following the introduction of internment without trial in August 1969, a small group of suspected subversives were signalled out for special treatment designed to force them to reveal information it was believed they each had about the activities and personnel of the Irish Republican Army (IRA). The five techniques of sensory deprivation that were deployed against the men (wall-standing, hooding, continuous noise, deprivation of food, and deprivation of sleep) were afterwards condemned as 'inhuman and degrading treatment' and as a breach therefore of Article 3 of the European Convention on Human Rights.[5] Even if the case had gone the other way, the damage had been done. The British army's reputation for fairness and impartiality, so important to its self-confidence as a supposedly neutral peace-keeping

---

[1] See, in particular, *A v Secretary of State for the Home Department (No 2)* [2005] UKHL 71, [2006] 2 AC 221.

[2] In general terms, such engagement should be permitted as part and parcel of the open culture of the host democracy.   [3] Police and Criminal Evidence Act 1984, s 76(2) and (8).

[4] For an elaboration of this background see the speech of Lord Bingham of Cornhill in *A v Secretary of State for the Home Department (No 2)*, n 1 above, paras [10]-[14].

[5] *Ireland v United Kingdom* (1978) 2 EHRR 25.

force in Northern Ireland, was permanently shattered. The international standing of the UK was greatly reduced. And while it was not clear that any useful information had been obtained from any of the victims of the abuse, what was obvious to all was that political violence had greatly increased in the aftermath of the implementation of these internment and sensory deprivation policies. There can be little doubt that the serious mistakes made in the name of counter-terrorism in the early 1970s in Northern Ireland have been widely recognized in police and military as well as in political and legal cultures, and one of the consequences of this has been to reinforce the strong official antipathy to torture that is to be found (one hopes more than merely ostensibly) within these shores.

THE DUTY NOT TO TAKE LIFE

The civil liberties approach to the right to life stresses not only its prohibitory but also its mandatory power. It is a command to the state both not to act and to act, to forbear from threatening or taking life on the one hand, and to act to protect individual lives from the attentions of angry third parties on the other. Each has a political dimension and I shall take them in turn, dealing with the duty not to take life in this section and the duty to protect life in the next.

As far as the negative command is concerned, the issue ought to be straightforward. It is as clear as day that it is quite wrong for the state through any of its servants deliberately to take life. If it does so, as with torture there are a myriad of ways in which those responsible can be held to account. These include criminal prosecutions, civil actions, and various other disciplinary processes and state-sponsored investigations (such as an inquest). The killing of a protestor or other kind of political actor by the authorities in Britain is a major event and its infrequent occurrence is a testimony not only to the restraint of the authorities but to the depth of the taboo against this level of politically motivated violence that is presently embedded in our society.[6] It is this culture of respect for life that the rival narrative rooted in counter-terrorism threatens to dilute. As was the case with torture, the record of disquiet is rooted at present in the activities of the state in Northern Ireland, engaged in at a time of serious disorder and violent, IRA-related subversion. But what the state did then—in an altogether not-too-distant past—ought to be a reminder of the kind of

---

[6] The death of Blair Peach in Southall on 23 April 1979 is remembered to this day: for an account of the incident, see National Council for Civil Liberties, *Southall. 23 April 1979. The Report of the Unofficial Committee of Inquiry* (London: National Council for Civil Liberties, 1980).

extremist reaction into which counter-terrorism can quickly plummet. The evidence of recent events is that this is more likely with regard to the right to life than with regard to the prohibition on torture.

There are four kinds of victims of state killings that raise civil libertarian concerns germane to this book. First, there are the deaths of members of subversive organizations who are killed by the police, army, or security services in the course of a criminal action, an 'encounter killing' as Whitty, Murphy, and Livingstone usefully describe it.[7] The *locus classicus* is the shooting dead of eight IRA members (and one bystander) in Loughgall, Northern Ireland in May 1987: the dead men were in the course of attacking a police station when they were surprised by the security forces. The facts of such events will often be disputed with the authorities saying that in the circumstances an arrest was impossible and the supporters of those killed asserting that the shootings were deliberate and unnecessary. Such deaths raise civil libertarian issues to the extent that there is a suspicion that activists engaged in criminal activity have been unnecessarily killed but such incidents are usually at the margins of our subject and with an event like that of Loughgall arguably outside it altogether. That event involved politically motivated violent acts rather than the kinds of peaceful communications in which our subject specializes. The second category of state killing, the 'planned operation'[8] is of much more obvious concern. This is where the authorities set out, either directly or through intermediaries ('death squads'), to kill civilians whom they judge to be involved in terrorist activity: sometimes it is said they have been shot in the course of some criminal operation, sometimes this is not even asserted, the suspect being gunned down at a check point or (if a paramilitary group has been given the job) at their home or place of work.

The outstanding example of such grim and destructive counter-terrorism is the 'shoot-to-kill' scandal involving senior Northern Ireland police officers which became a major story in the late 1980s.[9] In one of the failed prosecutions from that period the trial judge commended the police defendants for their 'courage and determination' in bringing the three men they had shot at a police checkpoint 'to justice; in this case to the final

---

[7] N Whitty, T Murphy and S Livingstone, *Civil Liberties Law: The Human Rights Act Era* (London: Butterworths, 2001), p 139.

[8] Ibid.

[9] KD Ewing and CA Gearty, *Freedom under Thatcher* (Oxford: Oxford University Press, 1990), pp 230–5. See J Stalker, *Stalker* (London: Harrap, 1988). And for a damning report about more recent activities, see the *Statement by the Police Ombudsman for Northern Ireland on her Investigation into the Circumstances Surrounding the Death of Raymond McCord Junior and Related Matters* (22 January 2007).

court of justice'.[10] What is particularly outrageous about this judicial intervention was its failure to appreciate that such killings directly challenge the decision by Parliament to remove the death penalty. It is deeply subversive of the whole democratic process for members of the executive branch to take upon themselves the responsibility of deciding to impose a penalty on suspected criminals which the elected representatives themselves have decided to prohibit—and to do so in such cases without even the pretence of a trial. That a judge could so openly support such malignant counter-terrorism beggars belief. Much more in line with civil liberties was the extremely brave European Court of Human Rights decision in *McCann v United Kingdom*,[11] where the Strasbourg court held, albeit by the narrowest of margins,[12] that the UK had infringed the right to life of three IRA operatives by managing a counter-terrorism operation so carelessly that the soldiers on the ground had no practical alternative other than to kill the three suspects when the moment of attempted apprehension came. The suspicion in that case had been that a high-level direction to kill the suspects had come from senior figures in the government but the court did not accept that the killings were deliberate in this sense. But its ruling, reaching past the moment of shooting to address the structure of the security operation which made such fatal action inevitable, has been a very important one in the European-wide human rights law on police powers.

The third kind of victim of official killings conducted under the excusatory label of 'counter-terrorism' is one that is to be found all too often in such incidents: the entirely innocent. The aftermath of such killings share a distressing pattern. There are the initial claims of a great security success which in some versions is linked to an assertion about how an enormous terrorist calamity has been heroically foiled. There is then a period of silence before a new, humbler version of events is revealed, and various explanations offered for the mistake that it is now accepted has been made. John Stalker recounts that it was the killing by a soldier of an innocent teenager, Michael Tighe, that caused him enormous personal distress when he was first commissioned to examine controversial security force killings in Northern Ireland.[13] The world of counter-terrorism might see these fatalities as collateral damage; the civil libertarian sees them as at worst murder, at best reckless manslaughter. Shortly after the attacks on London by four suicide-bombers on 7 July 2005, the Metropolitan Police Service found itself embroiled in exactly this kind of killing

<hr>

[10] *Freedom under Thatcher*, ibid, p 233. Three years later the judge in the case, Gibson LJ, and his wife were killed by the IRA in an attack on their car when travelling through Northern Ireland.
[11] (1995) 21 EHRR 97.   [12] Ten to nine.   [13] *Stalker*, n 9 above.

when it emerged that the individual whom officers had shot at Stockwell underground station was not, in fact, a terrorist intent upon mass murder as they believed but rather an innocent Brazilian, Jean Charles de Menezes. The immensely disturbing aspect of this killing from a civil libertarian viewpoint was the emergence afterwards of the fact that the police had put in place a new 'shoot-to-kill' policy for certain of their counter-terrorism operations, Operation Stratos. The analogy with Northern Ireland was disturbingly clear. The language of counter-terrorism is what led the officers involved in the operation, from those who formulated the policy through to the officers who pulled the trigger, to believe that the ordinary law did not apply in the normal way to such suspects.[14]

We come finally to the fourth category of victim, the one closest to the core of our subject whose killing is bound to raise the greatest civil libertarian concern of all. These are those fatal victims of authority (or the agents of authority) whose only fault has been to engage in political activity or to associate as supporters or legal advisers of persons involved in or suspected of paramilitary activity. One of the reasons why the killings by the army of 13 civilians in Derry on 30 January 1972 have been immortalized as 'Bloody Sunday' surely lies in the fact that the victims had been among a large group of nationalists whose reason for having gathered together was the public protest in which they had just participated. The anxiety of the authorities in the immediate aftermath of the event was to establish that those killed had themselves been shooting at the army, to turn the event into what we would now describe as a Loughgall-style incident rather than the attack on peaceful demonstrators that it appears in truth to have been.[15] This is the context in which the killings of members of the lawful political party Sinn Féin rightly attracted civil libertarian attention in the late 1980s and 1990s: such murders were a direct assault on the democratic process which was utterly unjustified by any claim of connection (even if it was true in specific cases) between those killed and IRA paramilitary activity. The same is true of the killings of lawyers well-known in the Province for their work for (among many other clients) those suspected of involvement in IRA-related subversion. In this context it hardly matters whether the

---

[14] For another example, fortunately not fatal, see 'Intelligence behind raid was wrong officials say', *Guardian*, 6 June 2006, p 1: the story concerned a pre-dawn raid on a property in Forest Gate in London which had reportedly involved 250 officers including armed teams and government scientists.

[15] See *Report of the Tribunal Appointed to Inquire into the Events on Sunday 30 January 1972 which led to Loss of Life in Connection with the Procession in Londonderry on that Day* (Chairman: Lord Widgery) (HL 101, HC 220). For the latest and probably most authoritative official version of events we have to await the Report of the Saville Inquiry.

murder of the lawyer Rosemary Nelson in 1999 or of the solicitor Patrick Finucane in 1988 were the work of state agents directly or paramilitary groups working to their command.[16] The death of the latter followed a mere 26 days after an assertion made by a government minister under cover of parliamentary privilege that there were 'in Northern Ireland a number of solicitors who [were] unduly sympathetic to the cause of the IRA'.[17] It is to be hoped that the distinguished parliamentarian who made those comments has come to appreciate how reckless, perhaps even malicious, they were, uttered at that moment by a person of such a stature.

The counter-terrorism operations that have followed 11 September 2001 have yet to approach the levels of official impunity that were achieved during the darkest hours of the Northern Ireland conflict. It may well be that they will never do so. As we have seen the torture prohibition is well-entrenched in UK law and the strongly adverse reaction to the Stockwell killing in 2005 was an indication of how serious the general public are likely to take such deaths. On the other hand, contemporary levels of subversive violence are remarkably low and we cannot be sure what the state's response—or public opinion—would be if the current 'War on Terror' were to progress from dealing with the occasional atrocity to confronting a systematic, IRA-style campaign of violence. What is certainly true is that there are far better safeguards in place against official killings than there were in Northern Ireland (or for that matter Britain) 20, even 10 years ago. The de Menezes shooting attracted the immediate attention of an independent and properly empowered police complaints commission whose analysis of the incident has led directly to a prosecution under health and safety legislation. The state's obligation properly to investigate deaths by its agents has been transformed by the European Court of Human Rights, one of the leading cases having been the result of proceedings taken by the widow of Mr Finucane.[18] Under the influence of the Strasbourg court, the House of Lords has imposed a much wider set of duties on coroners in situations of disputed fatalities.[19] In Northern Ireland there is a police ombudsman whose current incumbent, Mrs Nuala O'Loan, has shown herself to be independent of the police in fact as well as in theory. All civil

---

[16] See *Cory Collusion Inquiry Reports into the deaths of Patrick Finucane* (HC 470), *Robert Hamill* (HC 471), *Billy Wright* (HC 472) and *Rosemary Nelson* (HC 473) (1 April 2004).

[17] For the full exchange in which this remark was uttered see Official Report, Standing Committee B, Prevention of Terrorism Bill, 17 January 1989, cols 508, 509, and 519.

[18] *Finucane v United Kingdom* (2003) 37 EHRR 656. See also *Jordan v United Kingdom* (2001) 37 EHRR 52.

[19] The leading cases are *R (Middleton) v H M Coroner for the Western District of Somerset* [2004] UKHL 10, [2004] 2 AC 182; *R (Sacker) v H M Coroner of West Yorkshire* [2004] UKHL 11, [2004] 1 WLR 796; and *Re McKerr* [2004] UKHL 12, [2004] 1 WLR 807.

libertarians must hope that these structures will be robust enough to protect democracy and the rule of law if ever the need arises for them to be defensively invoked in the name of freedom.

THE DUTY TO PROTECT

I turn now to the second of the kinds of obligations to be found in Article 2, the positive duty on the state to act to protect life. In the context of civil liberties it is useful to link this to another provision of the Convention, the Article 5 guarantee of the right to security of the person. The leading British case on the Article 2 requirement is *Osman v United Kingdom*, where the Strasbourg judges laid down their approach in the following terms:

> The Court notes that the first sentence of Article 2(1) enjoins the State not only to refrain from the intentional and unlawful taking of life, but also to take appropriate steps to safeguard the lives of those within its jurisdiction. It is common ground that the State's obligation in this respect extends beyond its primary duty to secure the right to life by putting in place effective criminal law provisions to deter the commission of offences against the person backed up by law enforcement machinery for the prevention, suppression and sanctioning of breaches of such provisions. It is thus accepted by those appearing before the Court that Article 2 of the Convention may also imply in certain well-defined circumstances a positive obligation on the authorities to take preventive operational measures to protect an individual whose life is at risk from the criminal acts of another individual.[20]

It would be fair to say that this dicta, reflecting a long and well-developed aspect of the European court's jurisprudence and now translated into UK law via a range of judicial decisions under the Human Rights Act 1998,[21] has helped greatly to improve the rights of persons threatened by criminal wrongdoing. It has been used to help prisoners, school children, and other, vulnerable, members of the general public.

In the context of civil liberties it has a particular application of the first importance. Fused with the positive obligation to ensure the security of the person in Article 5, it becomes a duty to protect the physical integrity of the purveyors of unpopular political views. The obligation arises where a person is engaged in some political act, usually involving speech and invariably held in public, which stimulates from the listening audience or spectators neither applause nor approbation but rather a level of hostility that borders on and threatens to overflow into the criminally aggressive. It may be that the speaker knew that this would be the response to his or

---

[20] *Osman v United Kingdom* (1998) 29 EHRR 245, para [115].
[21] The inquest cases, n 19 above, for example.

her words, indeed that the causing of such a reaction was exactly what the utterances were designed to achieve. Or it could be that there is no such inflammatory purpose and that the political actor has simply wandered into the wrong community at the wrong time, saying exactly the wrong sorts of things. At the other end of the spectrum, it may be that the unruly listeners have gone to some lengths to find the speaker, knowing that he or she was involved in a public event and determined to be affronted by what they knew he or she would say or do. Where do civil liberties stand in each of these sets of circumstances? There is an instinct in favour of allowing political speech to proceed, come what may. On the other hand, one of those eventualities might be the death of or at least a severe assault upon the speaker, particularly likely if he or she is greatly outnumbered by the mob. What are the police to be advised to do in such circumstances?

   The problem has frequently arisen in the past, with civil liberties scholars seeking to explain the cases within the narrow bands of freedom of expression and assembly when deployment of this fairly new-fangled idea of an obligation to protect in tandem with those rights helps greatly to clarify the issues involved. In the old case of *Humphries v Connor*,[22] the plaintiff had chosen to walk down the main street of Swalinbar County Cavan (in Ireland) sporting an emblem on her lapel that she knew would be hugely provocative to many of those who happened to be on the street at the time. Sure enough a large crowd gathered and trouble was brewing when PC Connor happened upon the incident. His way of defusing the potential trouble was to remove the offending emblem from the lady. The crowd dispersed and Mrs Humphries' subsequent action for damages was unsuccessful. The court held in favour of the officer. This was surely the right decision. The issue was not solely one of the free expression of political views. The state had also a responsibility to consider how to pro-tect the plaintiff in light of her determination to ventilate her opinion in this emblematic but provocative way. On the facts, the only way this could be done was by taking the immediate action that PC Connor took. He was on his own, the incident was an unplanned one, the police were unpre-pared, and there was no time to call for reinforcements. Neither did the 'expression' involved have any great merit, being designed simply to offend rather than to communicate a particular point of view.

   The well-known case of *Beatty v Gillbanks*[23] shows the circumstances in which the law can legitimately operate in the opposite direction. The expression of the political point of view in that case was by the Salvation Army which was determined to parade its opposition to alcoholic

---

[22] (1864) 17 ICLR 1.   [23] (1882) 9 QBD 308.

consumption in a series of lively marches accompanied by the music of the Army's brass band. In Weston Super Mare, this activity excited the hostile attentions of the local brewers who combined together to create a band of hooligans, the 'Skeleton Army' to disrupt the Salvationists. This rival army duly sought by the threat of violence to make it impossible for their opponents to engage in their public processions. Faced with this threat to order, the local magistrates ordered that the marching stop. When the Salvation Army persisted, they were judged to have been involved in an unlawful assembly and their leaders were bound over to keep the peace.

The matter came before the High Court which declared the binding over order void and insisted on the Salvation Army's right to march: the group had associated together 'for religious exercises among themselves, and for a religious revival' so it was clear that no one could 'say that such an assembly [was] in itself an unlawful one'.[24] If the procession were stopped, this was the equivalent of saying 'that a man may be convicted for doing a lawful act—there is no authority for such a proposition'.[25] In modern terms we would say that the obligation to protect the life and/or personal security of the Salvationists extended to guaranteeing their right to march, and this was for four reasons in particular, all taking them outside the facts of the *Humphries v Connor* case: first, they were expressing in a *prima facie* lawful manner a political point of view the purpose of which was not to inflame but to communicate a perspective which they hoped would prove persuasive; second, the court considered the content of their message to be designed to a laudable end; third, those opposing the processions had no goal other than to prevent their occurrence by the use of unlawful violence, a particularly extreme case of a heckler's veto; and, fourth, the law enforcement authorities had had the capacity to protect the march and had chosen not to do so—each procession had been given plenty of advance publicity; the activities of the Skeleton Army were already notorious—this was by no means a case (as *Humphries v Connor* had been) of a police constable stumbling upon an insipient riot provoked by a reckless or malicious individual. The duty to protect pointed in the direction of supporting, not subverting the Salvationists' right to freedom of expression.

If this analysis is correct it follows that *O'Kelly v Harvey* has to be regarded as wrongly decided.[26] Certainly it is a very dangerous case from a civil libertarian point of view. Decided very shortly after *Beatty*, the Irish

---

[24] (1882) 9 QBD 308, p 313 per Field J.   [25] Ibid, p 314 per Field J.
[26] (1883) 15 Cox CC 435.

Court of Appeal upheld a decision by local magistrates to ban a long-arranged meeting in the north of Ireland solely on account of the fact that an unruly gang had organized itself to attack it when it took place. All the ingredients of *Beatty* were present. The meeting was for a clear political purpose, the reform of land law in favour of tenants' rights. It was being held in a hostile part of the country, it was true, but the purpose of the occasion was to propagate a new version of the truth in unpromising territory, to evangelize rather than to inflame. There had been sufficient notice of the meeting for the local law enforcement officers to arrange for its protection: certainly they knew all about the trouble that was expected, which was why they chose to break up the meeting. It is hard to resist the conclusion that the event was being effectively banned on account of the views that it was certain to express. It was simply not enough for the Irish Lord Chancellor to say of *Beatty* that he 'frankly' admitted that he did 'not understand' the decision.[27] In modern terms, what had happened here was that the authorities had discharged their duty to protect the demonstrators in a disproportionate way, by forcing silence upon them rather than ensuring that their point of view could be heard.

The duty to protect/free speech paradigm that we can see in embryo in these nineteenth-century cases has been played out in the new statutory contexts provided by twentieth-century law. Early local legislation prohibiting inflammatory words which cause others to react with violence has been on the legislative books for generations, allowing prosecutions such as that of Pastor George Wise for anti-Catholic rabble-rousing in Liverpool in 1902.[28] Similar national legislation passed in 1936 led to the important case of *Jordan v Burgoyne* in 1963.[29] The defendant, a person of extreme Right-wing views, addressed a crowd of some 5,000 people at a public meeting in Trafalgar Square. A group of 200–300 young people, mainly communists, members of the Jewish faith, and advocates of nuclear disarmament, were gathered immediately in front of the speakers' platform. They were aggressively hostile to all those who were participating in the meeting. When the defendant used words in his speech which were particularly offensive to this group, there was complete disorder, an outcry, and a general surge forward by the crowd. The defendant was afterwards convicted under the relevant provision (s 5 of the Public Order Act 1936), and this was upheld in the divisional court. He had engaged in no acts of violence himself: his offence lay in the fact that what he had chosen to say caused others to react in a criminal manner.

---

[27] Ibid, p 446 per Law LC.   [28] [1902] 1 KB 167.   [29] [1963] 2 QB 744.

Speaking for a unanimous court, Lord Parker CJ held that every such
speaker was required to take his or her audience as he or she found it:

[I]f in fact it is apparent that a body of persons are present—and let me assume in
the defendant's favour that they are a body of hooligans—yet if words are used
which threaten, abuse or insult—all very strong words—then that person must
take his audience as he finds them, and if those words to that audience or that part
of the audience are likely to provoke a breach of the peace, then the speaker is
guilty of an offence.[30]

It may be that his Lordship is expressing his ruling in the case in unduly
wide terms. The defendant here was clearly engaged in provocation rather
than communication, at least as far as the angered part of the audience was
concerned. The police might have judged that the only plausible way of
ensuring the speaker's safety (and the safety of others) was by asking him
to desist and then arresting him when he refused. On the other hand, there
is the undoubted fact that the group agitated to violence had come to the
event expecting to be provoked. It would seem that underlying the case is
an evaluation of the nature of the speech in relation to which the protection was being claimed. It may be that racist and anti-Semitic speech are
rightly to be regarded as on a uniquely offensive plane, justifying strong
restrictive measures, even at some cost to traditional civil liberties, at least
in those situations where their utterance is as a matter of fact producing a
violent reaction in others. Why should the police go to great lengths to
protect the purveyors of such hate speech not only in situations where
their only means of protecting the speaker is by calling a halt to what he
or she is saying but also even where they do have a range of operational
alternatives available to them?

Nevertheless, there is a slippery slope here which it is as well to notice.
Parliament has recently been immersed in controversial discussion over
whether the criminalization of speech aimed at stirring up religious
hatred—without the need for any violent reaction—is an illegitimate
intrusion into civil liberties and fundamental freedoms. The debate has
been similar to the discussions which preceded enactment of the incitement to racial hatred legislation in the 1960s and I shall look at both laws
in a later chapter on freedom of expression. Many believe that hate
speech—even hate speech that is so disgraceful that it moves its hearers to
violence—deserves to be protected by the authorities, or at least to be
defended to the greatest extent possible by the police. Such absolutists
argue that today's hate speech might be tomorrow's common sense and

---

[30] [1963] 2 QB 744, p 749.

that every utterance should be given the best chance to trade up in the market place of ideas, even where it causes not just anguish in the listeners but such offence as to provoke a risk to the security of the speaker in today's climate. *Hammond v Director of Public Prosecutions*[31] is a case in point. The defendant was an evangelical preaching a strong, morally conservative message in public in Bournemouth. Among his props was a sign designed to bring his message home: it had inscribed on it 'stop immorality' and (rather more specifically and therefore controversially) 'stop homosexuality' and 'stop lesbianism'. Thirty to forty people gathered, a number of whom were hostile and water was poured over the preacher's head. He (rather than the water-thrower) was promptly arrested and charged under public order law. This decision was upheld at the magistrates' court and again on appeal to the High Court: the defendant's sign had been insulting and his overall behaviour unreasonable. No human rights or (as we would say civil liberties) principle was found on the facts to operate in his favour.

Thirty years before, the nature of the communication would need to have been completely inverted to have produced a similar outcome: then it was the 'pro-gays' who risked the wrath of the mob to get their message across. Many who make today's human rights weather would applaud them for what they did and regard it as of the first importance that the law should have offered them protection. Is it social progress that that same law now seems to have declared open season on the losers of the moral wars of past generations, penalizing them when their persistence in holding to past orthodoxies exposes them not just to ridicule but to possible physical assault? It could be argued that quite apart from the content of the defendant's speech, the police constable who happened upon the threat to order had no alternative other than to act as he did. It was more a case of there being no alternative than the police officer choosing to join in the general persecution of an isolated pioneer for a speedy return to the past. The better guide to current practice is *Redmond–Bate v Director of Public Prosecutions*.[32] Here, three women Christian fundamentalists were preaching to passers-by from the steps of a cathedral. More than 100 people had gathered when a police officer, fearing a breach of the peace, asked them to stop preaching and arrested them when they refused. They were duly convicted for obstruction of a police officer in the execution of his duty and the women's subsequent appeal to the Crown Court was dismissed. There had been some hostility expressed towards the preachers but at the same time there had been no indication of any imminent violence.

---

[31] [2004] EWHC 69 (Admin), [2004] *Crim Law Rev* 851.
[32] [1999] *Crim Law Rev* 998, (1999) 7 BHRC 375.

On these facts, the Queen's Bench Division (Sedley LJ and Collins J) found the conviction to have been incompatible with Convention case law and with the decision in *Beatty*. The appeals were allowed and the convictions quashed.

In some of the cases discussed above we have seen how the content of the communications has affected official judgments as to the extent of protection that should be offered. With the possible exception of race and religious 'hate speech', an approach to the control of provocative (but otherwise in itself non-criminal) speech which is based on an evaluation of what is being said rather than on the capacity of the authorities to protect the speaker is likely to be subversive of civil libertarian principle. The main complaint behind the police protection of fascist marches in the 1930s and again in the 1970s lay in the alleged partiality that it was said was shown by the police—keen to uphold constitutional rights where extreme Ringwing protestors were involved; markedly less so when it was the radical Left whose views were provoking their opponents' peace-breaching wrath.[33] This was why national legislation passed first in 1936, added to in 1986, and again in 1994 has allowed the police to control processions, if necessary banning them outright if they judge there to be a risk of serious public disorder, but only in general rather than march-specific terms. Such an approach helps to reduce the risk of an unacceptable, content-based restriction on freedom of assembly. But in its laudably indiscriminate reach lie other dangers. In *Kent v Metropolitan Police Commissioner*,[34] both the High Court and the Court of Appeal upheld the police decision to ban almost all marches in London for 28 days. The ban was imposed during a period of high tension, sparked by levels of inner-city rioting which were extremely serious by British standards. The risk of disorder arising from the prohibited procession by the Campaign for Nuclear Disarmament (which led to the legal challenge) came not from the marchers themselves nor even from their opponents, but rather from '[h]ooligans and others [who] might attack the police',[35] but this was enough to justify the police action.

The upshot of the case was that a very important political perspective, traditionally expressed through public rather than parliamentary protest, was prevented from getting off the ground. This was despite the fact that at the time there was great anxiety over an escalating nuclear arms race that had been inspired by a newly elected and hawkish US President

---

[33] KD Ewing and CA Gearty, *The Struggle for Civil Liberties* (Oxford: Oxford University Press, 2000), chs 5 and 6; *Freedom under Thatcher. Civil Liberties in Modern Britain*, n 9 above, ch 4.
[34] *The Times*, 15 May 1981.   [35] Ibid, per Lord Denning MR.

Ronald Reagan. With decisions like *Jordan* and *Kent*, it has now become normal to regard a concern about order in general, and anxiety about speakers' and protestors' physical security in particular, as sufficient to underpin controls on all forms of public protest, both 'on the spot' (as in *Jordan* and *Hammond*) and prophylactic (as in *Kent* and long before it *O'Kelly v Harvey*). This is not so much a matter of law as of policing culture. Old cases like *O'Kelly*, *Humphries* and *Wise v Dunning* show that a combination of common law and locally applicable Westminster legislation allowed preventive action to be taken to protect the security of unpopular speakers long before the advent of nationwide public order laws like those enacted in 1936, 1986, and 1994. Similarly, the decisions of *Beatty* (1882) and *Redmond-Bate* (1999) show that another approach is possible, one that prioritizes free speech even at the price of forcing the authorities to discharge their obligation to protect in a way that is consistent with free speech principles. From a civil libertarian perspective it is clear that this will generally be the right route down which to go.

6

The Rights to Liberty and Due Process

The common law has long maintained that a principle of individual liberty is one of the presumptions that lies at its heart, informing the development of judge-made law and guiding the courts in their interpretation of statutes.[1] Since 1950 (and in Britain since 2000), the European Convention on Human Rights has reflected this commitment through Article 5, a provision declaring a right to liberty that is available to all regardless of national or ethnic background. Of course, such a freedom cannot be absolute and various limitations have long been permitted, with it being a moot point how far the judges have actually cared about the freedom, something to which I shall need to return to frequently in the course of this chapter. As far as Article 5 is concerned, all such permitted restrictions must be 'in accordance with a procedure prescribed by law'. A number of the exceptions that are then set out do not relate directly to our subject: they raise issues concerning detention for immigration, educational, or health purposes, all of which fit better within the more general framework of human rights. Two connect specifically to the criminal process, however, and have a direct relevance to civil liberties, as does a third concerning legal obligations. Each needs briefly to be noted now.

The first of these are those legitimate deprivations of liberty that follow from 'the lawful arrest or detention of a person effected for the purpose of bringing him before the competent legal authority on reasonable suspicion of having committed an offence or when it is reasonably considered necessary to prevent his committing an offence or fleeing after having done so'.[2] As a way of ameliorating the consequences of this executive power, the Convention goes on to assert a right to bail[3] and to trial within a reasonable time,[4] and offers as well a further entitlement 'to take proceedings by which the lawfulness of [one's] detention can be decided speedily by a court and his release ordered if the detention is not lawful'.[5] The second relevant exception arises after a trial process has come to an

---

[1] *Wheeler v Leicester City Council* [1985] AC 1054.   [2] Article 5(1)(c).
[3] Article 5(3). Note that release 'may be conditioned by guarantees to appear for trial'.
[4] Article 5(3).   [5] Article 5(4).

end, when liberty may be removed by 'the lawful detention of a person after conviction by a competent court'.[6] The third allows 'the lawful arrest or detention of a person for non-compliance with the lawful order of a court or in order to secure the fulfilment of any obligation prescribed by law'.[7] Under Article 5(5), '[e]veryone who has been the victim of arrest or detention in contravention of the provisions of this article' is assured 'an enforceable right to compensation', a clause denoting how seriously the entitlement to liberty is taken in the Convention scheme of rights.

Complimenting Article 5, and again echoing traditional common law safeguards,[8] Article 6 concerns itself primarily with the criminal process, and it is this that makes it also potentially relevant to civil liberties. The basic procedural rights available to accused persons in a criminal setting are set out in Article 6(2) and 6(3), with the overarching guarantee of fair procedures at the trial itself to be found in paragraph (1). This last provision encompasses but (unlike the rest of the Article) is not limited to the criminal sphere:

In the determination of his civil rights and obligations or of any criminal charge against him, everyone is entitled to a fair and public hearing within a reasonable time by an independent and impartial tribunal established by law. . . .

Article 6 has proved the most fruitful of all the articles in the Convention as far as the generation of litigation is concerned, with many of the cases concerned with the interface between the civil and the criminal, there being a wider set of guarantees with regard to the latter as compared with the former process.

Important though the rights to liberty and due process are, neither the criminal trial nor the police actions that may have preceded it are in themselves at the core of civil liberties. Were they so, the subject would find itself drifting too far into the realms of substantive and procedural criminal law. At this juncture I should recall a claim that was made initially in Chapter 2 and which runs as a theme through the course of this book: civil liberties as the term has been interpreted here is not inherently an anarchic subject. It does not oppose all laws that touch upon an individual's personal liberty. Far from being antagonistic to such restraints as a matter of course, those committed to political liberty often need law precisely in order to underpin the social advances which they are seeking either to procure or to protect through the democratic process. In any effective

[6] Article 5(1)(a).   [7] Article 5(1)(b).
[8] On which Article 6 was largely based: see AWB Simpson, *Human Rights and the End of Empire: Britain and the Genesis of the European Convention* (Oxford: Oxford University Press, 2001), chs 13 and 14.

democratic system, law will be a necessary means of enforcing community judgments that might be anathema to some, not least on account of how they inhibit personal choices or otherwise restrict action on pain of a penal sanction that might well involve the deprivation of liberty. The criminal law is therefore essential; deployed fairly and impartially it is a vital feature of any society run on the representative principle.

This is not to say that all civil libertarians feel obliged always to respect the law. There is a spectrum here, across history and contemporary practice. As we saw in Chapter 3, it is clear that various degrees of lawlessness have been a significant feature in the forging of the basic democratic structures that are taken for granted in Britain today. Along the way this has involved not just unlawful assemblies and occasional acts of sedition but engagement with much heavier forms of criminality, through treason via insurrection, and including what we would now call acts of terrorism (or even, as with William of Orange, 'international terrorism'). Sometimes the practitioners of such subversion have been successful and escaped punishment altogether. On other occasions they have been summarily executed, fired upon by the armed forces, or jailed or executed after a trial so deficient in fair procedures as to have amounted to a foregone conclusion. Only very unusually in the pre–democratic era would an entirely fair trial have been achieved prior to the punishment of such wrongdoers: it was possible and did occur in eighteenth–century England but it is a difficult commitment for state power to stick to without the disciplining effect of proper legal and political accountability.[9] It is in the democratic era that the idea of impartial police practices and the concept of a fair trial for all have reached the zenith of their influence.

The successful embedding of the basic structures of democratic government does not mean, however, that the law and practice of civil liberties is henceforth necessarily required to restrict itself to action that is always certain to be within the law. This was one of the paradoxes that I discussed at length in Chapter 3: while some politically engaged citizens might indeed say that Britain's democratic culture is now sufficiently defined to make action outside the law unnecessary and therefore no longer excusable as a necessary indiscretion *en route* to a better future, to others the creation of a new set of truths that changes the political culture and in due course produces enforceable legislative action cannot be left to any set of legislators, even those that are fairly elected by voters.

---

[9] The jury trial is so important in England precisely because it provided a potential protection against tyrannical police and state practices at a time when there was no more direct form of accountability for abuse of power.

An important part of the law and practice of civil liberties is about how activists with the latter sort of inclination have fared in their interaction with the law. It is clear that sometimes the mainstream criminal law will be directly breached by their actions, and at its extremes this can involve crimes as serious as murder, manslaughter, and criminal damage with intent to endanger life. The study of civil liberties is not primarily concerned with such wrongdoers, regarding their conduct as more within the realms of criminal justice or anti-terrorism law.

'Direct action' is the name given to strong forms of political engagement which actively court interaction with the authorities as a way of promoting their point of view, but which manages to do so without ever spilling into mainstream criminal, or core (in other words, violent) 'terrorist' action. Further across the scale, there is the kind of civil libertarian conduct that might appear unobjectionable on its face, but which cannot always be guaranteed to be legally watertight: the march down the high street that interferes with traffic; the shouting at the picket line that could conceivably be characterized as a noise nuisance; the handing out of pamphlets that others might characterize as littering. It is in relation to these last two forms of political engagement, 'direct action' and peaceful protest of uncertain legality, that the law and practice of civil liberties does, indeed, have a particular interest. Whether the mass cycle demonstration, the disruption of the local hunt, the sit-in or the picket of an animal testing laboratory set out to court trouble or seem to be and claim to be innocuous, they cannot always be certain of being able to resist the gaze of a scrupulous police officer intent upon finding a legal basis for bringing them to a speedy end, a gaze that would not light upon them if there were not already built into the official mind a prior distaste for their behaviour.

The breadth and range of law available to designate public protest as part of the criminal law and then to act against it—through an arrest initially and then through the deployment of the rest of the criminal process if needs be—is very wide indeed. The civil libertarian does not ask on his or her account for all such laws to be removed. Instead, he or she is on guard against the unfair application of the law, its deployment against a protestor or demonstrator when another person in exactly the same position but without an unfavoured political message to relay would be, and is, left completely untouched. The central concern of this chapter is therefore with the ways in which the criminal law is used against civil libertarian activists in an unfair and discriminatory way so as to inhibit or curtail their political engagement in society. The European Convention on Human Rights is once again important here. We have seen that Article 5 contains exceptions but Article 14 protects against the abuse of these by stating that the 'enjoyment of the rights and freedoms set forth in this Convention shall be secured *without discrimination on any ground* such as sex, race, colour, language, religion, *political or other opinion*, national or social origin, association with a national minority, property, birth or other status'. The emphasis is added to bring home how well Convention rights and civil liberties law intersect.

This question of discrimination runs through our subject. All studies of the substance of civil liberties protection are concerned not only with the way in which the authorities can negate such freedoms in particular cases but also with this issue of the unfair—because discriminatory—exercise of discretion. But as we shall see in the chapters that follow, in those cases where the freedoms of expression, assembly and/or association are being directly curtailed by legislation, the contentious issue will be as likely to gravitate around the inherent repugnance of the impugned law as much as it does around the alleged abuse of discretion under it. In those sections of the book we will find plenty of evidence of civil libertarians objecting in principle to this or that censorship or public order or pro-scription law: such provisions have protest in their sights rather than merely in their periphery, while they focus on some agreed social mischief. In contrast, the kind of laws I am discussing here are ostensibly aimed at matters that civil libertarians accept need to be dealt with by law and there-fore cannot be criticized merely on account of their existence. We do need a law to regulate obstructions of the highway, to curb litter, to control noise, and so on. Liberty does need on occasion to be curtailed; enthusiasm for due process presupposes a prior commitment to the legitimacy of the process whose fairness is in issue. The concern of this chapter is with how such laws, unexceptional on their face, are in practice deployed in a parti-san manner so as unfairly to deprive political activists of their liberty or to punish them via a criminal process that is sloppy or even malevolent in its exercise in comparison with its deployment against ordinary suspects.

In what follows I look first at how these issues of discretion and due process have played out in mainstream civil liberties law and practice, con-sidering initially the problems associated with the power of arrest and the discretion to prosecute that often falls to be exercised following such depriv-ations of liberty. I then look specifically at the binding-over power which has major civil libertarian implications and which has been the subject of two important judgments of the European Court of Human Rights. I then turn to a new development of potentially great significance for our subject: the emergence of a hybrid criminal/civil process leading to the imposition of punitive anti-social behaviour orders, better known as ASBOs. Here we have a new kind of legal form aimed at bad behaviour whose breadth makes it unsettlingly easy to be deployed against political expression. Finally, recalling our general discussion in Chapter 3, I assess the way in which terrorism laws, once again aimed at an agreed mischief (serious subversive violence), have been used in the UK to erode the rights of the politically engaged to liberty and to due process. As we shall see, this is a subject in which developments are coming thick and fast—many of them fundamentally challenging to our subject.

ARREST AND DETENTION

No law is safe from partisan deployment, no matter how apparently neutral. The criminal law wrestles frequently with the problem of the malicious or improper exercise of police powers, and the study of the judicial review of administrative law involves many cases where an improper purpose or a wrong motive is central to the proceedings.[10] Where such actions engage political expression, broadly defined, the interests of civil liberties law are engaged. A case we looked at in Chapter 5, *Beatty v Gillbanks*, was just one of a series of decisions from the late nineteenth century involving the Salvation Army; many of the others dealt with efforts by the organization to challenge noise control laws, ostensibly aimed at peace and tranquillity but in fact contrived as a means of forcing the Army to cease a vital part of its campaigning operations, the making of music.[11] One of the most important cases on free speech in the US Supreme Court arose out of a challenge to a noise control ordinance[12] and it was under the Control of Pollution Act 1974 that animal rights protestors at Club Row street market were forced to halt their anti-pet-sales agitation.[13] It is because of this potential for abuse in the application of such a wide criminal law that civil libertarians have always been wary of permitting a power of arrest to follow as a matter of course whenever a crime is suspected.

One of the most controversial aspects of the Police and Criminal Evidence Act 1984 was its extension of such a power (albeit in limited circumstances) to 'non-arrestable' as well as 'arrestable' offences.[14] Included among the former was obstruction of the highway—a necessary crime

[10] A leading case is *Holgate-Mohammed v Duke* [1984] AC 437.
[11] See DGT Williams, 'The Principle of *Beatty v Gillbanks*: A Reappraisal', in AN Doob and EL Greenspan (eds), *Perspectives in Criminal Law. Essays in Honour of J Ll J Edwards* (Aurora, Ontario: Canadian Law Books, 1985), pp 105–31.
[12] *Saia v People of the State of New York* 334 US 558 (1948).
[13] *Tower Hamlets London Borough Council v Manzoni and Walder* [1984] *Journal of Planning Law* 437: see R. Macrory, 'Street Noise—The Problems of Control' [1984] *Journal of Planning Law* 388. Cf; *Hackney London Borough Council v Rottenberg* [2007] EWHC 166 (Admin).
[14] Police and Criminal Evidence Act 1984, s 25.

certainly but one which many protesters might consider to be a *sine qua non* of any effective demonstration. The distinction seems merely quaint today with arrest now generally available and routinely used by the police as a start rather than end-point in their investigations. As a result of recent amendments to the 1984 Act, one of the grounds for arrest for *any* offence now judged sufficient is 'to allow the prompt and effective investigation of the (suspected) offence or of the conduct of the person in question'.[15] Pretty well every crime no matter how innocuous could lead to arrest under this provision. With arrest come various powers of search of the person and his or her home (and to a more limited extent other places), of seizure of property, and of course interrogation and possible extensions of detention without charge for up to four days.[16] Even leaving aside any special rules for terrorism, to which I shall turn later, the implications of these new, and by the standards of the late twentieth century Draconian, police powers have yet to be absorbed. The provisions have still to be blooded in a nationwide conflict between the police and demonstrators such as has been provided in the past by CND, the anti-apartheid movement, and peaceful mass picketing in the context of industrial disputes. But subject to the view taken by the police, which may yet be more benign and civil libertarian than the law allows, these new arrest powers have the potential to wipe out—or at least dramatically disrupt—public protest, turning the technical breaches of the law that are practically inevitable on such occasions into platforms for disproportionate police action. A key factor in how the law develops will be the attitude taken to it by the courts and the prosecuting authorities: as long as there is a memory of the provisions having once been viewed as Draconian the authorities will probably oversee their application with great care. It is what happens after the powers come to seem routine that will be critical.[17]

A reminder of quite how far the potential for deployment of ordinary law in an anti-civil libertarian way can go is the well-known case of *Arrowsmith v Jenkins*.[18] The defendant was a campaigner for a variety of radical causes. Her public meeting on a street in Bootle in April 1962 caused a total obstruction of the highway for five minutes and a partial block for a further 15. This is the kind of inconvenience that occurs frequently for a variety of reasons across the country. Yet Arrowsmith's

---

[15] Serious Organised Crime and Police Act, s 110, amending s 24 of the 1984 Act: see now s 24(5)(d).

[16] Police and Criminal Evidence Act 1984, s 44(3)(b).

[17] For a thoughtful analysis see the speech of Sir Ken McDonald to the Criminal Bar Association (2007) (copy with author).

[18] [1963] 2 QB 561.

conviction for obstruction of the highway was unanimously upheld in the divisional court in a short extempore judgment delivered by Lord Parker CJ. The case is not a 'one-off'. In *Broome v Director of Public Prosecutions*,[19] the House of Lords unanimously held that a strike picket who stood in front of a lorry urging its driver not to proceed in a certain direction could validly be convicted of obstruction of the highway, notwithstanding that the then industrial relations law gave such demonstrators certain rights in relation to the peaceful persuasion of non-striking workers. In a similar case in 1983, the divisional court allowed an appeal against an acquittal of hospital employees who had blocked an entrance to a hospital in pursuit of their claim for higher wages.[20]

THE BIND-OVER POWER

Once a protestor is charged with an offence, various further inhibitions on conduct may then entirely legitimately be imposed. The most obvious of these is detention in custody pending trial, but this is generally unusual in civil liberties cases of the two types that we are discussing, the demonstrator and the purveyor of 'direct action'. Much more frequently, the freedom to protest or to demonstrate is formally inhibited by the imposition of bail conditions, specifically designed to prevent the conduct that gave rise to the charge in the first place. In a fast-moving situation of the type that often arises where public protest is involved, such conditions can fatally deprive a demonstration of activist support at key moments, turning the attendance at certain events of named individuals into an infraction (the breach of a bail condition) which can lead without more to what could then easily become a substantial deprivation of liberty. Charges need not then even be proceeded with it when things calm down—they will already have done their suffocating work without need of actual prosecution. The practice surfaced in controversial terms during the miners' strike in 1983-4,[21] but it is a routine and highly effective piece of anti-civil libertarian weaponry in the armoury of the authorities. The virtue of the procedure from the police point of view is that no offence need ever be proved. Thus in September 2006, 25 protesters involved in a peaceful demonstration at Nottingham East Midlands Airport were arrested after having occupied the airport's taxiway for four hours. The protest was part

---

[19] [1974] AC 587.
[20] *Jones v Bescoby*, unreported, 8 July 1983 (divisional court), quoted in *Hirst and Agu v Chief Constable of West Yorkshire* (1987) 85 Cr App Rep 143.
[21] *R v Mansfield Justices, ex p Sharkey* [1985] QB 613.

of the 'Plane Stupid' campaign targeting the aviation industry's contribution to the pollution causing climate change. Some of the protesters were
reportedly held in solitary confinement for up to 36 hours and released
with a bail condition requiring they not speak to each other.[22] Examples
like these can be multiplied many times over: they are a staple of police
control of public protest.[23]

At the time of writing the 'Plane Stupid' activists face trial on charges
of aggravated trespass, causing a public nuisance, and entering a restricted
area of an airport without permission. Even if charges in cases such as
these are not pursued or not sustained, yet another controlling devise is
nevertheless available, this time via the magistrates who have had responsibility for the proceedings: the ancient jurisdiction of bind-over. The
famous decision in *Beatty v Gillbanks*[24] to which I have already referred
in this chapter is one such example. The case got to the High Court as
a challenge to a binding-over order which had been imposed on the
Salvationists. This antique procedure had caused them to be bound over
to be 'of good behaviour', on pain of immediate further sanction if they
were not. The open texture of such proceedings makes them an ideal vehi-
cle for local prosecution authorities intent upon disrupting protest of
which they disapprove, all the more so now that legal authorities subsequent to *Beatty* have gone on to make clear that no proof of a prior legal
infraction of a more specific nature is required before such an order can be
wheeled into action.[25] Lurking below the radar of the official law reports—
and therefore largely unnoticed by the those scholars whose attentions are
restricted to the law reports—these orders have harassed and restricted
generations of civil libertarians intent upon extra-parliamentary action.

The suffragettes secured their fair share and stimulated a rare exposure
of the process to higher scrutiny, in *Lansbury v Riley*.[26] The plaintiff, a
well-known political figure on the Left had urged the suffragettes to continue breaking the law in pursuit of their political agenda. As a result of
this generalized call to lawlessness, he was bound over, with the court
requiring him to enter into his own recognizances in the then enormous
sum of £1,000 and also to find two sureties for his good behaviour, each to
be bound in the sum of £500 with the threat of three months' imprisonment if these sureties not be found. The procedure came into its own in
the inter-war period when it was extensively deployed to inhibit the political expression of Communist Party members and other radical agitators.

---

[22] *The Observer*, 8 October 2006.
[23] A compendium of such records is the monthly *Statewatch* bulletin.
[24] (1882) LR 9 QB 308.   [25] *Wilson v Skeock* (1949) 113 *Justice of the Peace* 294.
[26] [1914] 3 KB 229.

The strong words of three members of the Party, expressed at a political meeting in Birmingham in 1924, led to their being bound over to keep the peace, with each such stipulation being backed by the threat of prison.[27] Ernest Woolley, the leader of the Young Communist League, was bound over for 12 months in Manchester in September 1925, with his 'crime' having been to start a public meeting without permission.[28] It was because he refused to be bound over following a speech he made at Hyde Park in May 1926 that the Communist MP for North Battersea, Shipurji Saklatvala, was imprisoned for two months in May 1926.[29] Other victims included Tom Mann and Emryhys Llewellyn, two of the leaders of the National Unemployed Workers' Movement which enjoyed great popularity in the early 1930s.[30] The repressive technique then invariably used was to initiate proceedings based on the breach of some heinous law related to seditious meetings or mutiny or the like, but then to resile from these and to tempt those whose political activities it was sought to curb with the much milder but vaguer idea of being 'bound over' to keep the peace. It became a point of principle with many such protestors not to preserve their liberty on such terms.

This discussion of the binding-over order in past eras of agitation should not blind us to its continued relevance today. As was the case with bail conditions, these orders popped up in the course of the bitter industrial dispute over the closure of coalmines in 1983–4,[31] and they have been a prominent feature of recent police action in controlling political protest. Under an ancient statute they have been capable of being deployed not only where a breach of the peace has been in issue—a concept which is itself dangerously vague and flexible—but also where a magistrate judges a person's behaviour to have been *contra bonos mores*.[32] The Law Commission was surely right in 1994 to condemn the latter jurisdiction as 'certainly . . . contrary to elementary notions of what is required by the principles of natural justice'.[33] The same body thought the breach of the peace power to be 'very arguably'[34] in the same position but it would seem clear that both are sufficiently objectionable in civil libertarian terms for the whole bind-over concept to be regarded as unacceptable, not only in

[27] KD Ewing and CA Gearty, *The Struggle for Civil Liberties. Political Freedom and the Rule of Law in Britain, 1914–1945* (Oxford: Oxford University Press, 2000), pp 132–3.
[28] Ibid, p 133.   [29] Ibid, p 201.   [30] Ibid, pp 226–8.
[31] KD Ewing and CA Gearty, *Freedom under Thatcher. Civil Liberties in Modern Britain* (Oxford: Oxford University Press, 1990), p 109.
[32] Justices of the Peace Act 1361.
[33] Law Commission *Binding Over* (1994), para 4.34. See also para 6.27.
[34] Ibid, para 4.34.

practice but as a matter of principle. The potentially repressive effect of such orders, the way in which they seek to curb political freedom by the threat of criminal sanction (often including deprivation of liberty) without the discipline of a trial for a substantive offence, and their vulnerability to discriminatory application all make them at very best a highly dubious way of purportedly securing public order. Any kind of binding-over order without prior proof of clear criminal conduct is surely wrong.

The European Court of Human Rights has intervened in this area in two important cases in recent years, with decidedly mixed results. The later of these, *Hashman and Harrup v United Kingdom*,[35] did not directly engage the right to liberty but its progressive ruling has important implications for the future of this basic freedom. As was often the case in the 1990s, the trenchant civil libertarians before the court were activists devoted to ending the practice of hunting foxes with dogs. They were seen blowing a hunting horn and generally making noise with a view to disrupting the activities of the well-known Portman Hunt. They were not arrested but a complaint was afterwards made to magistrates that the applicants should be required to enter into a recognizance with or without sureties to keep the peace and be of good behaviour. Invoking their medieval jurisdiction the magistrates duly obliged, binding the applicants over for 12 months on pain of forfeiting £100. In upholding the order the Crown Court conceded that no breach of the peace had occurred or been threatened but that nevertheless the order had been rightly made as the conduct of the applicants had been *contra bonos mores*: they were deliberately trying to interfere with the hunt and would do so again if not inhibited by the law.

This was not criminal behaviour it was true but it was considered sufficiently bad in broader moral terms to warrant the issuance of this order. By a vote of sixteen to one the European Court of Human Rights thought this jurisdiction too vague to be a valid legal exception to the right to freedom of expression. The judges were particularly unimpressed by the definition of conduct *contra bonos mores* as behaviour which is 'wrong rather than right in the judgment of the majority of contemporary fellow citizens'.[36] Nothing could sum up more succinctly than this why this was a power that had to go. The jurisdiction is no longer available to magistrates in the way that it was.[37] And hunting foxes with dogs—rather than trying to stop such hunting—is today's conduct *contra bonos mores*, albeit properly

---

[35] (1999) 30 EHRR 241.   [36] Ibid, para [38].
[37] Attorney General, *Points for Prosecutors* (The Legal Secretariat to the Law Officers, 2000), pp 10–11.

prohibited by law rather than via an arbitrary jurisdiction dating from Plantagenet times.[38]

The earlier of the Strasbourg cases is less praiseworthy from a civil libertarian perspective. In *Steel and others v United Kingdom*,[39] the right to liberty was directly engaged. The three stories that gave rise to this challenge to the breach of the peace/bind-over power tell us much about the reality of the policing of civil libertarian activists in contemporary Britain. Like Hashman and Harrap, Helen Steel was committed to animal rights. Together with some 60 others, she took part in a concerted attempt to disrupt a grouse shoot on a Yorkshire moor. When a police order to stop these activities was ignored, 13 of the protesters were arrested, including the applicant for what was described as 'breach of the peace'. According to the police what she had been doing was 'intentionally impeding the progress of a member of the shoot by walking in front of him as he lifted his shotgun to take aim, thus preventing him from firing'.[40] Having been held for 44 hours, the applicant was eventually charged with having 'behaved in a manner whereby a breach of the peace was occasioned', and a charge under public order legislation was added the following day. At a court hearing two days after her arrest, she was released on conditional bail, the condition being that she was not to attend any game shoot in North Yorkshire while on remand. Both the magistrates and later the Crown Court upheld the charges and when Steel refused to agree to be bound over to keep the peace she was committed to prison for 28 days.

All the details are of interest here: the police involvement; the vague basis for the original arrest; the long period of detention before charge; the emergence of a statutory public order offence late in the day; the conditional bail; and eventually the bind-over order. The second applicant in the case Rebecca Lush had a similar story. Her protest was against the building of a motorway extension which had led her and others to occupy one of the proposed road's construction sites. Her arrest had come while she was standing under the bucket of a large digger and the reason was that her conduct was judged likely to provoke a disturbance of the peace. When she, too, refused to comply with the subsequent binding-over order imposed by local magistrates, she was likewise committed to prison, albeit for a shorter period (seven days) than Helen Steel. The three remaining applicants, Andrew Needham, David Polden, and Christopher Cole, fell into a different category altogether in that all they were doing was holding a banner and handing out protest leaflets in front of a large conference centre within which was being held a meeting concerned with the sale of fighter helicopters.

---

[38] Hunting Act 2004.   [39] (1998) 28 EHRR 603.   [40] Ibid, para [8].

Yet they, too, were arrested for 'breach of the peace' and detained for some hours before being brought before magistrates. In their case, however, all charges were eventually dropped when the matter came back before the magistrates the following month.

In Strasbourg, all three sets of applicants complained that their detentions had not been authorized by any of the exceptions set out in Article 5(1) and that even if they had been, the deprivations of liberty had not been 'in accordance with a procedure prescribed by law' as the article also required. The court was, however, unsympathetic on the first of these points; '[b]earing in mind the nature of the proceedings in question and the penalty at stake . . . breach of the peace must be regarded as an "offence" within the meaning of Article 5(1)(c)'.[41] As far as the lawfulness of the procedure was concerned, the case law of the court made clear that this meant not only that there should be 'full compliance with the procedural and substantive rules of national law, but also that any deprivation of liberty be consistent with the purpose of Article 5 and not arbitrary'.[42] Furthermore, 'given the importance of personal liberty, it [was] essential that the applicable national law [meet] the standard of "lawfulness" set by the Convention, which requires that all law, whether written or unwritten be sufficiently precise to allow the citizen—if need be, with appropriate advice—to foresee, to a degree that is reasonable in the circumstances, the consequences which a given action may entail'.[43] It might have been supposed that with dicta like this the death-knell for the breach of the peace/bind-over jurisdiction was being sounded. But this was not the case.

Relying on recent decisions in the English courts which had 'now sufficiently established that a breach of the peace [was] committed only when an individual causes harm, or appears likely to cause harm, to persons or property or acts in a manner the natural consequence of which would be to provoke others to violence',[44] the Strasbourg court concluded that 'the relevant legal rules provided sufficient guidance and were formulated with the degree of precision required by the Convention.'[45] On the much less far-reaching issue of the application of the Convention law to the particular facts, the court found the arrest and detention of Steel and Lush to have been justified but those of Needham, Polden, and Cole not to have been— the protest of the last three had been 'entirely peaceful' and there had been no 'indication that they significantly obstructed or attempted to obstruct those attending the conference, or took any other action likely to provoke

---

[41] (1998) 28 EHRR 603, para [49].   [42] Ibid, para [54] footnote omitted.   [43] Ibid.
[44] Ibid, para [55] citing in particular *R v Howell* [1982] QB 416 and *Nicol and Selvanayagam v Director of Public Prosecutions* (1996) 160 *Justice of the Peace Reports* 155.
[45] Ibid.

those others to violence'.[46] All this was, of course, true but leaves open the mystery of why—if English law on breach of the peace was so clear—they had been arrested in the first place. The facts of this third case seem to undermine the way the court disposed of the first two. Whatever about this or that divisional court decision, the 'breach of the peace' power is construed by the police as an open-ended way of dealing with people (including protesters) who ought in their view to be dealt with. This leaves political protest far too vulnerable to immediate police action, and it is a matter of great regret that the Strasbourg court did not take this opportunity to say so.

The case is also disappointing on the challenge Steel and Lush made to their detention following their refusal to be bound over. Again, here was a chance to dispense with an unacceptable legal practice which the European judges refused to seize. The court held that the detentions were validly made under Article 5(1)(b), which it will be recalled allows deprivation of liberty 'for non-compliance with the lawful order of a court or in order to secure the fulfilment of any obligation prescribed by law'. And, '[h]aving considered all the circumstances, the Court [was] satisfied that, given the context, it was sufficiently clear' that the binding-over orders were asking the applicants 'to refrain from causing further, similar, breaches of the peace during the ensuing 12 months'.[47] There was nothing objectionably uncertain about them sufficient to give cause for concern under Article 5. It is hard for the civil libertarian not to agree with the opinion of Judges Valticos and Makarczyk, dissenting in the case of Helen Steel:

We cannot regard these measures as being compatible with the letter and spirit of the Convention. In the first place, the judge did not in this instance really act judicially, convicting someone on account of an offence she had committed, but, by seeking assurances from her that were drafted in very vague terms, and on pain of criminal penalties, he exercised a kind of '*imperium*' conferred on him by the Act, and in our view this type of order, which is not moreover regarded as a criminal penalty, goes beyond the concept of judicial decision to which the Convention refers.[48]

THE RIGHT TO A FAIR TRIAL AND ANTI-SOCIAL BEHAVIOUR LEGISLATION

Civil libertarians have always been vulnerable to trials which have been based on trumped-up charges and then conducted with such unfairness and hostility that the chances of acquittal have been rendered practically nugatory. The early nineteenth-century Irish radical MP Daniel O'Connell

---

[46] Ibid, para [64].   [47] Ibid, para [76].   [48] Ibid, p 651.

was once sufficiently confident of the conviction on sedition charges of his client that he constructed a speech to the jury so inflammatory in its attack on his client's persecutors that it turned legal defeat into political victory.[49] In the democratic era, the guarantee of a jury trial has been a strong safeguard against such abuse, so much so that one of the controversies attending direct action from time to time has been the way in which prosecutors have sought to pursue charges which have allowed matters to be dealt with summarily, despite the defendants' desire to be judged by their peers.[50] Even with a jury trial, however, there is the possibility of institutional interference: the jury-vetting system in place to weed out 'extremists' only became public knowledge as a result of revelations that occurred during the course of the prosecution of the senior civil servant Clive Ponting in 1985 (on charges under the Official Secrets Act for having supplied official information about the sinking of the Argentinian vessel the *General Belgrano* to the MP Tam Dalyell). The jury nevertheless acquitted, uncowed as well by the trial judge's evident enthusiasm to secure the opposite result.[51] Like the politically motivated prosecutor, the phenomenon of the partisan referee is something with which civil libertarians have also had to become familiar over the years, although, as with the trial process generally, there can be little doubt that viewed overall criminal proceedings are much fairer now than they were in the past. The reasons for this are beyond the remit of this book: we might perhaps note in passing that as far as the power to bring charges is concerned, the Crown Prosecution Service now provides an independent voice that did not exist in the past, and furthermore it has been a long time since anyone accused the judges of being in the pocket of the executive on matters concerning civil liberties.

The emphasis—and controversy—in recent years has not been on securing convictions via the criminal process but rather on designing whole new systems to achieve similar ends by a speedier, more efficient, but procedurally lighter means. The intention behind the anti-social behaviour legislation pioneered by the new Labour government in 1998,[52] and solidified further in 2003,[53] has been to pursue the kinds of low-level bad behaviour which the criminal law has generally ignored in the past but which have frequently made the lives of the local communities subject to

---

[49] See the gripping account in Sean O'Faolain, *King of the Beggars. A Life of Daniel O'Connell* (Swords: Poolbeg Press, 1980), pp 154–78.
[50] By insisting, for example, on bringing charges for criminal damage against CND activists for less than the threshold amount after, which a jury trial would become a right.
[51] *Freedom under Thatcher*, n 31 above, pp 144–6.   [52] Crime and Disorder Act 1998.
[53] Anti-Social Behaviour Act 2003.

them a misery. Under s 1 of the Crime and Disorder Act 1998, an ASBO can be obtained by application by the local authority or police[54] to the magistrates' court where a person is said to have acted 'in an anti-social manner, that is to say, in a manner that caused or was likely to cause harassment, alarm or distress to one or more persons not of the same household as himself' and 'that such an order is necessary to protect [relevant] persons from further anti-social acts by him'.[55] The Order, which is regarded by the courts as a civil matter and therefore as not something which attracts the criminal burden of proof,[56] can be as broad as is the authorities' want, prohibiting the defendant 'from doing anything described' in it, and it must remain in place for a minimum of two years. Swingeing punishments can result if the order is breached: a fine and (if tried by jury) a sentence of up to five years in jail.

ASBOs and their younger sibling acceptable behaviour contracts (ABCs) have been among the most controversial initiatives in the entire lexicon of New Labour. Generally popular with voters, they have been regarded with great hostility by civil liberties organizations and by many of those involved in human rights law. Issues of liberty and of due process are clearly directly engaged. As the system has bedded down, the scale and variety of the kinds of orders sought and obtained appears to have increased, with newspapers and legal journals carrying regular stories on this or that extreme example which has been presented as either disproportionately Draconian or eccentrically misguided or both. The remit this book has set for itself means that it does not have to enter the more general debate that still surrounds the legitimacy of the ASBO and ABC process. Our concern is with their potential deployment against those engaged in political protest. The strong orientation of the orders towards anti-social conduct, backed by government advice that has accompanied their application, has so far helped steer the procedure away from any application in the arena of public demonstrations and freedom of speech.[57] However, as we shall see it has provided a template for the (from a civil liberties point of view) far more dangerous anti-terrorism control orders.

Even though we do not have the range of evidence on the point yet, there is no certainty that, in some future period of civil libertarian stress,

---

[54] And some other authorities in specified circumstances: s 1(1A).

[55] Relevant persons are those within the area of responsibility of the body making the application: s 1(B).

[56] *R (McCann) v Manchester Crown Court; Clingham v Kensington and Chelsea Royal London Borough Council* [2002] UKHL 39, [2003] 1 AC 787.

[57] See the ringing denunciation of a local authority's attempt to obtain an ASBO against veteran peace campaigner Lindis Percy in May 2005. In one newspaper it was described as an attempt to 'use a club to beat down the expression of legitimate comment and the expression of views on matters of public concern', *Guardian*, 18 May 2005, p 5.

ASBOs and ABCs will not be turned to as a way of imposing political con-
formity on pain of criminal sanction. That there is such potential is evident from the decision of *R (Singh) v Chief Constable of West Midlands
Police*.[58] The case arose in the context of dispersal orders which were
introduced by the Anti-Social Behaviour Act 2003. The legislative goal
here was to tackle general rather individual thuggery and loutish behaviour, with a superintendent or more senior officer able to secure a general
authorization to issue a dispersal order if he or she had 'reasonable
grounds for believing that any members of the public [had] been intimi-
dated, harassed, alarmed or distressed as a result of the presence or behaviour of groups of two or more persons in public places . . . and that
anti-social behaviour [was] a significant and persistent problem' in that
area.[59] Armed with such an authorization, to which the local authority
must have consented, the police officer on the beat is then empowered to
order groups to disperse without waiting for an offence or even the likeli-
hood of one: a reasonable expectation of intimidation, harassment, alarm,
or distress to members of the public is sufficient. As with ASBOs, ignor-
ing the order carries penalties, a fine or (in this instance) a jail sentence of
up to three months.[60]

The potential deployment of these powers in the arena of public protest
will be immediately obvious and when enacting the law Parliament made
clear that it did not intend public processions under the Public Order Act
or action being taken as part of a lawful trade dispute to be caught by it.
This still left stationary public protests vulnerable. It was inevitable that
human rights law would eventually be drawn into a legal dispute about the
provision's breadth, though it is a matter for regret that it should have
occurred in a case with facts so intertwined with public disorder as those
that gave rise to the decision in *Singh*. A series of attempts had been made
by members of the Sikh community in Birmingham to disrupt the staging
of a play which it was perceived was bringing dishonour to their religion.
After some days of rising tension, some 30 to 40 protesters secured entry
to the theatre complex where the play was being shown, refusing to leave
and angrily demanding that it be stopped. After the men had been ejected
(they were all men), they remained outside the building, where together
with some others they continued to shout abuse and to push and shove at
police lines. Rejecting the use of more conventional criminal tools against
particularly aggressive individuals (such as arrest for public order offences

---

[58] [2006] EWCA 1118, [2006] 1 WLR 3374 affirming the divisional court: [2005] EWHC 2840
(Admin).
[59] 2003 Act, s 30(1).   [60] Ibid, s 32(2).

or for breach of the peace), the police inspector on the scene used his power under s 30(4) of the 2003 Act to give a verbal order to the group to disperse. When the appellant refused to obey the order he was arrested (as was one other) and taken to the local police station, where he was released with a caution.

In this case two s 30 authorizations had been in place, designed to deal with general pre-Christmas rowdyism and a particular skateboarding nuisance, respectively. Neither made any mention of the need to curb any other kind of protest. The applicant argued that as a matter of principle the power could not apply to public protest at all, that it was intended to apply to anti-social behaviour, that protest for political purposes was a different kind of conduct altogether to which the Public Order Act alone applied. The point drew powerful support from a well-known dictum of Lord Hoffmann's which seemed directly in point:

. . . the principle of legality means that Parliament must squarely confront what it is doing and accept the political cost. Fundamental rights cannot be overridden by general or ambiguous words. This is because there is too great a risk that the full implications of their unqualified meaning may have passed unnoticed in the democratic process. In the absence of express language or necessary implication to the contrary, the courts therefore presume that even the most general words were intended to be subject to the basic rights of the individual.[61]

The applicant submitted that the threshold permitting control under the anti-social behaviour legislation was so low that directing it at political assemblies would have the potential to destroy protests that could not otherwise be truncated or prohibited under the existing statute or common law that dealt directly with such matters. The essential point was that this particular statutory weapon had no legitimate basis for being fired off against him; other more specifically conduct-based public order law was what should have been considered and, if thought applicable, deployed.

Neither the divisional court nor the Court of Appeal was persuaded. It was 'compellingly clear' to Lady Justice Hallett that 'Parliament did intend that the dispersal regime under section 30 should apply to protests'.[62] What did for the appellant was not only the exemptions specifically in place for other kinds of protest—Parliament must have thought about it and deliberately left out assemblies—but also the general violent context in which the right to protest was here being asserted. The dispersal order was one of the milder weapons in the police arsenal, with far stronger action against the appellant than that actually taken having been likely to

[61] *R (Simms) v Secretary of State for the Home Department* [2000] 2 AC 115, p 131.
[62] See para [79]. Both Wall and Wilson LJJ agreed with Hallett LJ.

have been justified on the facts. Nevertheless, the breadth of the reasoning of the judges is disturbing from a civil libertarian point of view, in particular their willingness to accept that 'alarm' or 'distress' can do the same work as 'intimidation' and 'harassment' as far as underpinning the power is concerned.[63] It was true that '[o]ne or two particularly sensitive members of the public may be alarmed or distressed by conduct that would not or should not offend others' with all of us 'who have the privilege of living in a free and democratic society [having] on occasions [to] suffer some inconvenience caused by protests and protesters', but these were matters to be left to the particular circumstances of any particular incident: '[p]olice officers must act proportionately and sensibly, as the officers claim they did here'.[64] As we shall see when we look directly at public order law in Chapter 7, the version of events supplied by the police officer on the spot is rarely contradicted in later judicial review proceedings. These dicta hardly stand as ringing endorsements of the right to protest. The prevailing mood of 'common sense' is rarely an ally of freedom in the particular case.

ANTI-TERRORISM CONTROL ORDERS

The impact of terrorism laws on the rights of liberty and due process has a long history in the UK.[65] The most infamous example was the deployment of the power of internment by the regional government of Northern Ireland in August 1971. The majority of those detained appear not to have had any direct or even indirect involvement with political violence and the overall effect of the policy, ham-fistedly executed as it was, was greatly to exacerbate community tensions and radically to deepen nationalist alienation from the state. (In the first sweeps of suspects, only nationalists were apprehended.)[66] It goes without saying that a Draconian power like this, aimed exclusively at one particular community, was bound to have had—and did have—a chilling effect on political freedom, albeit the effect of the chilling in the particular context of Northern Ireland was to drive activists into subversive violence rather than sullen silence.[67] Subtler but almost as problematic from a civil libertarian perspective was the diluted criminal

---

[63] See para [88] per Hallett LJ.
[64] See para [89] per Hallett LJ. The judges found that on the particular facts of this case the power had been properly exercised under s 30.
[65] For a general discussion of the terrorism laws see pp 42–8 above.
[66] See J Bowyer Bell, *The Irish Troubles. A Generation of Violence, 1967–1992* (Dublin: Gill and Macmillan, 1993), ch 7.
[67] Ibid.

process to which the state had resort when the counterproductive impact of the internment option could no longer credibly be denied. Through the 1970s and 1980s, the politics of Anglo-Irish relations were dominated by disputes over the integrity of the Diplock court system. This was the framework of non-jury courts, equipped with special procedures, relaxed rules of evidence and an ever-expanding range of statutory crimes, with which the British government—by this time now directly responsible for governance in Northern Ireland—sought to tackle IRA and other paramilitary crime within a framework of some kind of rule of law.[68]

The story of the Diplock courts, fast approaching its closing chapter it would seem,[69] is beyond the remit of this chapter. A comprehensive analysis of it would take us into the realm of criminal justice. There were certainly frequent claims of the targeting of political activists within the Republican movement and no doubt this was true to at least a significant extent. On the other hand, it could hardly have been otherwise at a time when the political movement concerned moved so seamlessly between the legitimate (Sinn Féin) and the illegitimate (IRA violence). Republican protestations about human rights abuses were perhaps often sincere but such aggressive partisanship by the state in the field of law was in some ways an inevitable downside to the organization's otherwise (from its perspective) tactically astute intermingling of the political with the criminal. From the standpoint of this chapter, it is the legacy of the Northern Ireland problem—in the form of a much wider and broader criminal law than would otherwise have existed—that is of the greater importance. The Terrorism Act 2000 drew from the Northern Ireland precedent numerous criminal offences of great breadth and with severe penal sanctions. Examples include the crimes of: directing 'at any level . . . the activities of an organization which is concerned in the commission of acts of terrorism' (for the which the maximum penalty is life imprisonment);[70] possessing 'an article in circumstances which give rise to a reasonable suspicion that [such] possession is for a purpose connected with the commission, preparation or instigation of acts of terrorism' (10 years maximum imprisonment);[71] and inciting 'another person to commit an act of terrorism overseas' (up to life in prison, depending on what is being incited).[72] When

---

[68] Northern Ireland (Emergency Provisions) Act 1973 and subsequent legislation: see, generally, CA Gearty and JA Kimbell, *Terrorism and the Rule of Law* (London: Civil Liberties Research Unit, King's College London, 1995).
[69] Northern Ireland Office, *Replacement Arrangements for the Diplock Court System. A Consultation Paper* (August 2006).
[70] Terrorism Act 2000, s 56.   [71] Ibid, s 57. There are defences: see subss (2) and (3).
[72] Ibid, s 59.

we recall the breadth of the statutory definition of terrorism in this Act,[73] it will be clear how such a prosecutorial power can potentially be deployed against civil libertarian activists as well as the criminally violent subversives at whom it is ostensibly aimed.

The anti-terrorism control orders were not to be found in the 2000 Act, nor in the Anti-terrorism, Crime and Security Act 2001 that was enacted in the months that followed the attacks by Al-Qaida on New York and Washington on 11 September 2001. The latter measure came up with a different way of aggressively controlling suspect terrorists, and this involved a *de facto* return to internment. The words *de facto* are pertinent here: the executive detention envisaged in Part IV of the 2001 Act extended only to 'suspected international terrorists' as defined in the Act[74] and even these presumptively dangerous trouble-makers could leave the country if they chose to do so and could find a place willing to take them without the threat of torture or other ill-treatment. In persuading Parliament to enact a measure that drew invidious comparisons with the failed policies of Northern Ireland in 1971, the government stressed that it was only acting against a tiny band of non-nationals whom it would prefer to have expelled but whom the extra-jurisdictional reach of the European Convention on Human Rights (as interpreted by the Strasbourg judges[75]) had made it impossible to remove. This focus on foreigners, and the claim that the measure was a result of rather than in defiance of human rights law, made good politics at the time but proved the eventual undoing of the policy.

When the scheme of the Act eventually reached the House of Lords for a definitive ruling, in December 2004, it was unequivocally declared a breach of Articles 5 and 14 of the Convention and one moreover which had not been successfully protected by the derogation under Article 15 upon which the government had thought it could confidently rely.[76] As we have seen,[77] this latter provision insists not only that any departures from the right to liberty be on account of a 'war or public emergency threatening the life of the nation' but that all such government actions under it should also be proportionate, with this term including within it a requirement for a rational relationship between the means of implementing the policy and the goal that it was ostensibly designed to achieve. Their Lordships could largely accept the first (the emergency) but they were on the whole dismissive of the second (the rationality of the means

---

[73] See pp 46–7 above.   [74] See s 21.
[75] *Soering v United Kingdom* (1989) 11 EHRR 439; *Chahal v United Kingdom* (1996) 23 EHRR 413.
[76] *A v Secretary of State for the Home Department* [2004] UKHL 56, [2005] 2 AC 68.
[77] See p 32 above.

deployed): why pick on foreigners only when Al-Qaida could just as easily emerge from within Britain was the question which the failure adequately to answer eventually did for the government's case. One possibly convincing answer, that they were a minority that had been easy to get at without too much political blowback, was not one that could within the scheme of human rights law be given. The ruling of their Lordships in the Belmarsh case (so called after the prison in which the detainees were held) is rightly celebrated as a high-point in the story of the judicial protection of unpopular and uninfluential minorities; preceding the July 2005 London bombings (the work of native Britons) by just over six months, its stature has grown as the wisdom of its analysis has been vindicated by events.[78]

The judges were not able to declare the law invalid, such frontal assaults on primary legislation not being allowed under the Human Rights Act 1998 (as we saw in Chapter 2). Instead, their Lordships issued a declaration of incompatibility which the government was, of course, legally free to ignore entirely. However, the political reaction to the decision, the departure of the key minister from the Home Office at exactly this time for unrelated reasons,[79] and the government's own image of itself as a human-rights-abiding administration made such sullen quietude impossible. The upshot was the new idea of anti-terrorism control orders, introduced, after a most tremendous political quarrel, in the Prevention of Terrorism Act 2005, the Royal assent for which was obtained on 11 March 2005. The object of the Act, which crucially reached British and non-British persons alike, was 'to provide for the making against individuals involved in terrorism-related activity of orders imposing obligations on them for purposes connected with preventing or restricting their further involvement in such activity . . . '.[80] The Act intends that these obligations replace the indefinite detention that their Lordships had ruled out against foreigners only and which Parliament had not even been asked to extend to the population as a whole.

Two sorts of orders are envisaged under the Act. The more restrictive of the two are 'derogating control orders'. These impose obligations on individuals which are so severe that they amount to a breach of the Convention and can therefore only be validly done if a derogation from the Convention, under Article 15, is in place and adequately covers the case. Amounting at its extreme to house arrest (clear breach of Article 5 and, depending on

---

[78] See CA Gearty, 'Human Rights in an Age of Counter-Terrorism: Injurious, Irrelevant or Indispensable?' (1995) 58 *Current Legal Problems* 25; TM Poole, 'Harnessing the Power of the Past? Lord Hoffmann and the *Belmarsh Detainees* Case' (2005) 32 *Journal of Law and Society* 534.
[79] David Blunkett.   [80] Part of the long title of the Act.

circumstances, the right to respect for privacy in Article 8) no such orders have as yet been made. The second kind of order, the non-derogating control orders, have been resorted to, albeit not so frequently as was first feared by opponents of the proposed regime.[81] The Secretary of State may make such an order against an individual if '(i) he or she has reasonable grounds for suspecting that the individual is or has been involved in terrorism-related activity; and (ii) he or she considers that it is necessary, for purposes connected with protecting members of the public from a risk of terrorism, to make a control order imposing obligations on that individual.'[82] The suspicion of terrorism does not need to be of specific acts[83] and the obligations thereby permitted can be any that the Secretary of State 'considers necessary for purposes connected with preventing or restricting involvement by that individual in the terrorism activity'.[84] The Act goes into extensive (but non-exhaustive) detail on what these obligations might entail: prohibition of or restriction on the possession or use of certain articles, services or facilities; controls on paid professional activities; restrictions on association, residence, travel, and movement; an obligation to allow entry, search, and seizure powers to be deployed by specified persons; submission to electronic tagging; reporting restrictions; and much else besides.

The Act envisages different procedural routes for the making of these two kinds of orders. Whereas derogating control orders must be made by a court (albeit in an initial hearing of which the subject need not be informed and thereafter with the civil rather than criminal standard of proof),[85] the non-derogating order is the formal responsibility of the Secretary of State, albeit subject to the securing of judicial permission for its promulgation.[86] Such an order can last for up to 12 months but may then be indefinitely renewed, subject only to the Secretary of State being satisfied as to its continued necessity.[87] The suspicion of terrorism that can keep a control order of this sort in place does not have to be the same as that which underpinned the original decision; indeed, it is 'immaterial for the purposes of determining what obligations may be imposed by a control order made by the Secretary of State, whether the involvement in terrorism-related activity to be prevented or restricted by the obligations is connected with matters to which the Secretary of State's ground for

---

[81]   See Lord Carlile of Berriew's second independent review of the Prevention of Terrorism Act 2005 (Home Office, 19 February 2007).

[82]   Prevention of Terrorism Act 2005, s 2(1). For a definition of 'terrorism-related activity' see s 1(9).

[83]   Ibid, s 1(9).   [84]   Ibid, s 1(3).   [85]   Ibid, s 4.

[86]   Ibid, s 3(1). Permission can be dispensed with if matters are urgent: s 3(1)(b).

[87]   Ibid, s 2(6).

suspicion relate'.[88] While there is a provision dealing specifically with review,[89] there is a real danger here of a drift towards a casual, bureaucratic kind of authoritarianism, with individuals lost to public view by non-derogating control orders which are then maintained in perpetuity as much by repressive momentum combined with over-cautious risk-assessment as by any genuine and continuing societal need. In this way the scheme resembles the pernicious exclusion orders under which Irish persons—from both North and South—found themselves expelled from Britain on suspicion of terrorism and without proper due process: it is hard now to believe that an end to this power was one of the key demands of Tony Blair as shadow Home Secretary when he was in other ways positioning himself and his party as more responsive to the needs of terrorism law than in the past.[90]

The courts had precious little role with regard to the old Irish-related exclusion orders[91] and in this respect the 2005 scheme is a distinct improvement. The central role of the courts in the making of derogating control orders has already been noted. As far as non-derogating orders is concerned, the Secretary of State does make the order but in the ordinary course of events only after he or she has received the permission of the High Court. This curious formulation is the result of much parliamentary energy having been expended on the question of who exactly should be making these orders: the answer for the sponsors of the measure remains the minister, while for its critics it is in practice the courts. But this concession to parliamentary opponents of the proposal exacted a high price in the very light standard of review that the court can then bring to the question of whether to grant or refuse permission. The function of the judge with regard to any putative order 'is to consider whether the Secretary of State's decision that there are grounds to make that order is obviously flawed'.[92] This hearing need not involve the subject of the order, who does not need to be informed of it in advance: nor if he or she does learn of it is there any obligation to allow him or her to make representations.[93] Such an opportunity to engage with the process comes after rather than before the order has been made,[94] with the test at this later stage now being whether the decision was 'flawed' (rather than 'obviously flawed'). Testing for such a defect is to be by reference to 'the principles applicable on an application for judicial review'.[95]

[88] Ibid, s 2(9).   [89] Ibid, s 7 and see also s 10.
[90] Home Office, *Legislation against Terrorism. A Consultation Paper*, Cm. 4178 (London: The Stationery Office, 1998), ch 5.
[91] *R (Stitt) v Secretary of State for the Home Department* (1987) *The Times*, 3 February.
[92] Prevention of Terrorism Act 2005, s 3(2)(a).   [93] Ibid, s 3(5).   [94] Ibid, s 3(7).
[95] Ibid, s 3(10) and (11).

The control order regime is a major departure from the normal criminal law in that it provides for the imposition of quite severe restraints on persons on the basis of a suspicion that would not necessarily form the basis of a criminal charge[96] and after a process that, like the ASBO regime that preceded it, lacks many of the vital safeguards associated with the criminal trial. Much depends on how it is implemented in practice. On the one hand, it may be very rarely deployed and gradually fall into the background, a reminder of how far Parliament was prepared to go under pressure at a time of particular stress, like some of the provisions of the Northern Ireland emergency legislation. On the other hand, its use could become a familiar part of the counter-terrorism scene: first a few non-derogating orders; then some more of these; then derogating orders; and with the net of subjects gradually widening from the obviously culpable through to the sorts of political activists whose conduct is already within the range of the terrorism laws. We are nowhere near entering such a spiral of civil libertarian decline at the present time. Whether we ever do may well depend on the future levels of terrorist violence: contemporary political leaders have yet to be tested by the kind of systematic and consistent levels of political violence achieved by the IRA in the 1980s and early 1990s. If the pressure to use the Act does grow, then much will depend on the judgment of the statutory appointee whose job it is to review the operation of the Act,[97] and on the opinion of parliamentarians who will have sight of such a reviewer's reports and who must vote on any extension of the Act beyond the one year achieved by the legislation itself.[98]

And what of the courts? It is on account of the senior judges' commitment to human rights, manifest in the Belmarsh decision, that this framework has been put in place. The role of the High Court on a case-by-case basis has already been identified, but there is also the broader question of whether the regime as a whole breaches the due process guarantees of Article 6. In the first case that came before it, the High Court did, indeed, come to this conclusion. Upholding the control order before him, but issuing a declaration of incompatibility with regard to the law under which it had been made, Sullivan J was as emphatic as the conventions of legal discourse could credibly allow:

Standing back and looking at the overall picture, there can be only one conclusion. To say that the Act does not give the respondent in this case, against whom a

---

[96] Indeed, if the Secretary of State suspects that some terrorism-related crime may be involved he or she has a duty to consult the police as to whether a prosecution might be possible: s 8(1) and (2) see further; *Secretary of State for the Home Department v E & S* [2007] EWCA Civ 459.
[97] Prevention of Terrorism Act 2005, s 14(2).   [98] See s 13.

non-derogating control order has been made by the Secretary of State, a fair hearing in the determination of his rights under Article 8 of the Convention would be an understatement. The court would be failing in its duty under the 1998 Act, a duty imposed upon the court by Parliament, if it did not say, loud and clear, that the procedure under the Act whereby the court merely reviews the lawfulness of the Secretary of State's decision to make the order upon the basis of the material available to him at that earlier stage [is] conspicuously unfair. The thin veneer of legality which is sought to be applied by section 3 of the Act cannot disguise the reality. That controlees' rights under the Convention are being determined not by an independent court in compliance with Article 6.1, but by executive decision-making, untrammelled by any prospect of effective judicial supervision.[99]

The appeal of the Home Secretary against this ruling was, however, successful. Viewing the procedure as a whole and recognizing that only civil rights were in issue (there being no criminal charge involved), the Court of Appeal saw a more engaged judicial role than Sullivan J had considered to be the case, and was as a result clear that the determination of civil rights involved had not been in violation of Article 6.[100] The reasoning of the learned judge had not supported the 'robust conclusion'[101] set out above. Matters will no doubt wind their way to the House of Lords for a definitive ruling. If the Court of Appeal is upheld, and if the use of these powers does stray into the realm of the political, then civil libertarians may have to prepare themselves for a fight over an issue of principle on which human rights law may well be on the opposite side.

---

[99] *Secretary of State for the Home Department v MB* [2006] EWHC 1000 (Admin), para [103]; Further strong decisions on the point have emerged: *Secretary of State for the Home Department v AF* [2007] EWHC 651 (Admin), *Secretary of State for the Home Department v Abu Rideh* [2007] EWHC 804 (Admin).

[100] *Secretary of State for the Home Department v MB* [2006] EWCA Civ 1140, [2006] 3 WLR 839. Compare *Secretary of State for the Home Department v JJ; KK; GG; HH; NN; and LL* [2006] EWCA Civ 1141, [2006] 3 WLR 866, where the finding of the same judge that six non-derogating control orders had, in fact, infringed the Article 5 liberty rights of those subject to them was upheld. These orders had required those subject to them to remain within their place of residence at all times, save between 10 am and 4 pm.

[101] *Secretary of State for the Home Department v MB*, ibid, para [31].

7

The Right to Freedom of Expression

It is only in relatively stable societies that restrictions on freedom of expression are regarded as the most serious conceivable breach of civil liberties. It is true that in Britain the guarantee of free speech is 'often regarded as iconic for civil liberties'[1] and that to many, including the influential former law lord, Lord Steyn, it is the 'primary right', the very 'lifeblood of democracy'.[2] But it is only when other entitlements have been secured, when it is possible to vote and engage in political activity without fear of death, disappearance, torture, or incarceration, that the civil libertarian has the time and freedom to be exercised by inhibitions on his or her power of communication. The freedom to express oneself, understood here to include not just the deployment of words but also of physical action in lieu of or complementary to words (protest as well as talk), is certainly central to civil liberties in the sense that it is impossible to imagine a free political culture without it. But such a society is equally unfeasible without the right to vote, or with state-controlled death squads and torture chambers. Freedom of expression has an important place in civil liberties law—but it is a place and not the whole story.

This point needs to be made not only because of the false primacy that freedom of expression is occasionally given by its devotees but also because the concept itself is more problematic than is often realized. The idea of free speech is clearly much wider than political communication, embracing as it clearly does different varieties of expression—the justifications for these (if they exist at all) must rest on other than the kinds of democratic arguments that are being mustered in this book.[3] It will quite often be the case that speech of this sort should be controlled: incitement to murder is rightly punished; the creator (and downloader) of images of

---

[1] N Whitty, T Murphy and S Livingstone, *Civil Liberties Law: the Human Rights Act Era* (London: Butterworths, 2001), p 380.
[2] *R (Simms) v Secretary of State for the Home Department* [2000] 2 AC 115, p 126.
[3] See, generally, E Barendt, *Freedom of Speech* (2nd edn) (Oxford: Oxford University Press, 2005). Also of interest from the theoretical point of view is L Alexander, *Is there a Right to Freedom of Expression?* (Cambridge: Cambridge University Press, 2005).

children being abused is subject to criminal sanction; to report the classic example, the false cry of fire in a crowded cinema correctly lands the prankster in the dock for any damage that might follow. As we saw in Chapter 3, even in the sphere of political speech, civil liberties theory does acknowledge *in extremis* the right of a free society to defend itself against elements inclined to use such a culture's freedoms in order more effectively to destroy it: 'no free speech for fascists' can in the right circumstances be a civil libertarian rather than an oppressive slogan.

The 'necessary in a democratic society' and public emergency caveats of the European Convention on Human Rights capture this point well and permit limitations to political speech as well as to speech generally, in these particularly dangerous circumstances. Even political speech that is not subversive of the status quo might need to be truncated for the greater, civil libertarian good of all: we saw in Chapter 4 how controls on the financing of election campaigns have come to be seen as a vital part of political freedom, preventing disproportionate influence flowing to the powerful through their capacity to buy the voters' attention. It is also clear that where the expression involves a physical protest in the form of a procession or demonstration, then there are broader considerations of public interest that inevitably must be taken into account: this kind of expressive doing is more at risk of being unreasonably inconveniencing than the saying or printing of words.

In recognizing that these qualifications on political speech are necessary, we should also at the same time remind ourselves that they can be abused. The demands of societal survival are particularly likely to be exaggerated by those whose inclination it is to see in all change potentially destructive forces at work. Such people may well feel that public protest demanding radical transformation of some sort or another is a step too far down the road to public disorder: as we saw in Chapter 3, the line between 'changing' a society and 'destroying' it will often depend on who is doing the drawing. Persons inclined to see much of the former as the latter have often been to the fore in government, in the senior judiciary, and in the police and security forces. This may explain a further problematic dimension to this chapter's subject, which is the gulf that exists between the rhetoric of free speech and the law and practice on the subject. On the whole, we are right when we say that people mainly have the vote in this country and that political activists are neither arbitrarily imprisoned nor systematically ill-treated on account of their activism. However, to engage in the 'wrong kind of speech'—a term that (as we saw in Chapter 2) a Home Secretary once used when justifying a crackdown on the

Communist Party[4]—has always been to court trouble. To say as Lord Justice Judge has done[5] (and he is not alone[6]) that free speech is, as he put it, 'bred in the bone of the common law' is to invite a reminder of exactly the opposite point, of quite how restrictive of speech the common law has consistently been, both generally—inventing new crimes,[7] putting conservative glosses on restrictive laws[8]—and particularly, in the sphere of political expression. Concerning the latter, it is impossible to ignore the vast evidence against Judge's claim: the plethora of cases under the official secrets legislation, the public order laws, and the defence of the realm acts; the enthusiastic development of common law crimes and powers in a way which has undermined political speech; above all the paucity of cases in which sterling judicial utterances in favour of free speech have made the slightest difference to the outcome of any case.[9]

The European Convention on Human Rights has had something of a double-edged effect in this regard. Articles 10 and 11 cover the basic rights of freedom of expression and of assembly respectively, with 'everyone' being declared the possessor of both the 'right to freedom of expression' (Article 10) and the 'right to freedom of peaceful assembly' (Article 11). (Association, which is also in Article 11, is dealt with in the next chapter.) It is true that the range of legitimate grounds upon which each of these rights can be restricted is very broad indeed, in Article 10 covering 'the interests of national security, territorial integrity or public safety, . . . the prevention of disorder or crime, . . . the protection of health or morals, . . . the protection of the reputation or rights of others, . . . [the prevention of] the disclosure of information received in confidence, [and the maintenance of] the authority and impartiality of the judiciary', and in Article 11 extending to all of these apart from territorial integrity and reputation and the final two about confidentiality and the judiciary. However, all of these restrictions

---

[4] Sir William Joynson-Hicks. See p 35 above. For the full story see KD Ewing and CA Gearty, *The Struggle for Civil Liberties. Political Freedom and the Rule of Law in Britain, 1914–1945* (Oxford: Oxford University Press, 2000), p 139.

[5] *R v Central Criminal Court ex parte Bright* [2001] 2 All ER 244, para [87].

[6] *R (Simms) v Secretary of State for the Home Department*, n 2 above, per Lord Steyn; Lord Hoffmann, ibid, p 131; *Verrall v Great Yarmouth Borough Council* [1981] QB 202, p 205 per Watkins LJ.

[7] *Shaw v Director of Public Prosecutions* [1962] AC 220; *Knuller v Director of Public Prosecutions* [1973] AC 435.

[8] See, for example, the judge's summing up in *R v Ponting* [1985] Crim Law Rev 318 and the decision of a unanimous House of Lords in *R (Brind) v Secretary of State for the Home Department* [1991] 2 AC 696.

[9] See generally, *The Struggle for Civil Liberties*, n 4 above and for the Thatcher period KD Ewing and CA Gearty, *Freedom under Thatcher. Civil Liberties in Modern Britain* (Oxford: Oxford University Press, 1990).

are in both articles required not only to be 'prescribed by law' but also, as I have earlier noted, to be 'necessary in a democratic society'.

On the one hand, it is clear that in its interpreting of these articles, and the phrase 'necessary in a democratic society' in particular, the European Court of Human Rights has been mindful of the need to protect political expression above all other kinds of free speech. The Strasbourg court has not only been more ringing than its English counterparts in its commitment to 'pluralism, tolerance and broadmindedness without which there is no "democratic society" ' but also more alive to the importance of freedom of expression as 'one of the essential foundations of a democratic society'.[10] Its application of these principles has also been much less disappointing in the political sphere than has been the case in the UK, with the court being readier to challenge governmental power,[11] less quick when determining the breadth of necessity to see societal survival as at issue, and more imaginative in the way it has sought to incorporate protections for the non-print media into the body of Article 10.[12]

On the other hand, the Strasbourg court's reading of democratic necessity has on occasion embraced political censorship which has run counter to the spirit of civil liberties—the effect of this compliance with the Convention has made restrictive action by the executive politically easier than would otherwise have been the case.[13] The European court's commitment to free speech has also sometimes worked to destabilize democracy—we saw the potentiality of this in Chapter 4 when I considered how, in an unequal society, it will sometimes be necessary to curb the speech of the powerful in order to achieve a fair electoral battleground for all parties, and yet how nervous the European Court of Human Rights has invariably been about such civil libertarian 'censorship'.[14] A further complication is the Convention's simultaneous solicitude with the need to ensure that 'everyone has the right to respect for his private life . . .' (Article 8)—this risks sending the law off on a different and, in the context of democratic freedom, dangerous tack. Although replete with the same kinds of exceptions as we have just noted in relation to Articles 10 and 11, and also (so far at least) habitually downgraded by the Strasbourg court when confronted by political speech, this privacy guarantee has percolated steadily into UK law and its benign (because as yet non-existent) impact on political speech cannot be guaranteed in perpetuity.[15]

---

[10] *Lingens v Austria* (1986) 8 EHRR 407, paras [41]–[42].
[11] *Observer and the Guardian v United Kingdom* (1991) 14 EHRR 153.
[12] *Jersild v Denmark* (1994) 19 EHRR 1.   [13] See pp 132 and 153 below.
[14] *Bowman v United Kingdom* (1998) 26 EHRR 1; see p 70 above.
[15] Discussed further, see p 128 below.

The cases in the European Court of Human Rights have frequent walk-on parts in the description of British law that follows, more often cast in the role of the wise tribunal intervening to correct the censorious tendencies of the British state than that of the disturber of political freedom of which it is also capable. There is very recent evidence as well that the existence of these rights in legal form may have stimulated a new kind of liberalism among senior British judges.[16] It is to be hoped that this is the case, for the fact is that, depressingly, it is one of our main jobs in this chapter to catalogue the precise ways in which radical political speech has been subject to control in Britain, at the hands of all three branches of the state and informally via the private sector as well, and in the present time as well as the distant (and not-so-distant) past. In the first and second sections, I examine the preventive powers available to the authorities to restrict expression, via (to take them in the order in which I analyse them) controls on political speech and on the right of public protest. These are the most serious interferences with free speech because they are able to destroy an idea before it even gets off the ground. The third and fourth categories of legal regulation to be considered are those offences which are specifically designed to control expression and which threaten anyone who speaks out in contravention of such laws with criminal sanction: such punishment after the event can be as restrictive through its deterrent effect as pre-emptive action. I deal in successive sections with such laws insofar as they impact on speech and public protest, respectively. In concluding the chapter, I briefly move beyond the legal to mention the array of informal mechanisms that the British state also has available to it to limit the circulation of political ideas—in historical terms this has been one of the most important ways in which political speech has been controlled in this country. I also consider at this point the impact of private sector constraints on political speech which, as we shall see, has been not inconsiderable.

PREVENTIVE CONTROLS ON SPEECH

The general position taken by British law is that preventing political speech before it is uttered is a bad thing. Unlike many principled propositions in this area, this is one that—with a couple of exceptions to which I shall turn in a moment—is broadly reflected in the case law. There is some restriction of cinema and the broadcasting media which certainly has an impact on what is transmitted via these modes of communication: we saw an example of this in Chapter 4 when we discussed the litigation

---

[16] *R (Laporte) v Chief Constable of Gloucestershire* [2006] UKHL 55, [2007] 2 AC 46.

over the party political broadcast by the ProLife Alliance that the BBC and its commercial equivalent had refused to transmit in the form in which it had been submitted.[17] But restrictions here have flowed out of the particular nature of the medium involved rather than out of any desire to exert formal political control.[18] The potential of the law of libel for those who have wanted to stop political discussion in advance on the ground that what was about to be said was defamatory has also, happily, never been realized. This is on account of the settled law that if a defendant intends to plead justification or fair comment on a matter of public interest, and the defence is not self-evidently preposterous, the courts allow the publication to take place, with the claimant being left to sue for damages if he or she is still as certain of the injustice to them as they are of the affront to their reputation.[19]

When the Human Rights Act 1998 was being enacted, legislators felt so strongly about the need to protect free speech from preventive action, and sufficiently anxious about the capacity of the new Article 8 right to respect for privacy in the Convention to intrude in this way, that they insisted on inserting the following provision (now s 12) into the Act:

(1) This section applies if a court is considering whether to grant any relief which, if granted, might affect the exercise of the Convention right to freedom of expression.

(2) If the person against whom the application for relief is made ('the respondent') is neither present nor represented, no such relief is to be granted unless the court is satisfied—
    (a) that the applicant has taken all practicable steps to notify the respondent; or
    (b) that there are compelling reasons why the respondent should not be notified.

(3) No such relief is to be granted so as to restrain publication before trial unless the court is satisfied that the applicant is likely to establish that publication should not be allowed.

(4) The Court must have particular regard to the importance of the Convention right to freedom of expression and, where the proceedings relate to material which the respondent claims, or which appears to the court, to be journalistic, literary or artistic material (or to conduct connected with such material), to—
    (a) the extent to which—
        (i) the material has, or is about to, become available to the public; or
        (ii) it is, or would be, in the public interest for the material to be published;
    (b) any relevant privacy code.

---

[17] See pp 71–5 above.　　[18] Informal control is a different matter: see pp 153–4 below.
[19] *Fraser v Evans* [1969] 1 QB 349, p 360 per Lord Denning MR, citing *Bonnard v Perryman* [1891] 2 Ch 269.

The newspaper industry, in particular, had keenly campaigned for incorp-
oration of the European Convention on Human Rights into UK law
largely because the Convention had come to be widely perceived as a charter for free speech.[20] It was only during passage of the Bill that the potential reach of Article 8 into the private as well as the public sector became
apparent, on account of the (so far as the press was concerned) hitherto
unnoticed reach of cl 6(3)(a), which included courts and tribunals within
the definition of the public authorities required under cl 6(1) to act compatibly with the Convention rights. Section 12 was a consolation provision
conceded by government to those who (somewhat ambitiously, it has to be
said) had wanted a more explicit exclusion of the media from the potential
constraints of the Act.[21]

It remains to be seen how far the courts will allow Article 8 to reach into
the public arena and if it does how willing they will be to deploy s 12 to
protect political speech: as mentioned earlier there are as yet no substantial developments to report on this front of the free speech battleground.[22]
The print and broadcast media and their parliamentary supporters were
not only concerned about the hypothetically deleterious effect on their
work of the Convention's right to respect for privacy. They were reacting
as well to a dramatic story of attempted state censorship that had been the
focus of much debate and discussion in the late 1980s and the early 1990s,
and which had played an important part in the creation of that climate of
informed opinion that had led many to come to believe in the need for a
charter of rights in the first place. This was the *Spycatcher* affair,[23] exem-
plar of the first of our two exceptions to the rule against prior restraint. The
author of a book of this name, Peter Wright, was a retired security service
officer who from the safety of his home beyond the reach of UK law made
a number of serious allegations in his memoirs about the activities of his
former employers in the security service.

When Wright sought to publish his book in Australia, the UK government promptly commenced legal proceedings to secure a restraining
injunction. Two British newspapers, the *Guardian* and *The Observer* ran
news reports about the case, and in particular about the allegations that the
book was said to contain—sensational claims about the conduct of certain
security officers. Inevitably, given that he had launched the Australian

---

[20] See *Freedom of Speech*, n 3 above, ch 12.
[21] A very useful book of extracts from the parliamentary debates has been published:
J Cooper and A Marshall-Williams, *Legislating for Human Rights. The Parliamentary Debates
on the Human Rights Bill* (Oxford: Hart Publishing, 2000). For discussion of the press and the
Bill, see pp 168–76.
[22] Article 8 is, however, continuing to expand: *Ash v McKennitt* [2006] EWCA Civ 1714.
[23] For an account of the drama up see *Freedom under Thatcher*, n 9 above, pp 152–69.

proceedings, the English attorney-general found himself seeking injunctions against these two papers as well. He obtained restraining orders on an interim basis, and persisted with them even after the legal action in Australia had failed, and the book had been published not only there but in the US as well. This was what caused matters to take on a surreal complexion with the government finding itself engaged in series of aggressive law actions to control the dissemination of allegations that—thanks to the publicity generated by the legal battle and the practical availability of the book— were increasingly in the public domain.[24] At a time when the daily news was taken up with the collapse of the Soviet empire and with the dissent of anti-Communists across Eastern Europe, it seemed to some at least that Britain had stumbled upon its very own piece of authoritarian extremism.

With the benefit of hindsight, the whole story now seems much tamer than it did at the time. Having insisted on upholding the interim injunctions, and incurring vast opprobrium for doing so, the House of Lords eventually succumbed, holding that there was no call for permanent injunctions in view of the fact that the material in the book was already largely known. Whereas it was the case that security service personnel did owe a life-long duty of confidentiality which could be enforced by means of injunction against both such persons themselves and any third party to whom such material was wrongly passed, it was nevertheless the case that the general availability of the book outside Britain and the impossibility as a practical matter of curbing the dissemination of its content within the country meant that the public interest argument in favour of such an injunction simply could not be sustained.[25] This was a line that the Strasbourg court had earlier taken when the interlocutory injunctions had come before it,[26] unfortunately declining the opportunity to declare prior restraints like these to be bad in principle but focusing instead on the fact of American publication having already tilted the balance against the injunctions. So it was the US's first amendment guarantee of free speech, introduced into the UK via Strasbourg, that eventually destroyed the government's litigation strategy.

It is unlikely that a cause célèbre of *Spycatcher* proportions will ever occur in the future: the case stands on the cusp of the internet era and from the perspective of users of the World Wide Web, the litigious efforts of the authorities appear not merely to be ill-judged but to belong to a different era. Nevertheless, the legacy of the *Spycatcher* series of cases remains with

---

[24] See, in particular, *Attorney-General v Guardian Newspapers Ltd* [1987] 1 WLR 1248.
[25] *Attorney-General v Observer Ltd; Attorney-General v Times Newspapers Ltd* [1990] 1 AC 109.
[26] See n 11 above.

us. The legal weapon that was used to secure the injunctions was the equitable concept of breach of confidence. Developed in commercial law, the idea that you could prevent political speech by alleging a breach of confidence at some point in the chain from communication to publication had been accepted in principle in the early 1970s, in a case concerning the publication of the diaries of the cabinet minister Richard Crossman.[27] It was the conjunction of this jurisdiction with the deployment of temporary forms of relief designed for the business rather than fast-moving media world that made the *Spycatcher* case so incendiary. Each technique of restriction remains available today, albeit with s 12 now bound to be a factor in any such proceedings. It has been through an expansionary tweaking of this notion of breach of confidence that Article 8's command to the courts to ensure respect for privacy has been formulated as a *de facto* substantive right; it may be that this imaginative growth in the jurisdiction could not have occurred without the flexibility that it had already been shown to have in the Crossman diaries case and especially in the various *Spycatcher* proceedings. Another enduring consequence of the decision is the confirmation that it produced (in yet another House of Lords ruling[28]) that all media outlets are bound to obey court orders of which they have notice, on pain of being prosecuted for contempt of court. This means that an injunction against one newspaper or television channel can be made binding against all, as long as the fact of the order is brought to the attention of these third parties.

At a still broader level of generality, the efforts of the state authorities to prevent Peter Wright's allegations from reaching the public domain demonstrate how vulnerable even political speech is where there is a determined campaign to prevent it, and how wrong it is simply to assume that the courts can be relied on to stand up even for this supposedly 'iconic' freedom. Of course, the exact matrix of *Spycatcher* will not be repeated, but who is to know from where the next pressure point will arise? The Prime Minister of the day, Margaret Thatcher, was committed to curbing Peter Wright and it was her equal determination to deny militant Irish republicans any credible broadcasting platform for their views that gave rise to the second large exception to the general rule against prior restraint on political speech. As a matter of formal law this one now more clearly belongs to the history books even than the *Spycatcher* case but its contemporary focus—terrorism—makes its return to prominence as a

---

[27] *Attorney-General v Jonathan Cape Ltd and Times Newspapers Ltd* [1976] QB 752. The government lost on the facts and the book was published.

[28] *Attorney-General v Times Newspapers Ltd* [1992] 1 AC 191.

precedent for new restrictions on speech not at all impossible. The 'media ban' issued by the then Home Secretary Douglas Hurd in October 1988 in the form of a notice to both the BBC (under its charter) and to the Independent Broadcasting Authority (IBA) (under the relevant provision of the Broadcasting Act 1981)[29] required both organizations to:

Refrain from broadcasting any matter which consists of or includes—any words spoken, whether in the course of an interview or discussion or otherwise, by a person who appears or is heard on the programme in which the matter is broadcast where—

(a) the person speaking the words represents or purports to represent an organization specified in paragraph 2 below, or
(b) the words support or solicit or invite support for such an organization, other than any matter specified in paragraph 3 below.

Paragraph 2 extended the ban to all the Northern Ireland-based groups that were then proscribed under the Province's emergency laws, the Irish Republican Army, the Irish National Liberation Army, the Ulster Volunteer Force, the Ulster Freedom Fighters, the Red Hand Commando, Fianna na hEireann, Cumann na mBan, and Saor Eire. But it also embraced three lawful political organizations—Sinn Féin, Republican Sinn Féin, and the Ulster Defence Association. In a nod in the direction of political freedom, para 3 exempted from the strictures of the ban 'any words spoken—(a) in the course of proceedings in Parliament, or (b) by or in support of a candidate at a parliamentary, European Parliamentary or local election pending that election'.

During its relatively brief life, the broadcasting ban attracted a fair degree of mockery as well as the predictable opprobrium of the journalists and activists who were affected by it. Its oddly tentative drafting allowed broadcasters to evade its central purpose by engaging professional actors to speak the words of banned persons, with the synchronicity of these thespian words with the lip movements of the banned speaker on television being the *reductio ad absurdum* that eventually, after an initial hesitancy on the part of the broadcasting authorities, became almost (but not quite) routine. When its removal became one of the first indicators of *rapprochement* by the government in the aftermath of the IRA ceasefire of 1994, the ban was already widely perceived to have been no more than an irritant to those at whom it had been aimed, and certainly not the knockout blow for censorship that might have been the hope of at least some elements within the government of the day.

---

[29] Broadcasting Act 1981, s 29(3).

Its malign impact on civil liberties should not, however, be underestimated. First, it confirmed a practical constraint that already applied to members of banned organizations, and went further than this by making impossible any direct broadcasting of their views, something that had happened from time to time during the years before 1988. Second, it attacked the political speech of unbanned political organizations, ostensibly punishing them for their association with paramilitary groups but in reality seeming to be seeking their political annihilation by a process of censorious suffocation, the denial of the 'oxygen of publicity' to which Margaret Thatcher had once so memorably referred.[30] Third, the ban extended beyond the members of these organizations effectively to encompass within its remit non-members whose political views happened to coincide with the aims of any of the censored groups. Politicians with strong nationalist views on the Irish question found themselves under pressure to control their tongues lest they caused the outlet broadcasting their words to fall foul of the ban. The levels of self-censorship—by speaker and media providers alike—were worryingly high during the Thatcherite heyday of the ban's determined operation.[31]

Lastly—and here I return to the point with which I began discussion of the ban—there was the lamentable performance of the judges. When the divisional court was invited to rule on the ban's lawfulness, it concluded not only that the control 'was not perverse or absurd or a decision which no reasonable minister properly directing himself in law could reach'[32] but also that it was compatible with the European Convention on Human Rights in that it fell within the 'necessary in a democratic society' exception to Article 10(1). In the House of Lords (to which the case speedily progressed) the same view was taken on the lawfulness of the measure, their Lordships at times seeming to regard the ban as, if anything, irrationally lenient rather than the other way around.[33] To many critics at the time the litigation showed the need for Britain to incorporate the European Convention into UK law so that the guarantees set out in Article 10 could be brought directly into play, but this view took a severe knock with the upholding of the ban by the European Commission on Human Rights in 1994. In a vindication of the severe assessment of the divisional court, the issue was found to be so clear that the complaint under Article 10 was assessed as 'manifestly ill-founded' and therefore not deserving of the attention of the full court.[34]

---

[30] G. Edgerton, 'Quelling the "Oxygen of Publicity": British Broadcasting and "The Troubles" During the Thatcher Years' (1996) 30 *Journal of Popular Culture* 115.

[31] See *Freedom under Thatcher*, n 9 above, pp 241–50.

[32] *R (Brind) v Secretary of State for the Home Department* (1989) 139 *New Law Journal* 1229.

[33] *R (Brind) v Secretary of State for the Home Department*, n 8 above.

[34] *Brind v United Kingdom* (1995) 18 EHRR CD 76.

Could something like the media ban happen again, toughened up perhaps so as this time to eliminate the concessions to political speech that it had contained? While the Northern Ireland question has faded into the political background, the general issue of terrorism has come more and more to the fore. The 'enemy within' is not now the Irish republican activist; rather it is the politically engaged radical member of the Islamic community, one who either sees it as his or her duty to defend his or her co-religionists from attack (in Britain or more to the point, abroad) and/or who is determined to spread a particular version of the Islamic faith within the local or national community of which he or she is part. The media ban came as a direct result of government's desire to respond to the killings in Ballygawley of eight servicemen, and there is no guarantee that the 'politics of the last atrocity' will not return to drive policy in repressive directions once again. Just six days after the London bombings in July 2005, the then Prime Minister Tony Blair proposed new anti-terror laws which he said would aim to 'pull up this evil ideology by its roots' by tackling incitement to terrorism. He announced a two-week consultation on a variety of measures, including how the law against those 'glorifying' terrorism could be tightened.[35] After this brief period, a proposed new criminal offence emerged. Aware of the difficulties of definition, the draft Bill required the Home Secretary to create a list of historical 'terrorist' events which under the new regime it would be a crime to glorify. The proposal was eventually diluted and is now to be found, minus the list and with various other safeguards, in the Terrorism Act 2006, where the wrong is described as the 'encouraging' rather than glorifying of terrorism. Parliament did its work in the end, preventing the enactment of a law that would have prohibited in advance whole areas of political discussion involving the 'celebration' (whatever that might entail) of certain past acts of political violence. But it was a close run thing and a salutary reminder of how vulnerable free speech is to a frontal assault by a Prime Minister determined to put his or her own highly particular ideas about how to defeat terrorism above the principle of free speech.

PREVENTIVE CONTROLS ON CONDUCT

It is not surprising that the law has been more sympathetic to prior restraint where the communication of political ideas has been via words and conduct or through conduct alone. Marches and demonstrations are certainly a vital part of political freedom, advertising a solidarity which

---

[35] S Jeffrey, 'Q and A: the glorification of terrorism'. *Guardian Unlimited*, 15 February 2006 is good on the background.

deepens the power of the thought being expressed, and enjoying a liberating freedom from dependence on power and money—there is no editor to please nor proprietor to pay for this opportunity to speak to the world at large. But as we have already noted, the potential for inconvenience is greater than with print or broadcast media. Roads can be cluttered by throngs of protestors in a way that makes ordinary life impossible for the thoroughfares' co-users. The fact of the gathering of a political crowd carries its own risks as well: tempers can flare, solidarity can spill over into defiance, the demo can transform itself quickly into a mob. In a democracy, the law is anxious to facilitate the expression of political points of view via public protest but at the same time it carries within its genetic code a programmed suspicion, rooted in past chaos, of any such gatherings of the masses.[36] This latter anxiety leads it to do more than merely vigilantly police demonstrations with a view to swooping upon trouble-makers as soon as disorder begins. In Britain, all public authorities have long enjoyed powers to control public protest in advance, either acting to prevent such events entirely or allowing them to proceed only on a highly conditional basis.

In Chapter 5 we saw how the old binding-over power was used in an attempt to constrain the Salvation Army,[37] unlawfully as it turned out in that case because it had been an opposing rabble rather than the Army itself that had been threatening the peace. No one doubted that had the authorities judged the marchers themselves to have been likely to have been violent then this power with its strong preventive implications would have been available to them. It is this kind of situation, rather than the one in which an admittedly peaceful protest is attacked, that is the concern of this chapter. The power to ban or truncate public protest in advance on nebulous grounds of threatened violence or disorder is one that is clearly open to abuse, and the record shows that it has often been deployed illegitimately to limit the communication of political ideas judged unacceptable to the authorities. The growth of national legislation in this area has been a feature of the law only since the 1930s, it having been under local Acts of Parliament and by-laws that opportunities were frequently taken in the nineteenth and the first decades of the twentieth centuries to curb demonstrations in particular places.[38] I turn to the recent plethora of general statutes on the subject shortly. First, I need to notice the continuing effect of the pre-democratic, indeed ancient, power to act with regard to actual and apprehended breaches of the peace. This has managed to avoid being

[36] See pp 41–2 above for further discussion of this paradox.
[37] *Beatty v Gillbanks*, above, pp 89–90.
[38] *The Struggle for Civil Liberties*, n 4 above, pp 305–6.

supplanted by legislative alternatives and as a result has survived into the modern era as an attractive because very flexible basis for the control of protest. However, its breadth has been the subject of an immensely important Lords' decision at the end of 2006 which, if properly followed, will greatly reduce its capacity to do civil libertarian harm and produce a correspondingly increased reliance on statutory powers.[39]

At first glance, the crime under cover of which the breach of the peace power operates—obstructing a police officer in the execution of his or her duty[40]—sounds as though it has no preventive dimension whatsoever. But this is deceptive. The problem arises from the breadth of the discretion afforded a police officer who reasonably believes that a breach of the peace is in the offing, with the crime then being committed by refusing to do whatever he or she says (is duty-bound to say) is necessary to stop the occurrence of the anticipated disorder. Despite occasional efforts to tie the language down,[41] the courts have been extremely reluctant to challenge an officer's judgement not only as to what might happen in the future and as to when it might happen but also as to what must now be done to prevent it. There are few problems with the police officer who stumbles upon a situation of tension and potential violence. In such circumstances sensible precautions can be taken to calm tempers, and this is the case even if political speech is controlled as a result. In a case we have already discussed in Chapter 5, *Humphries v Connor*,[42] the removal of an inflammatory political emblem from the lapel of the plaintiff was rightly judged by the court in subsequent civil proceedings for assault to have been justified by the need to quell the disorder that the wearing of such a piece of provocative apparel was threatening to occasion. The same is surely obviously the case if the violence is on the verge of emanating from the protestor himself or herself. It is an altogether different situation if there is a policy decision taken by the police, at a senior level, to stop an organized political event on the basis of a breach of the peace by some or all of its participants, which is anticipated only by the officers themselves and the evidence for the prospect of which is nowhere clearly to be seen. This is thinly disguised political censorship, made all the more serious by the fact that it occurs under a common law power (backed by statutory sanction) which has never been properly scrutinized by the legislature, and

---

[39] *R (Laporte) v Chief Constable of Gloucestershire*, n 16 above.
[40] Police Act 1996, s 89(2). Section 89(1) covers assaulting a police officer in the execution of his or her duty.
[41] Reviewed in *R (Laporte) v Chief Constable of Gloucestershire*, n 16 above, especially the speech of Lord Bingham of Cornhill, and see further p 138 below.
[42] (1864) 17 ICLR 1, discussed pp 89–90 above.

which lacks all the safeguards that elected representatives might have imposed had the matter ever come before them for proper scrutiny before becoming part of the law.

It is a depressing fact that the history of civil liberties in the UK abounds with examples of the misuse of the breach of the peace power in exactly this kind of political context. Until the path-breaking Lords' decision at the end of 2006, to which I shall turn properly in a moment, efforts to challenge the discretion in court had proved not only unhelpful but entirely counter-productive as well, sanctioning that which previously had been at least a little doubtful. In *Duncan v Jones*,[43] the defendant had attempted to address a protest meeting outside a training centre for the unemployed. When she refused to shift proceedings 175 yards down the road to an altogether more innocuous venue where she was likely to attract few listeners, she was promptly arrested for obstructing the officer in the execution of his duty. As the case made its way up the judicial hierarchy, the paucity of the evi-dence of any prospect of the outbreak of violence was increasingly laid bare, and close examination of the wider context showed how frequently the police had broken up peaceful protests against mass unemployment in exactly this way. In fact, *Duncan v Jones* was an early 'test case', with the protesters determined to create facts which would allow them to challenge this brand of habitual police repression. But in the High Court the actions of the authorities were thoroughly vindicated, with the Lord Chief Justice of the day (Lord Hewart) being joined by two senior colleagues in uphold-ing the obligation of the police to keep the peace as they saw fit. In vain did leading counsel for Mrs Duncan draw attention to *Beatty v Gillbanks* and the ostensible commitment of English law to the protection of civil liberties: to Hewart, that decision was 'somewhat unsatisfactory' and 'apart from the present case'.[44] In any event English law did 'not recognize any special right of public meeting for political or other purposes'.[45]

Decided just before *Duncan*, *Thomas v Sawkins* produced a similarly negative result for the civil libertarian activist who had initiated the case by prosecuting for assault a police officer who had resisted what he had believed were efforts to have him removed from a public meeting at which he and his colleagues had insisted on being present.[46] The occasion of this indoor rally had been to call for the dismissal of the local chief constable as well as to rally support against a Bill on incitement to disaffection that was then going through Parliament. With Lord Hewart prominent once again,

---

[43] [1936] 1 KB 218; *Struggle for Civil Liberties*, n 4 above, pp 261–70.
[44] [1936] 1 KB 218, p 222.   [45] Ibid.
[46] *Thomas v Sawkins* [1935] 2 KB 249. For the full story see *Struggle for Civil Liberties*, n 4 above, pp 289–95.

the High Court upheld the right of the police to enter and remain on private property where they reasonably anticipated a breach of the peace or any offence whatsoever including (from a puisne judge Avory J) the making of seditious speeches. These examples of the forging of a repressive common law in the bleak atmosphere of class conflict in 1930s Britain cannot be dismissed as relevant to this period alone: their precedent value has dogged the protection of civil liberties in Britain, being deployed to close down protest at key moments on a regular basis ever since. Now and again, glimpses of how this street level official power works can be seen from the law reports. In *Piddington v Bates* the courts permitted the police to use the breach of the peace power to impose restrictions on the number of pickets that could be deployed in the course of a trade dispute.[47] In the bitter industrial dispute of 1983–4, efforts to express solidarity with striking members of the National Union of Mineworkers were foiled by the simple expedient of refusing to allow suspected picketers to leave the motorways they were using at the exits they needed to use in order to reach the protests they were intending to join.[48] The judges were clear that provided senior police officers present 'honestly and reasonably form[ed] the opinion that there [was] a real risk of a breach of the peace in the sense that it is in close proximity both in place and time, then the conditions exist for reasonable preventive action including, if necessary, the measures taken in this case'.[49]

If followed in spirit as well as on the exact legal point it decided, the ruling of their Lordships in *R (Laporte) v Chief Constable of Gloucestershire* promises a sea-change in the whole approach of the authorities to the breach of the peace power.[50] The facts of the case were that a large-scale protest had been planned outside a particular air base and the police had made a variety of plans and invoked a number of legislative powers in order to be able effectively to manage the event. When the local force became aware that included among the protesters travelling in three coaches from London were a handful of members of a 'hard core activist anarchist group'[51] known as the Wombles,[52] the senior officer in charge arranged for the stopping and searching of these coaches, some way from their destination. He then could not resist also insisting that the buses—with nearly all of the passengers still on board—return to London, ensuring that this in fact occurred by arranging for a police escort all the way back to the city. This preventive action was done not under any explicit

---

[47] [1961] 1 WLR 162.   [48] *Moss v McLachlan* [1985] IRLR 76.   [49] Ibid, p 78.

[50] *R (Laporte) v Chief Constable of Gloucestershire*, n 16 above.

[51] Ibid, para [5] per Lord Bingham of Cornhill.

[52] While Overalls Movement Building Libertarian Effective Struggles.

statutory power but ostensibly by invocation of the breach of the peace jurisdiction, despite the decision-making officer's candid (and as it transpired critical) admission that no breach of the peace was imminent at the precise moment that he had decided to turn the coaches back. Marooned in London, the claimant and many other non-Womble protestors found they had been denied their chance to protest. One of them, Jean Laporte, took judicial review proceedings, claiming that the police had acted unlawfully in both stopping the coaches from proceeding and in requiring them to return to London.

The latter of these actions was too much for all the courts that considered the question, but both the High Court and the Court of Appeal considered the refusal to allow the buses to proceed to have been within the general discretion of the police to act to prevent reasonably apprehended breaches of the peace.[53] Here they were merely following in the long line of cases (some mentioned above) which had fairly blindly but consistently supported police judgements on breach of the peace. But in an unexpected ruling just before Christmas 2006, the Lords overturned this finding, unanimously ruling that the stopping had itself also been wrong because no breach of the peace had been about to occur or had in any sense been imminent. The vague ruling in *Piddington v Bates* under which the police had done serious civil libertarian damage for over 40 years was condemned by Lord Bingham as an 'aberrant decision'[54] and even *Moss v McLachlan*—so important to the operational defeat of the miners' union in 1983–4 and to the stifling of CND and other protests for nearly two decades—was practically confined to its own facts, albeit with the different law lords striking individual notes as to how exactly they viewed the case.[55] Particularly important was the ruling in *Laporte* that the police actions had not been 'prescribed by law'. This was because the preventive powers the police enjoyed in this area only kicked in when a breach of the peace was imminent, with there being no sliding scale of police power that hinged on how likely, or reasonably apprehended, a particular breach of the peace was. In dispensing so unequivocally with a muddy line of dicta which the police have worked to their advantage for generations, the law lords have struck a highly significant blow for the right to protest. The effect of their incisive determination on the 'prescribed by law' point, furthermore, was that the whole case did not resolve itself into a fact-specific assessment of what was

---

[53] *R (Laporte) v Chief Constable of Gloucestershire Constabulary* [2004] EWCA Civ 1639, [2005] QB 678.

[54] *R (Laporte) v Chief Constable of Gloucestershire*, n 16 above, para [47].

[55] Usefully summarized by Lord Brown of Eaton-under-Heywood, ibid, para [116].

'necessary in a democratic society'—in the new Human Rights Act era, it was the wide power itself that was illegitimate.

How important is the *Laporte* case likely to be? The facts were good ones on which to fight the point of principle. Their Lordships clearly thought the police had gone over the top in denying the occupants of all three coaches their rights merely on account of a degree of anxiety over a few mildly dangerous Wombles. If it had been asserted that a breach of the peace had been imminent, the second-guessing of this discretion would have taken more courage; as it was, the police assertion, made contemporaneously, of exactly the opposite of that made the ruling very much easier. The implications of the decision will be worked through in future situations of conflict; only then will it be possible to know how successfully its liberal perspective has been embedded in the law. But whatever happens, it stands as a massive vindication of those who argued that a change in hostile judicial attitudes to political liberty was not only necessary but also possible. The emphasis on freedom and on the need for restrictions on liberty to be proportionate to be found in the Human Rights Act 1998 certainly helped here. Also a factor might well have been the judges' empathy with the protestors—they were seeking to oppose an invasion of which the vast majority of the public had heartily disapproved. A vital factor in the mind of the senior law lord, Lord Bingham, and his colleagues clearly was that the authorities had had available to them a range of statutory provisions which they had already used to impose a wide range of conditions on the planned protest: falling back on the common law power was unnecessary, a power too far as far as their Lordships were concerned. It is to this array of parliamentary controls on protest that we now turn. As indicated earlier, after the battering that the common law power has suffered at the hands of their Lordships in late 2006, it may be that the statute law in this field will become even more important in future than it has been in the past.

The first national legislation providing for a power to ban or impose conditions on marches was the Public Order Act 1936. The overall measure was a belated response to the challenge to political authority posed by the fascist followers of Sir Oswald Mosley, with its main clauses prohibited the wearing of political uniforms and the conducting or managing of quasi-military associations.[56] Section 3 allowed conditions or an outright ban to be imposed on a procession where a chief officer of police was of opinion, 'having regard to the time or place at which and the circumstances in which any public procession is taking place or is intended to take place and to the route taken or proposed to be taken by the procession' that

[56] Public Order Act 1936, ss 1 and 2.

there was 'reasonable ground for apprehending that [it] may occasion serious public disorder'. The power was immediately deployed upon enactment to clamp down on protest marches across London in the late 1930s. Designed to control the fascists, the reach of such orders had necessarily to be more general, with Parliament having deliberately chosen not to allow the police to pick and choose which protesters they wanted to facilitate and which to repress. (The contrast with the common law here is particularly marked.) The same civil libertarian sentiment was evident in the fact that the s 3 powers only kicked in where 'serious public disorder' was perceived to be in the offing and in the exemption altogether of stationary meetings from the reach of the Act. Perhaps reflecting a continuing societal taboo against banning orders and the like, the power was rarely invoked after the first flurry of energy against the fascists had died down, with the controversies of the 1960s and 1970s being more about the police allowing processions (by, for example, the National Front) than banning them.

The atmosphere changed in the early 1980s. Since then we have seen a loosening of the civil libertarian controls on these statutory powers and a (perhaps consequent) dramatic rise in their deployment by the police. The Public Order Act 1986 made three important changes: for the first time at national level it required advance notice of processions to be given to the police;[57] it expanded the power to impose conditions on processions in the 1936 Act to include stationary assemblies as well;[58] and it widened the criteria under which processions (and now these non-marching protests as well) could be made the subject of conditions, to include not only serious public disorder but also a reasonable apprehension that an event would occasion serious damage to property, serious disruption to the life of the community, or the intimidation of others 'with a view to compelling them not to do an act they have a right to do, or to do an act they have a right not to do' (so long as such intimidation is the purpose behind the protest).[59] As we saw in Chapter 3, the 1980s and first half of the 1990s was the period in which societal solidarity with civil liberties began its decline.[60] The 1980s began with the CND protests against cruise missiles, saw large-scale industrial conflict in its middle years and ended with the poll tax revolt that was eventually to be a major factor in bringing down the prime minister with whom these years will always be associated, Margaret Thatcher. By the mid-1990s the Conservative Party she had led was still in power but the main opposition Party, Labour, had embarked upon a strategy of policy

---

[57] Public Order Act 1986, s 11. For a rare case see *Kay v Metropolitan Police Commissioner* [2006] EWHC 1536 (Admin).
[58] Public Order Act 1936, s 14.   [59] Ibid, ss 12 and 14.   [60] See above pp 49–57.

emulation in the 'law and order' field, under its enthusiastic shadow Home Secretary and (from 1995) leader, Tony Blair.

The results were extremely bad for the freedom of public protest. Pivotal in this regard was the Criminal Justice and Public Order Act 1994, on which the opposition Labour Party was agonistic but against which a huge head of protest was nevertheless mustered. This was the last occasion in Britain when a proposal with a strongly negative impact on the right of public protest was recognized as such, albeit to no avail. For the first time under statute law the police secured the power to order an end to protest meetings.[61] The device was via new controls on 'trespassory assemblies', meetings 'on land to which the public has no right of access or only a limited right of access'. As roads are for processing along and not stopping, this definition brought the public highway within its repressive remit.[62] The power kicks in where a chief officer 'reasonably believes' that such an assembly of 20 or more persons '(a) is likely to be held without the permission of the occupier of the land', and '(b) may result in (i) serious disruption to the life of the community; or (ii) where the land, or a building or monument on it, is of historical, architectural, archaeological or scientific importance, in significant damage to the land, building or monument'. With these conditions met, such an officer may apply to the local authority for an order prohibiting all 'trespassory assemblies' in the district or part of it for a designated period up to four days and within a radius of five miles of the specified centre.

In 2005, Parliament went further than this, prohibiting demonstrations carried out in its vicinity without the prior approval of the Metropolitan Police Commissioner, whose consent can be lawfully withheld for a variety of reasons.[63] Just as they sought to modify the effects of the 1994 Act with their narrow reading of what constituted trespass on the highway,[64] so the judges initially recoiled from the implications of the 2005 Act, particularly in relation to the extraordinarily persistent protest on Parliament Square of Brian Haw—a one-man crusade the constant sight of which was said to have precipitated parliamentarians into this repressive action.[65]

---

[61] Now Public Order Act, s 14A.

[62] Subject to the important decision of *Director of Public Prosecutions v Jones* [1999] 2 AC 240, which reaffirmed that within limits the holding of a public meeting on the highway was not necessarily a trespass.

[63] Serious Organized Crime and Police Act 2005, s 132.

[64] *Director of Public Prosecutions v Jones*, n 62 above.

[65] *R (Haw) v Secretary of State for the Home Department* [2005] EWHC 2061 (Admin), [2006] QB 359. But see *R (Haw) v Secretary of State for the Home Department* [2006] EWCA Civ 532, where Haw finally lost his battle to continue his protest on the scale into which he had developed it. On 23 May 2006 his protest was cut back by the police so as to conform to the new requirement, under the 2005 Act, that it be no more than 3 square metres.

142 Civil Liberties

But the courts do not have the flexibility to recant that they enjoy when reviewing their own common law creations, so any hopes for a *Laporte*-like change need to be directed towards the legislative rather than the judicial branch. This has now been confirmed by the Administrative Court decision in *Blum and others v The Director of Public Prosecutions*.[66] Two of the four appellants in the case had taken part in a deliberately unauthorized protest in Parliament Square on the day the law came into force. The third and fourth appellants took their action nearly three months later, choosing a Whitehall location opposite Downing Street to read out the names both of British soldiers who had been killed in Iraq and of Iraqi citizens who had died in the conflict. Authorization for the protest had been neither sought nor given. All four appellants were convicted of offences under s 132 in proceedings at Bow Street Magistrates' Court (and therefore without a jury). In rejecting their appeals against conviction, Waller LJ and Lloyd Jones J pointed to Strasbourg authority to the effect that to require prior authorization for a protest 'does not normally encroach upon the essence of the right' to demonstrate.[67] Since states had a 'right to require authorization, they must be able to apply sanctions to those who participate in demonstrations that do not comply with the requirement'.[68] This was because the 'impossibility to impose such sanction would render illusory the power of the State to require authorization'.[69] In vein did counsel for the appellants muster an array of authorities to seek to circumvent the 'compelling' logic of these observations.[70] In this instance Strasbourg provided guidance supportive of a legal framework that in the absence of such legitimation would surely have been more clearly seen for what it was, a serious invasion of civil liberties. The appellants might have been better advised to have sought permission and then to have attempted a judicial review of the denial that might (or might not) have followed.

PUNITIVE CONTROLS ON SPEECH

I have already observed that in a free society there is a large difference between preventing the communication of a political point of view on the one hand and punishing the speaker via the criminal or civil law on the other. In the second kind of situation, the sentiment has reached its target market, the point of view has been got out into the open and there is no way that it can now be rendered unsaid or forcibly unremembered. To accept

---

[66] [2006] EWHC 3209 (Admin).
[67] Ibid, at para [19] per Waller LJ referring to *Ziliberberg v Moldova*, application 61821/00, judgment of 4 May 2004, p 11.
[68] Ibid. [69] Ibid. [70] Ibid, para [21] per Waller LJ.

this distinction is not to say, however, that the punishment of political speech is something about which the law of civil liberties is relaxed. If the coercion is severe enough, and the procedures to secure free speech lax enough, then the chill caused by the breadth of the law can be such as to make it effectively a form of prior restraint. Free speech can be badly damaged, and democratic culture consequently eroded, by broad punishments for its exercise even where it would not be possible formally to stop the utterance in the first place. The point is an important one in the British context because of the remarkable contrast between the very few laws there are on prior restraint and the very great deal indeed that are available to punish the speaker after the event.

To lay out the vast range of ways that political speech can be punished in the UK is, without more, to seem to indicate that we already live in a police state. There are two depressingly long sections in the leading textbook, Bradley and Ewing's *Constitutional and Administrative Law*,[71] dealing with, respectively, 'offences against the state and public order' and 'state security and official secrets'. The first covers the old common law offences of sedition and blasphemy, the various statutory offences concerned with preventing incitement to disaffection in the armed forces, and the modern offence of incitement to racial hatred. The latter was the precedent that Parliament turned to in 2006 when it enacted a controversial new control on speech aimed at religious hate speech.[72] The second category of offences in Bradley and Ewing cover mainly those set out in the Official Secrets Act 1989. As though this menu of restraint were not enough, we should also recall that further controls on speech ostensibly designed to safeguard other important state interests (such as public morality, disruption of the peace, and the integrity of the administration of justice) are well capable of producing (and have produced) yet more inhibitions on political expression, via the laws of obscenity, criminal libel, and contempt, respectively—all also the recipients of careful attention in *Bradley and Ewing*.[73] The meagre space afforded to any kind of *right* to free speech—the legislative intervention in 1986 to ensure that unpopular speakers should get a chance to speak on university campuses being a rare example[74]—compounds the dismal story, and makes the enactment of the Human Rights Act 1998 with its guarantee of freedom of expression all the more important in this area.

---

[71] *Constitutional and Administrative Law*, 14th edn (Harlow: Pearson Education Limited, 2007), pp 551–5; 599–625.

[72] Racial and Religious Hatred Act 2006, s 1 and Sch 1, adding ss 29A–29N in a new Part 3A of the Public Order Act 1936.   [73] *Constitutional and Administrative Law*, n 71 above.

[74] Education (No 2) Act 1986, s 43. See *R (Caeser-Gordon) v University of Liverpool* [1991] 1 QB 124.

It is to this plethora of laws that defenders of free speech turn when they seek evidence for their argument that freedom is in decline in Britain and that free speech is, if anything and despite the Human Rights Act 1998, more vulnerable now than it has been in the past.[75] Such provisions also explain the sceptical response to judges' claims on free speech with which this chapter started. While conceding that there is plenty of room for civil libertarian anxiety, and recognizing also that the historical record reveals a number of groups that have been denied the freedom to engage in political debate on their own terms[76] (a point to which I return), it is nevertheless suggested that a thorough appraisal of the limits of free expression requires a broader approach than one rooted in mere citation of the fact of the existence of this or that restrictive law. The first point to make is that many of these restrictive laws are acknowledged even by their opponents to be necessary in principle—the libertarian may be against all controls on speech but the civil libertarian concedes that limits need to be set. The effect of this concession is that as far as many of these laws are concerned, the issue is as to the details of any such provision rather than the mere fact of its having been enacted. It follows that usually the right concern to have is not with the fact that the law exists so much as with how well it reconciles the (often reasonably uncontroversial) objective that has produced it with the underlying principle of free speech that it must necessarily (to some extent) subvert. The parliamentary record, aided from time to time by judicial interpretation, is not so bad in this regard as is sometimes supposed.

Examples of such legislative balancing acts abound. The necessity to empower the police to detect crime persuaded Parliament of the need for legislation to allow the authorities to force members of the media to divulge material which it was judged might be useful to an ongoing investigation.[77] However, a large number of inhibitions against reckless police action were written into the relevant legislation so as to prevent abuse, and the overall effect of the power has as a result been less damaging to journalistic enquiry than was initially feared.[78] In the same way, when Parliament set out to design a contempt of court law that would secure a fair trial for an accused without serious interference or pre-judgment of the outcome by the media, it balanced its strict liability rule (condemning as contempt all publications creating 'a substantial risk that the course of justice in the proceedings in question will be seriously impeded or prejudiced'[79]) with a

---

[75] See the regular columns in *The Observer* of Henry Porter; also the special issue of *Index on Censorship* on 'What New Labour did for Free Speech' (2007) 36 (2), *Index on Censorship*.
[76] For the inter-war record see *The Struggle for Civil Liberties*, n 4 above. For the 1980s see *Freedom under Thatcher*, n 9 above.
[77] Police and Criminal Evidence Act 1984, Part 2, esp ss 9–14 and Sch 1.
[78] *R v Central Criminal Court, ex parte Bright, Alton and Rusbridger* [2001] 1 WLR 662.
[79] Contempt of Court Act 1981, s 2(2).

variety of restrictions and defences designed to facilitate public discussion so far as was reasonably possible.[80] Robustly interpreted by the courts in a civil libertarian direction,[81] the overall effect of the Act has not been seriously negative for free speech, except insofar as it has inhibited particular comment on specific cases—exactly what the Act was designed to do. The same point could even be made, albeit more tentatively, about the Official Secrets Act 1989, passed by Parliament to replace the antiquated, much criticized and wide-ranging s 2 of the 1911 Act of the same name. The hesitancy here derives from the civil libertarians' unease about the actual purpose of the measure: stifling free speech in the name of national security is not as persuasive to such a person's ears as is the need to secure a fair trial. However, the range of safeguards embedded in the Act against its misuse have been sufficient to persuade the House of Lords in the leading case that its terms do not fall foul of the Human Rights Act 1998, and in particular that the right to freedom of expression set out in Article 10 of the Convention has not been breached.[82]

Where the free speech implications of a given proposal are not easily redeemed by a legislative aim that commands widespread approval, then Parliament is much more likely, if not to reject the provision altogether, then sharply to modify its terms, or to act in other ways that serve to signal the legislature's ongoing commitment to free speech. Two examples may be given here. The incitement to racial hatred laws were very controversial when they were first introduced in the mid-1960s, with their effect on free speech being the main basis for the critique to which the proposals were subjected when they were first mooted by the then Labour government of Harold Wilson. Persuaded by the force of the free speech argument, yet anxious not to reject the law, Parliament agreed a new criminal offence which required much more than mere hate speech to produce a conviction.[83] An element of intention and/or violent effect of the speech has remained part and parcel of the law ever since. The jurors that acquitted the leader of the British National Party (BNP), Nick Griffin, of charges under the current form of the Act in November 2006 may have been guilty not of an immoral sympathy with his views (as many seem to have assumed) but of merely regarding the ingredients of the offence with which he was charged with the appropriate degree of seriousness.[84]

---

[80] Schedule 1 and especially ss 4 and 5.
[81] In particular, *Attorney-General v English* [1983] 1 AC 116 and *re Lonrho plc* [1990] 2 AC 154.
[82] *R v Shayler* [2002] UKHL 11, [2003] 1 AC 247.   [83] Race Relations Act 1965, s 6.
[84] The acquittal was returned on 10 November 2006, after the jury had scrutinized on more than one occasion the whole of the video footage extracts from which had been at the core of the prosecution's case.

The second example are the controls on religiously motivated hate speech to which I have earlier referred, these were introduced amid great controversy in 2006, with many arguing that the original proposals heralded a quite unacceptable expansion of the legal control of free speech into the realm of freedom of conscience and of open political debate. The analogy with the race hate laws was not convincing to such critics—they saw in the proposal a potential threat to the proper discussion of a whole range of public issues. In the event, Parliament enacted a law which was not only hedged about with restrictions but which also contained a remarkable caveat, amounting almost to a cry not to be taken too seriously:

Nothing in this Part shall be read or given effect in a way which prohibits or restricts discussion, criticism or expressions of antipathy, dislike, ridicule, insult or abuse of particular religions or the beliefs or practices of their adherents, or of any other belief system or the beliefs or practices of its adherents, or proselytising or urging adherents of a different religion or belief system to cease practising their religion or belief system.[85]

Whether a law limiting free speech secures its passage through Parliament in an unqualified or qualified form, it still faces two further obstacles before it can be transformed into a reliably inhibiting measure on the ground. The first of these relates to the power formally to deploy the provision, in other words to initiate proceedings against alleged wrongdoers. In this sensitive area of free speech, Parliament routinely entrusts the prosecution decision to the authorities, usually the Director of Public Prosecutions but in relation to particularly important matters the Attorney General. Proceedings under the Incitement to Disaffection Act 1934, for example, require the Director's consent.[86] Race hatred prosecutions need the involvement of the Attorney General.[87] Sometimes no less a figure than a High Court judge must sanction what is proposed, as is the case with prosecutions for criminal libel.[88] Even if this kind of safeguard is not present, a member of the public seeking to unleash the force of the criminal law against someone on account of his or her views has still to persuade a magistrate to issue a summons: this was the basis on which efforts to prosecute the novelist Salman Rushdie for the common law offence of seditious libel were successfully stymied.[89]

---

[85] Public Order Act 1986, s 29J, added by Racial and Religious Hatred Act 2006, s 1 and Schedule. Note that the EU is involving itself in the general area: 'EU agrees new race hatred law', *Guardian*, 20 April 2007.

[86] Which was given in *R v Arrowsmith* [1975] QB 678.   [87] Public Order Act 1986, s 27(1).

[88] Law of Libel Amendment Act 1888, s 8. For a rare example see *Goldsmith v Pressdram Ltd* [1977] QB 83.

[89] *R v Chief Metropolitan Stipendiary Magistrate, ex p Choudhury* [1991] 1 QB 429. Cf *Whitehouse v Lemon* [1979] AC 617.

Second, and if all else fails, there is still the jury. Of course, for crimes carrying modest penalties the authorities can avoid the need to persuade lay people of the rightness of their cause: we saw this in relation to the convictions of the protestors in Whitehall in the *Blum* case. But we have also seen how the leader of the BNP was able to secure an acquittal on race hate charges by persuading the jury that tried him that he had not committed the offences with which he had been charged. It is the jury trial—sometimes compulsory; sometimes (as with encouraging terrorism) a *sine qua non* of a heavy punishment—that is the residual guarantor of free speech in Britain. The risk of an unexpected result from a 'perverse jury' is sometimes thought an argument in favour of their abolition; in fact it might be exactly the reason why they are essential.[90] By their willingness to refuse verdicts that are out of step with common sense or civil libertarian principle or both, and by their determination to do this whatever the law might seem to require, juries fulfil a vital role in taming the law. Their verdicts can defy the guidance of the trial judge and the comprehensiveness of the prosecutorial case. They are the common law's safeguard against the sort of zealous enforcement of the law that, if left unchallenged, can quickly drift into authoritarianism.

The point is an old one, with *Bushell's case* having established as early as 1670 the right of a jury to acquit against the evidence.[91] *Bushell* has its modern equivalent in *R v Ponting*, a celebrated official secrets prosecution in the mid-1980s in which a jury rejected the trial judge's demand that it treat the interests of the state as being solely what the government of the day said they were.[92] In the early 2000s, charges under the Official Secrets Act 1989 against a Government Communications Headquarters (GCHQ) employee Katherine Gun, for having allegedly leaked an email from US spies to their British counterparts were dropped, with the authorities being fearful that a jury would acquit (by finding a defence of necessity) out of a sense of sympathy with Gun—she was determinedly anti-war and prepared to argue that her actions had been designed to save innocent lives.[93] It is not only perverse juries that do civil libertarian work. As we have seen it might well have been the scrupulous care taken by Nick Griffin's jury that led to his acquittal, rather than any (from the law's point of view) eccentric empathy with the accused's supposedly (but only supposedly) criminal remarks. The convictions of Abu Hamza on six charges of

[90] See Lord Devlin, *Trial by Jury* (London: Methuen, 1966).
[91] See *R v Penn and Mead* (1670) 6 St Tr 951.   [92] [1985] *Crim Law Rev* 318.
[93] See the Standard Note on the case by Oonagh Gay (SN/PC/2023, House of Commons library, 8 March 2004).

engaging in a particularly heinous form of speech—soliciting murder—are all the more convincing for the fact that his jury also saw fit to acquit him of three similar charges.[94] There is a seriousness of purpose and a democratic dimension to jury trial that makes it not only a guarantor of free speech but also a dependable adjudicator—credible to all communities in Britain—on when the freedom has to give way to other societal demands.

It might be thought that there is an inconsistency in our treatment of the law here. At the start of the chapter I deplored the past record of the British state in attacking the free speech of certain elements within society. But now I seem to have mounted an argument that we should all be more relaxed about what appears in the statute book, on account of the fact that there are these layers of official good sense, moderation, and sensitivity to civil liberties that make the gap between law and the practice on the ground pleasingly wider than the civil libertarian critics allow. But the fact is that although these restraints operate most of the time, they do not always do so and it is when the full force of the law is unleashed on a marginal political grouping or individual that we see English law at its most repressively extreme. Examples that come to mind are the way in which the Communist Party of Great Britain and the National Unemployed Workers' Movement were treated in the inter-war period and the former organization, striking labour unions and Irish nationalist groups in the post-war decades, particularly (as far as Irish republicans were concerned) during the 1970s and 1980s. The risk with the current anxiety about the threat of political violence from Islamic groups is that it will loosen the constraints that are currently inhibiting the application of the law against a whole range of Islamic speech. If this were to happen it would be expecting a great deal of the Human Rights Act 1998, and therefore the judiciary, to do all the defensive work on behalf of free speech.

PUNITIVE CONTROLS ON PUBLIC PROTEST

The public interest in maintaining a degree of order on the streets is usually more evident than the need to suppress the written word. Controls on public protest are always more likely, and more likely to be uncontroversial, than controls on speech. In situations where violence has been threatened, or indeed occasioned, there can be little dispute about the use of the criminal law against those responsible. Thus charges of riot, violent disorder,

---

[94] See *R v Abu Hamza* [2006] EWCA Crim 2918. Note also the conviction of Umran Javed for soliciting murder and stirring up racial hatred during a demonstration outside the Danish embassy in London: *Guardian*, 6 January 2007.

and affray will only raise civil liberties issues if there is a suspicion that their deployment has been discriminatory, a way of punishing protestors disproportionately for bad behaviour that would not have attracted the same levels of attention had it been free of political content.[95] The closer a provision gets to encompassing non-violent action, the greater the potential for its partial application and therefore for civil libertarian abuse. Thus while the punishment of threatening, abusive, or insulting words or behaviour in s 4 of the Public Order Act 1986 might be uncontroversial on its face from a civil liberties point of view, on account of the clear requirement of a connection with violence,[96] the practical use to which the police have put the provision (and its predecessor, s 5 of the 1936 Act)—stimulated by its relatively open categories of bad conduct—has often attracted controversy.[97] The same is even more the case with ss 4A and 5 of the 1986 Act, where the consequence of the designated bad behaviour that attracts police attention need not be violence but rather nothing more than the intentional causing of 'harassment, alarm or distress' to a third party. In a similar vein is the Protection from Harassment Act 1997, a law which has been used to curb the campaigns of so-called animal rights groups against persons targeted for abuse on account of their involvement in animal experimentation, whether as employees, contractors, scientists, or even investors in companies with a commercial association with those involved in the practice.[98] The Criminal Justice and Police Act 2001 and the Serious Organized Crime and Police Act 2005 have added further provisions designed to curb the *ad hominem* campaigning of these quasi-militant anti-vivisectionists.[99]

While the Human Rights Act 1998 has done some effective work to curb the wider applications of these laws, in one well-known case leading to the quashing of a conviction where the defendant had desecrated the US flag in front of American soldiers,[100] it is unlikely that protest which deliberately seeks to cause distress as a way of communicating its perspective

---

[95] See now Public Order Act 1986, ss 1–3. For a controversial use of the riot charge see *R v Caird* (1970) 54 Cr App Reps 499.

[96] There must be an intent 'to cause that person to believe that immediate unlawful violence will be used against him or another by any person, or to provoke the immediate use of unlawful violence by that person or another, or whereby that person is likely to believe that such violence will be used or it is likely that such violence will be provoked'.

[97] See *Brutus v Cozens* [1973] AC 854.

[98] See *Oxford University v Broughton* [2004] EWHC 2490 (QB). See also *Daiichi Pharmaceuticals UK Ltd v Stop Huntingdon Animal Cruelty* [2004] 1 WLR 1503. The ordinary criminal law has also been to the fore: 'Animal rights activists involved in bid to shut lab among 30 arrested in raids', *Guardian*, 2 May 2007.

[99] In particular s 42 if the 2001 Act and ss 126 and 127 of the 2005 Act. Section 126 added a new s 42A to the 2001 Act, while s 127 amended s 42.

[100] *Percy v Director of Public Prosecutions* [2001] EWHC 1125 (Admin), [2002] *Crim Law Rev* 835.

will be able to use Articles 10 or 11 to shield itself from the attentions of these provisions.[101] This has certainly proved to be the case so far as the Protection from Harassment Act 1997 is concerned.[102] In any case, so long as they are narrowly focused, why should laws dealing with this kind of conduct be undone by a human rights charter? Consciously antagonistic behaviour of the sort that has stimulated these recent anti-harassment laws is a far cry from the traditional march or demonstration where solidarity rather than hostility is invariably the prevailing emotion. We are back in the world of direct action, which was last considered in Chapter 5. In its paradigmatic form, this kind of protest is deliberately designed to cause serious disruption, and as such it is impatient of compromise with the police and at the same time confidently insensitive to the countervailing interests of the general public. If the law is not deliberately broken by such protestors, then it is certainly flirted with in a disrespectful fashion. The point goes well beyond the animal rights activists. The anti-war Wombles whom the Gloucestershire police were keen to stop getting to the public protest on their patch fall into this category. So too do the many 'stop-the-city', eco-warrior and anti-motorway groups that have sprung up in the recent past. One of the main techniques of such protestors has been the mass trespass and this has led the law to a recent preoccupation with the need to control access to private property. Sit-ins,[103] collective trespasses,[104] trespassing in a designated site,[105] and engaging in a disruptive trespass[106] have all received close attention from Parliament in recent years, to the point where it has never been easier to transform an act of trespass into a criminal act. If it is not to condemn such laws out of hand, how should the law and practice of civil liberties regard them?

As a matter of principle, it must be right that those who set out to harass or abuse others should not be insulated from legal accountability solely on account of the purity of their (political) motivation. Equally, the right to

---

[101]   *Hammond v Director of Public Prosecutions* [2004] *Crim Law Rev* 851, *Norwood v Director of Public Prosecutions* [2003] *Crim Law Rev* 888 and *Director of Public Prosecutions v Collins* [2006] UKHL 40 show the limits of the Convention in this area. Cf *Morrow, Geach and Thomas v Director of Public Prosecutions* [1994] *Crim Law Rev* 58; *Director of Public Prosecutions v Clarke* (1992) 94 Cr App Reps 359.   [102]   *Oxford University v Broughton*, n 98 above.

[103]   Criminal Law Act 1977, ss 6–9. See *R v Jones* [2006] UKHL 16, [2006] 2 WLR 772. Another way of controlling such protests is via the Trade Union and Labour Relations (Consolidation) Act 1992, s 241 of which preserves an old Victorian provision from the Conspiracy and Protection of Property Act 1875 (s 7): *Galt v Philp* [1984] IRLR 156.

[104]   Criminal Justice and Public Order Act 1994, Part V.

[105]   Serious Organized Crime and Police Act 2005, s 128. Originally focused on military bases and nuclear power stations, designated sites have recently been expanded to include the Palace of Westminster, Chequers, and various royal residences. The new list took effect in June 2007: 'New powers against trespassers of key sites', *Guardian*, 24 March 2007.

[106]   Criminal Justice and Public Order Act 1994, s 68.

assemble to express a collective point of view can hardly entail the indefinite appropriation of another's property, regardless of the inconvenience caused to him or her. The law needs to be able to act in such circumstances. Whether it should actually do so in any particular case is, however, another matter. As we saw at the end of the last section there is—rightly—a gap between law and practice through which civil libertarian distance can be put between what the law seems to allow and what is actually done. The police need, on occasion, to lace their natural commitment to order with some compassion for the activist and a sense of balance. As with free speech law, much also depends on the intelligent exercise of the prosecutorial discretion (if criminal proceedings are involved) or on the good sense of the affected claimants (if a civil injunction is what is sought). In any of these cases, a court can be brought in to correct anti-civil libertarian excess at a later stage (either by declaring the initial police action unlawful or by refusing to convict or to grant the desired injunction in the terms sought); the test of proportionality which is required of all exceptions to the rights set out in Articles 10 and 11 can be mustered to good effect to provide a legal basis for exactly these kinds of pragmatic interventions. But those who chose harassment or trespass as their way of wrenching public sentiment in their direction need to acknowledge that they may be doing so at a price so far as their criminal records are concerned. This is not necessarily to say that they are wrong, it is merely to suggest that civil liberties theory does not require that their conduct be entirely immune from criminal or civil responsibility. Sometimes, even in a democracy, what is right and what is lawful need to be out of kilter.

CONCLUSION

At the end of the last section I noted in passing the role of civil actions in the control of types of public protest which are judged to have passed into unacceptable forms of direct action. The Protection from Harassment Act 1997, in particular, has invited in the affected parties as partners in the controlling exercise that the legislation makes possible. While this may be appropriate to the particular circumstances of Oxford University and Huntingdon Life Sciences, each of which successfully obtained injunctions against animal rights activists who were harassing their staff, there are two grounds for disquiet. The first anticipated above, relates to the potential breadth of the court orders obtained in such circumstances. In the *Oxford University* case, for example, the injunction against animal rights activists and animal rights organizations that was obtained encompassed members and employees of the university and their families, the employees and shareholders of an affected contractor (together with their families, servants, or agents), and also any person seeking to visit the laboratory or any premises or home belonging to or occupied by any such protected person.[107] Understandable though such a Draconian reaction to the harassment established in that case might have been, there are nevertheless serious questions about the chilling effect on political freedom entailed in such a wide court order. In *Oxford University v Broughton*, appeals to the Human Rights Act 1998 proved unavailing, with freedom having been more successfully protected before the Act was enacted, in the 1997 case of *Huntingdon Life Sciences Ltd v Curtin*. In this decision, the British Union for the Abolition of Vivisection managed to get themselves removed from those at whom an injunction under the 1997 Act (obtained ex parte) had been directed. Eady J was emphatic that the 1997 Act 'was clearly not intended by Parliament to be used to clamp down on the discussion of matters of public interest or upon the rights of political protest and public demonstration which was so much part of our democratic tradition'.[108]

This kind of human rights-based protection for political freedom is especially important in relation to the second ground of disquiet concerning these proceedings initiated by private parties. Unlike state law enforcers or prosecutors, those starting such civil actions have only their own interests in mind. Frequently, these will be either entirely or partly commercial: the claimant's business concern is being adversely affected by a public protest. Legitimate when narrowly focused on particular incidents of direct harassment or of abusive or grossly intrusive behaviour, such court orders have the potential to reach more widely than this, purposefully availing of the coercive power of law to stifle legitimate public discussion on matters of public interest. The inclination of the civil system to protect economic interests over non-monetizable, political concerns means that protest can be stifled by an injunction which though merely interim (or even ex parte) destroys the opportunity for protestors to strike at the most effective time for them. As any campaigner will tell you (but the law has been slow to realize) a demonstration postponed for a year or two (until trial of the full action) is as dead as one that has been properly banned. It is to be hoped that the effect of the Human Rights Act 1998 will be to make more difficult cases like the celebrated *Hubbard v Pitt*, in which a 1970s community group anxious about the gentrification of their borough were injuncted from distributing leaflets and displaying placards outside an estate agent they judged partly responsible for the change.[109] At a time when large corporations have quite consciously used aggressive legal methods to close down criticisms of their activities (strategic litigation

---

[107] See n 98 above. [108] Queen's Bench Division, 28 November 1997.

[109] [1976] QB 142. The decision contains a powerful dissent by Lord Denning MR. Cf *Thomas v National Union of Mineworkers (South Wales Area)* [1986] Ch 20.

against private parties or SLAPP[110]), such judicial vigilance—now empowered by the Human Rights Act 1998—is more important than ever.[111] The signs are not too unpromising in this regard. Apart from the welcome remarks of Eady J cited above, there have been the restrictions that have been imposed on claimants in defamation cases[112] and the famous Strasbourg decision involving the 'McDonald Two' the effect of which is to require state support for impecunious private parties where they are made defendants in libel actions initiated by large corporate entities.[113]

It is to be hoped that it is now clear that the level of protection for freedom of political speech in Britain is, as is also invariably the case elsewhere, only partly dependant on the law. As we have seen there are important roles for executive and judicial functionaries in moderating the potentially disproportionate impact of notionally illiberal laws. There is also a wider point about culture that needs to be made. The UK is a free society because those who live in this country think of themselves as free: the assumption becomes the norm that guides conduct, thereby solidifying that which was initially assumed to be the case. The various informal constraints on speech which exist in Britain but which we have not dealt with explicitly here—the DA (formerly D) Notice system under which the media are guided on reporting on national security issues;[114] the Press Complaints Commission's unenforceable code of practice; the political pressure that is sometimes put on the BBC[115]—all need to be understood against this background of a shared commitment to freedom of expression on the part of all those involved. To take an example from the world of legal regulation to make the point in a different way, the Broadcasting Code which regulates BBC as well as other broadcasters explicitly acknowledges that '[f]reedom of expression is at the heart of any democratic state'.[116] As long as this is the cultural assumption, then it is likely that freedom of speech will remain a real part of the practice of civil liberties in Britain.

The threat to that practice, then, is more from the atmosphere in the country than from any law in particular. As indicated a little while back in this chapter, there is a real risk that anxiety about terrorism will affect the culture's toleration of political perspectives coming from sources identified

[110] F Donson, *Legal Intimidation* (London: Free Association Books, 2000).
[111] But the Convention is not always reliable: see the depressing outcome of *Appleby v United Kingdom* (2003) 37 EHRR 783.
[112] *Reynolds v Times Newspapers Ltd* [2001] 2 AC 127; *Jameel v Wall Street Journal* [2006] UKHL 44.
[113] *Steel and Morris v United Kingdom* (2005) 41 EHRR 403.
[114] S Gallant and J Epworth, *Media Law: A Practical Guide to Managing Publication Risks* (London: Sweet and Maxwell, 2001) lays out the notices at pp 163–4.
[115] For example, the furore over the *Real Lives* television programme: see *Freedom under Thatcher*, n 9 above, pp 242–3.
[116] *Constitutional and Administrative Law*, n 71 above, p 549.

(rightly or wrongly) with such criminal acts. An ominous sign is the extent to which public fear of terrorism seems to remain high despite the historically very low levels of political violence in Britain, certainly as compared with the 1970s and 1980s. The 'War on Terror' may turn out to be less like the old IRA campaign and more akin to the suspicion of the 'enemy within' during the Cold War, a perpetual driving force in the culture, whatever the facts on the ground. If this does happen, then we may see a narrowing of the political space with consequent increased alienation from those who find there is no opportunity to assert their views. It was exactly this kind of potential in the glorifying terrorism provision that made the proposal so controversial when it was introduced. To be a true civil libertarian society, it is important not to repeat the mistakes of the past (with regard to Left wing and Irish nationalist speech in particular) and to show that a proper democratic state can be a broad church as far as discourse is concerned, while being fundamentalist when it comes to violence.

At a broader level there is great concern about the degree to which concentrations of media ownership in a few hands might adversely affect the political culture.[117] This is undoubtedly a serious matter; the way the public look at the world is certainly shaped to some extent by the providers of the data on which they make their assessments, and if there is bad faith in the delivery (a hidden political or commercial agenda) then the public discussion is skewed accordingly. But at the same time we see this trend towards greater control, there is the countervailing influence of the 'ubiquitous internet',[118] a 'flourishing non-market sector of information, knowledge and cultural production, based on the networked environment, and applied to anything that the many individuals connected to it can imagine'.[119] Already these breakthroughs in communication have greatly strengthened the campaign of a US presidential candidate (Howard Dean) and made easier the kinds of direct actions with which we have been concerned in an earlier section of this chapter. The working through of the implications for political freedom of this new world of communication are in their very earliest stages.[120] Political freedom has proved itself a highly robust creature in the past, and we may be witnessing another of its reconfigurations to fit within the latest, technologically driven model for effective communication.

[117] *Constitutional and Administrative Law*, n 71 above, pp 545–6.
[118] J Naughton, 'Blogging and the emerging media ecosystem', Background paper for an invited seminar to Reuters Fellowship, University of Oxford, 8 November 2006, p 5.
[119] Y Benkler, *The Wealth of Networks: How Social Production Transforms Markets and Freedom* (New Haven, CT: Yale University Press, 2006), p 7, cited by Naughton, ibid, p 1.
[120] See M Klang and A Murray, *Human Rights in the Digital Age* (London: Glasshouse Press, 2005). See 'Internet giants bow to human rights protest', *The Observer*, 28 January 2007.

8

The Right to Freedom of Association

The right of association for political ends is a strongly embedded entitlement in British political culture. It is a freedom that has been forged in past eras of repression, when the branding of a political association as unlawful was frequently turned to as a means of hindering the advance of the ideas for which its members stood. By the twentieth century, however, the liberty had managed to become well-established in the UK (apart from in Northern Ireland, on which see further below). Thus the generally severe defence of the realm regulations promulgated at the outset of and throughout the First World War empowered the authorities to harass in all sorts of ways the radical peace activists and trade unionists who were perceived to be a threat to national defence, but they did not take the short-cut of group censorship.[1] Nor did the government when faced with the new threat of a domestic Communist Party of Great Britain in the 1920s.[2] The emergency regulations of the Second World War era likewise tended to go for suspected persons rather than groups.[3] Through much of the liberal post-war period, the idea of banning political groups or other kinds of associations was more or less unthinkable in Britain.

This entrenchment of a previously highly contentious freedom may have been a benign side-effect of the large-scale battles that had been fought (and won) in the pre-democratic era to secure the right of working men and women to associate together in unions to defend their interests. Among other progressive results that victory had given birth to the Labour Party, and a further reason why governments and Parliaments have regarded banning groups as something of a taboo might lie in the strong link that exists in practice between democratic government and political parties: the former is hardly possible without the latter, a fact of which we may be sure all such parties are acutely aware. It has also long been the case

---

[1] KD Ewing and CA Gearty, *The Struggle for Civil Liberties* (Oxford: Oxford University Press, 2000), ch 2.

[2] Ibid, ch 3. It is arguable, however, that the sedition trial of the Communist Party leadership in 1925 was a de facto attack on the existence of the Party itself.

[3] N Stammers, *Civil Liberties in Britain during the 2nd World War: A Political Study* (London: Croom Helm, 1983).

that across the world the banning of rival factions—the criminalization of mere membership of a group for opposition to the government—is the clearest possible evidence in such a place of the decline of democratic freedom, something entirely different in kind from *ad hominem* prosecutions or even from such an extreme action as internment. Carrying these kinds of authoritarian overtones, it has become a correspondingly difficult step for a self-consciously democratic government to take.

To the extent that there are limitations on involvement in mainstream political associations in contemporary Britain, these tend to be designed to support rather than subvert democracy. Police officers are not permitted to engage in political activity.[4] Certain local government officials may not actively engage in party politics if they are in restricted posts, although even here membership (as long as it is passive) is not denied.[5] Judges and civil servants are also restricted in the individual contributions they can make in the political arena. It has long been the case as well that certain sensitive jobs in the public sector have been vetted and for much of the Cold War period membership of a radical organization (for example, the Communist Party of Great Britain) would have led to an individual being denied entry (or it might be advancement) on grounds of their unreliability.[6] Efforts to expand such controls were highly contested even during the Cold War. The alleged linkage between membership of a trade union and a threat to national security which underpinned the introduction of a prohibition on membership of such associations at GCHQ in 1984 was extremely controversial even at the time, with the revocation of the ban being among the first acts of the incoming Labour administration in 1997.[7] However, the contemporary anxiety relates to the threat of penetration of the public service and this has meant that some restrictions on access to the public service have remained in place.

So far the concern has been with actions that can be taken against individuals rather than the groups to which they belong. More directly concerned with associations as such, and motivated by a fear of allowing the development of a state within a state, are ss 1 and 2 of the Public Order Act 1936. The first of these provisions makes it an offence for any person in a

---

[4] See *Champion v Chief Constable of Gwent* [1990] 1 WLR 1.

[5] Local Government and Housing Act 1989, ss 1 and 2. The system has survived Strasbourg challenge: *Ahmed v United Kingdom* (1998) 29 EHRR 1.

[6] The even tougher approach of the German authorities on the same point was held by the European Court of Human Rights not to involve any Convention right, the right of access to the civil service not being within the Convention: *Kosiek v Germany* (1986) 9 EHRR 328; *Glasenapp v Germany* (1986) 9 EHRR 25. For the post-Cold War position see *Vogt v Germany* (1995) 21 EHRR 205.

[7] *Council of Civil Service Unions v Minister for the Civil Service* [1985] AC 374.

public place or at a public meeting to wear a uniform signifying association with a political organization or with the promotion of any political object. The second extends the reach of the criminal law to the organization or training of its members or supporters so as to allow them to usurp the functions of the police or the armed forces or to display force in such a way as to give rise to a 'reasonable apprehension' that this is indeed what they are about. Here are examples of the kind of legislative actions which, as we saw in Chapter 3, democracies feel capable of taking to defend themselves. The law emerged by way of a response to Mosley's British Union of Fascists and it has been used from time to time to control the tendency of many such factions to engage in fantasy law and order manoeuvres of a pseudo-military sort.[8] With the outbreak of serious disorder in Northern Ireland in the late 1960s these provisions were used from time to time to control the anything but frivolous displays of militant confidence by a re-emerging IRA. In *O'Moran v Director of Public Prosecutions*[9] the traditional salute at the graveside of an IRA member by former colleagues attired in black clothing and black berets was held by Widgery LCJ and his colleagues on the High Court bench to fall within the provisions of s 1(1) of the 1936 Act.

By the time the appeal in *O'Moran* was decided, however,[10] the authorities had a more direct legislative weapon to hand, in the form of the proscription of the IRA itself. This was a key part of the package of measures that had been rushed through Parliament in the aftermath of the Birmingham pub bombing in November 1974.[11] As suggested at the start of this chapter, the banning of associations had long been part of the repertoire of repressive laws available to the authorities in Northern Ireland. From its inception in 1922 until its abolition exactly 50 years later, the devolved administration in Belfast had used its autonomy in relation to law and order to push through a series of swingeing regulations against civil and political rights, and from the start these had included the condemnation as unlawful of a variety of nationalist associations.[12] A set of these powers were upheld (albeit by a bare majority of three to two) in a very controversial decision of the House of Lords in 1971.[13] So entrenched was the commitment to freedom of association in the rest of the UK that the IRA

---

[8] *R v Jordan and Tyndall* [1963] *Crim Law Rev* 124. Cf Terrorism Act 2006, s 6 (training for terrorism) and s 8 (attendance at a place used for terrorist training).
[9] [1975] QB 864.   [10] 11 December 1974.
[11] See D Bonner, 'Responding to Crisis: Legislating Against Terrorism' (2006) 122 *Law Quarterly Review* 602.
[12] *Struggle for Civil Liberties*, n 1 above, pp 381–2.
[13] *McEldowney v Forde* [1971] AC 632. For a modern ruling see *R v Z* [2005] UKHL 35.

was able to continue to enjoy a public presence while at the same time conducting a bombing campaign in Britain which was unprecedented in savagery for a period when the country was not formally at war. This changed in 1974.

True, initially, both government and informed public opinion were very anxious to limit the terrorism laws, both as to their substance and their duration. Gradually, under the pressure of events, this changed. As we have seen in Chapter 3 the legislation both persisted on the statute books and grew in size, and the groups banned under its repressive aegis began also inexorably to rise. The Irish National Liberation Army soon joined the IRA on the list, as did other Northern Ireland-based groups: by the time the comprehensive and now permanent Terrorism Act 2000 reached the statute book on 20 July 2000, no fewer than 14 such groups (from both the unionist and nationalist sides of the Northern Ireland argument) figured on the banned list—it might be thought somewhat bizarrely in light of the fact that the paramilitary ceasefires of 1997 and the ensuing Good Friday Agreement had already established a fairly secure peace across the whole UK. But the taboo against proscription was a thing of the past. Indeed, the constraint was by now all in the opposite direction: once banned it would take almost eccentric courage on the part of a mainstream political leader to take the risks inherent in making a de-proscription order.

The 2000 Act extended the reach of the terrorism laws, including the power of proscription, well beyond the affairs of Northern Ireland and into the realm of domestic and international terrorism. Given the way in which the civil libertarian principle had already been compromised by the Northern Ireland situation, it was inevitable that the reaction to the attacks of 11 September 2001 should see these powers being quickly deployed against associations suspected by the authorities of being involved in international terrorism. As is invariably the case with banning orders, the momentum has been in the direction of expansion. Twenty-one groups (including those from Northern Ireland) were proscribed even before 11 September,[14] with a further four being added in October 2002[15] and an additional 15 in October 2005.[16] Since then four more have been added, two under new powers taken in 2006 to clamp down on 'glorifying terrorism'.[17] Unsurprisingly, many of these associations are believed to be

[14] Terrorism Act 2000 (Proscribed Organizations) (Amendment) Order 2001, SI 2001/1261.
[15] Terrorism Act 2000 (Proscribed Organizations) (Amendment) Order 2002, SI 2002/2724.
[16] Terrorism Act 2000 (Proscribed Organizations) (Amendment) Order 2005, SI 2005/2892.
[17] Terrorism Act 2000 (Proscribed Organizations) (Amendment) Order 2006, SI 2006/2016.

involved in terrorism which is related either directly to the Al Qaida movement or to the achievement by violence of politico-religious goals which are shared with Osama Bin Laden and his followers. Others on the list have no connection with political Islam but are suspected of involvement in revolutionary violence in various places across the world: the Kurdistan Workers' Party (PKK), the Liberation Tigers of Tamil Eelam (LTTE), the International Sikh Youth Federation, and Basque Homeland and Liberty (ETA) are four such examples.

Some at least of the groups on the list draw support from a circle of followers who agree their aims while disavowing (or denying) their methods. Insofar as such persons seek to express their opinions in Britain then they are bound to be inhibited in their political engagement by the fact of proscription of the organization with which they are so closely associated. Others such as Hizb ut-Tahrir have been inhibited by the occasional threat that their banning is imminent.[18] The chill on conduct and speech generally is bound to be enormous: proscription can lead to a range of offences, involving membership, support, and the wearing of uniforms.[19] The financial effect can also be catastrophic, at not only the local[20] but also the EU and international levels.[21] Recognizing this, the Terrorism Act 2000 has set up a Proscribed Organizations Appeal Commission (POAC) to which banned groups can appeal.[22] The framework allows for legal representation for the affected organization and obligates the authorities to implement the Commission's rulings.[23]

So far, no domestic British group outside Northern Ireland has been proscribed. This is a reflection both of the gratifying lack of systematic violence from any such organization and the residual taboo against banning indigenous groups that persists in the minds of the authorities. It can be only partly on account of any constraints placed on such decision-makers by the legislation itself. The power may be exercised if the secretary of state 'believes' that an organization is 'concerned in terrorism'.[24] This belief is not required to be based on objective evidence or to be in any definable sense reasonable. To be condemned as 'concerned in terrorism' an organization does not have to be involved in acts of terrorism or in preparing for such acts; it is enough that it is believed to promote or encourage terrorism or that it 'is otherwise concerned in terrorism'.[25] Given what has gone before, it is hard to imagine what the term 'otherwise'

---

[18] See 'Blair drops ban on Muslim radicals', *The Observer*, 24 December 2006.
[19] Terrorism Act 2000, ss 11–13.   [20] Ibid, Part III.   [21] See Chapter 9 below.
[22] Terrorism Act 2000, s 5 and Sch 3.   [23] Ibid.   [24] Ibid, s 3(4).
[25] Ibid, s 3(5)(a)–(d).

might involve here. The oversight provided by the POAC only bites where the refusal of the secretary of state to deproscribe (on an application from the group) is 'flawed when considered in the light of the principles applicable on an application for judicial review'[26]—a tough hurdle for an appellant to negotiate in this security-oriented context.

In practice, the main avenue of attack will be for breach of the right to freedom of association set out in Article 11 of the Convention and now included in the guarantees set out in the Human Rights Act 1998—an acknowledgement of this mode of challenging a proscription is built into the very structure of the Terrorism Act 2000 itself.[27] But as with the other civil liberties in the Convention, the guarantee in Article 11 yields to what is 'necessary in a democratic society' and the Strasbourg jurisprudence is not so determined on behalf of political freedom as might have been supposed, with the emphasis of the European judges being more on the procedure under which such decisions are made than with their inherent unacceptability from the civil libertarian perspective.[28] The creation of POAC seems designed to avoid a defeat in Strasbourg and (it follows) in the domestic courts, to the latter of which disputed questions of law arising from the Commission's decisions can also be referred.[29] We are a very long way from having to fight banning orders again British-based 'direct action' or radical activist groups. It is a matter of regret that the framework for such an escalation of repression has been put in place, and that so many proscription orders have been littered on so many foreign political agitators based in Britain, making the idea of banned groups an almost routine, and certainly a familiar one in the minds of a public that within living memory thought the very idea inherent inimical to British liberty. It is this kind of shifting of perspective that makes later, deeper erosions of freedom easier to contemplate and less impossible to sell. If the price of keeping our liberty is vigilance, then one of the things that it is necessary to be vigilant about is the preservation of a well-based sense of indignation at how wrong it is to turn people into criminals merely because of the fact of their association with others.

---

[26] Terrorism Act 2000, s 5(3).   [27] See especially s 9.
[28] See e.g. *Refah Partisi (Welfare Party) and others v Turkey* (2001) 35 EHRR 56.
[29] Terrorism Act, s 6.

Part III

The International Dimension

9

Civil Liberties Beyond the Nation State

Thus far in this book I have been content to describe the law and practice of civil liberties in the UK in a way which (Strasbourg apart) has not required discussion of an international or regional dimension. There has been a deliberate air of unfashionable provinciality which in this chapter will now be at least partly deflated. The UK has always been an island only in the geographical sense. Once it was the ownership of large parts of France, and then the empire. Now the country is part of various twentieth-century orders outside itself: the EU, the Council of Europe, the United Nations (UN), the World Trade Organization, the World Bank, the International Monetary Fund, and many others besides. A large number of these bodies make rules which bind the behaviour of people within Britain, with some of them also possessing institutions whose job it is to oversee with intrusive vigilance how well or badly this country has implemented their decisions. Immensely important consequences flow from all this for the country's international standing, its economic health, and its cultural well-being.

This matters to lawyers insofar as it is generative of new frameworks of laws that need to be studied and critically assessed. But the impact of these international bodies on the law and practice of civil liberties is more restricted. For all its breadth and depth, the array of extra-jurisdictional involvements in which the UK is now entangled does not undermine the nation state in an important sovereign sense. It is technically a fact that the UK remains a self-governing, independent nation. The binding described above is provisional, not immutable. Any British government could perfectly lawfully withdraw from all international and regional associations tomorrow; indeed, there are political parties that are committed to just such a position in relation to the most important supranational body of all, the EU—and no one suggests they do not have a right to put their case. It follows that the precise involvement of the law and practice of civil liberties in this global environment must be carefully identified. In a representative democracy, the legal sovereignty of parliament is not capable of being diluted merely by being described as 'technical'. All the word

'technical' indicates here is that the exercise of that sovereignty in certain
ways is so unthinkable as to be beyond serious discussion. This is a political, a sociological, and an economic fact—but it is not a legal one.

Of course, there are some who say that civil liberties are restricted in the
UK to such an extent that it is impossible to get radical ideas (departure
from the EU; withdrawal from the World Trade Organization) onto the
political agenda—but this is a comment not on the international organizations themselves but rather on the state of our indigenous civil liberties
(combining as some might say with the relative weakness of these arguments). Our concern in this chapter is accordingly not with the various
international bodies whose decisions on trade and finance and the like, and
whose adjudications on such issues via judicial and quasi-judicial bodies,
affect the well-being of those living in this country. Rather, our interest lies
in the rather different matter of the extent to which the UK's ongoing
commitment to various supra-national bodies affects the political health
of this country. How is our right to vote affected, if at all? Can we continue
to engage in all the usual sorts of political activities or does membership of
any of these organizations curtail our freedom? Can the organs of international associations reach directly into the local jurisdiction to impede
political freedom? Have such bodies the capacity to order the executive
branch within Britain to do their illiberal work for them?

There is a large difference between, on the one hand, the fact of
membership of international and regional organizations circumscrib-
ing the content of what can be credibly discussed in a democratic polity
and, on the other, such bodies actually inhibiting the political discourse
by force of the exercise of their own legal powers. In this chapter I am
concerned with the second not the first of these, dealing initially with
international and then with regional bodies. As we shall see, what was
once a very small story has grown as the pressures of globalization have
caused the reach of many of these organizations greatly to expand, and
this has begun to engage civil libertarian issues in an important way.
There is a further dimension to internationalism that has become very
prominent at least since the 11 September 2001 attacks: the power of
the counter-terrorism narrative. The way in which concerns about terrorism have shaped the international political climate has lead—among
many other consequences—to the emergence of new forms of mandatory international and regional laws with clear implications, actual and
potential, for political freedom. It is these developments that have been
the driving force behind the various international legal regimes to
which I now turn.

THE INTERNATIONAL CONTEXT

Under Article 24(1) of the Charter of the United Nations, the member states of the UN 'confer on the Security Council primary responsibility for the maintenance of international peace and security, and agree that in carrying out its duties under this responsibility the Security Council acts on their behalf'. Article 25 declares that the members of the UN 'agree to accept and carry out the decisions of the Security Council in accordance with the present Charter'. Article 41 then goes on to say:

> The Security Council may decide what measures not involving the use of armed force are to be employed to give effect to its decisions, and it may call upon the Members of the United Nations to apply such measures. These may include complete or partial interruption of economic relations and of rail, sea, air, postal, radio, and other means of communication, and the severance of diplomatic relations.

In accordance with Article 48(2), the decisions of the UN Security Council concerning the maintenance of international peace and security 'shall be carried out by the members of the UN directly and through their action in the appropriate international agencies of which they are members'.

The United Nations Act 1946 sets out the basic approach of British law to its UN obligations. Headed 'Measures under Article 41', s 1 is as follows:

> If, under Article forty-one of the Charter of the United Nations . . . the Security Council of the United Nations call (*sic*) upon His Majesty's Government in the United Kingdom to apply any measures to give effect to any decision of that Council, His Majesty may by Order in Council make such provision as appears to Him necessary or expedient for enabling those measures to be effectively applied, including (without prejudice to the generality of the preceding words) provision for the apprehension, trial and punishment of persons offending against the Order.

Clearly, this is as a matter of law a discretionary power; however, as the opening clause makes clear it is one that would be capable of being exercised only at the behest of an international body. Indeed, it may even be the case that a refusal to heed the call of the UN Security Council in a particular instance might leave the government (acting—or not acting—as always on behalf of His or Her Majesty) open to judicial review.

This domestic legal environment is further shaped by the view that another supra-national actor, the EU, takes on such obligations. The relevant provision today is Article 307 of the EC Treaty. This gives precedence as a matter of principle to '[t]he rights and obligations arising from agreements concluded before the entry into force of this Treaty between one or more Member States on the one hand and one or more third countries on the other' by providing that they 'shall not be affected by the provisions of this Treaty'. UN obligations, of course, precede those of the European communities. The EU approach leaves with the national courts the job of ensuring that non-member countries' rights under earlier agreements are honoured, and that the various correlative obligations of member states are fulfilled.[1] It follows that a provision of national law which is judged necessary in order to ensure the performance by the member state concerned of any international obligation falling within Article 307 must be applied even though it conflicts with a provision of Community law.[2] But the EU also goes even further than this, since Article 307 'would not achieve its purpose if it did not imply a duty on the part of the institutions of the Community not to impede the performance of the obligations of Member States which stem from a prior agreement'.[3] Thus resolutions of the UN Security Council which are binding on the member states are also (on account of their impact on these states) treated as imposing an obligation on the EU itself to take all measures necessary to ensure that such resolutions are put into effect.[4]

It might well be objected that this UN capacity to invade the domestic legal sphere of the UK with dictates for action, whether via EU or domestic law, has only a tangential connection with civil liberties. After all, an organization which dedicates itself in its foundational charter to support for the rule of law and to the promotion of fundamental human rights is unlikely thereafter to commit itself to any legislation which is destructive of democracy, or damaging to free speech, freedom of association, and the other, vital political liberties. Whilst this is still largely true, the emergence of the counter-terrorism discourse mentioned in the introduction to this chapter should give pause for thought. How the system can potentially work to subvert civil liberties (and, indeed, human rights) can be seen from the impact of certain UN actions arising out of a desire to act against the Taliban government in Afghanistan. Even before 11 September 2001, the protection afforded Usama bin Laden had made that country a target

---

[1] Case 10/61 _Commission v Italy_ [1962] ECR 1, p 10; Case C-324/93 _Evans Medical and Macfarlan Smith_ [1995] ECR I-563; Case C-124/95 _Centro-Com_ [1997] ECR I–81, para 56. This section of the book draws heavily on the well-researched and authoritative judgment of Kenneth Parker QC (sitting as a deputy judge of the High Court) in _M and MM v Her Majesty's Treasury and Others_ [2006] EWHC 2328 (Admin); note that the appeal against the decision to the Court of Appeal has been unsuccessful: [2007] EWCA Civ 173.

[2] Case C-158/91 _Levy_ [1993] ECR I–4287, para [22].

[3] Case 812/79 _Burgoa_ [1980] ECR 2787, para [9].

[4] Opinions of Advocate General Jacobs in Case C-84/95 _Bosphorus_ [1996] ECR I-3953, p 3956, para [2] and Case C-177/95 _Ebony Maritime and Loten Navigation_ [1997] ECR I–1111, p 1115, para [27].

of Article 41 action. As part of the menu of measures contained in Resolution 1267 (1999), and in order better to enforce the sanctions regime that this resolution was establishing, the UN Security Council set up a committee made up of all its members to police member states so as to make sure they were all implementing the various financial and other actions that were required by this initiative. In summary the plan was to starve the Taliban of funds except those that might be authorized by the sanctions committee on a case-by-case basis on the ground of humanitarian need. Further and stricter resolutions followed, with the committee being instructed (in resolution 1333 (2000)) to maintain a list of individuals and entities designated as associated with Usama bin Laden (including the Al-Qaida organization) to which sanctions would then be applied. Needless to say, the punishment regime hardened enormously after 11 September 2001, with Resolutions 1390 (adopted on 16 January 2002) and 1452 (adopted on 20 December 2002) being particularly important in this regard.[5]

Taking its assumed responsibilities with regard to the UN seriously, the EU promulgated various regulations to give effect to the UN-inspired common positions it had adopted on the question of Afghanistan. Regulation (EC) No 337/2000 dealt with a flight ban and the freezing of funds and other financial resources under the control of the Taleban.[6] Regulation 467/2001 prohibited the export of certain goods and services to Afghanistan and strengthened further the measures that had been taken earlier.[7] A subsequent common position lead to yet more legislation, toughening up the regime generally and in particular imposing certain specific measures against named persons and entities identified as being associated with Usama bin Laden, the Al Qaida network and the Taliban.[8] As these various laws began to bite so their victims started to challenge their application in court. In *M and MM v Her Majesty's Treasury and others*,[9] each of the claimants was 'a housewife responsible for raising several children and [was] a person who qualifie[d] under statutory criteria to receive some or all of certain social security benefits, namely, child benefit,

---

[5] See the study commissioned by the UN Office of Legal Affairs, B Fassbender, *Targeted Sanctions and Due Process* (Office of the Legal Counsel, United Nations, 2006), esp p 4 where the breadth of the sanctions' regime is set out.   [6] [2001] OJ L67, p 1.

[7] [2001] OJ L277, p 25. This regulation superseded Regulation (EC) 337/2000.

[8] Regulation (EC) No 881/2002 [2002] OJ L139, p 9 superseding Regulation 467/2001. Regulation 881/2002 was itself later amended in some important ways by Regulation (EC) 561/2003, which was in turn generated as a follow-up to Security Council Resolution 1452 (2002).

[9] See n 1 above. To similar effect albeit engaging action outside the jurisdiction is *R (Al-Jedda) v Secretary of State for Defence* [2006] EWCA Civ 327.

child tax credit, income support, disability living allowance, carers allowance, housing benefit and council tax benefit'.[10] But each was also the wife of or lived with a person who was listed under the UN Security Council regime and who therefore was to be denied funds under the UN scheme. Under the 1946 Act, the Treasury had arranged a system whereby the claimants had to be licensed before they could receive these moneys— the idea behind the licensing was to ensure that none of the recipients of the benefits then deployed them in a way which violated the sanctions scheme.

When this framework was challenged in the Administrative Court, the argument turned on the EU regulations which underpinned it rather than the domestic law by reference to which the Treasury had acted. The line of attack of direct relevance to civil liberties was that which said that these EU laws were somewhat ambiguous and should and could be sharply modified by interpretation so as to remove the incompatibility with EU fundamental human rights which it was argued inevitably flowed from taking the wide view of their reach that had been the position adopted by the Treasury. This line of attack based on human rights is a well-known head of review of EU law; indeed, in the European Court of Justice it is possible to bring entire laws down by successfully establishing their inconsistency with general principles of community law (of which respect for fundamental human rights is one). The claimants appeared on strong ground in being able to point to fairly severe interferences with both their right to property and to fair procedures as well as (albeit to a lesser extent) to an incursion into their respective rights to family privacy. On its face the regulation under scrutiny was extremely broad, catching 'economic bene-fits of every kind, including but not limited to cash . . . ',[11] and the power of the UN sanctions committee to decide who to include in and exclude from its list was extensive, despite which it was subject neither to any pro-cedural obligations nor other forms of legal accountability. Nevertheless, the claimants were unsuccessful, with Kenneth Parker QC (sitting as a deputy judge of the High Court) finding 'no ambiguity, either as regards language or intention' in the regulations under scrutiny.[12] It followed that there was no room for any common law or EU-based presumption of com-patibility with human rights to operate.

Mr Parker went further than this, however, in a way that has potentially large implications for the future of our subject. Having reviewed the EU case law on the matter, his Lordship 'seriously doubt[ed] whether the

---

[10] *M v Her Majesty's Treasury*, n 1 above, para [1].

[11] Regulation (EC) 881/2002, Article 1.

[12] *M v Her Majesty's Treasury*, n 1 above, para [71].

common law principle (or the provisions of the ECHR) could have any application at all in the present context'.[13] This was on account of two cases, also involving challenges to the Afghanistan sanctions regime, which had been decided by the Court of First Instance in Luxembourg the previous year. In these, highly controversial rulings (which have yet to be confirmed by the court),[14] the second chamber sitting with an extended composition had rejected similar arguments based on property and due process to those in *M* and had endorsed the absolute supremacy of UN resolutions even when fundamental principle was engaged. This was how the European judges framed their decision:

266. Any review of the internal lawfulness of the contested regulation, especially having regard to the provisions or general principles of Community law relating to the protection of fundamental rights, would . . . imply that the Court is to consider, indirectly, the lawfulness of those resolutions. In that hypothetical situation, in fact, the origin of the illegality alleged by the applicant would have to be sought, not in the adoption of the contested regulation but in the resolutions of the Security Council which imposed the sanctions.

267. In particular, if the Court were to annul the contested regulation, as the applicants claim it should, although the regulation seems to be imposed by international law, on the ground that that act infringes their fundamental rights which are protected by the Community legal order, such annulment would indirectly mean that the resolutions of the Security Council concerned themselves infringe those fundamental rights. In other words, the applicants ask the Court to declare by implication that the provision of international law at issue infringes the fundamental rights of individuals, as protected by the Community legal order.[15]

This the judges in each case refused to do. The court had 'no authority to call in question, even indirectly' the lawfulness of the UN resolutions in light of Community law.[16] The only chink in this absolutism lay in the requirement that even UN Security Council actions needed to be consistent with '*jus cogens*, understood as a body of higher rules of public international law binding on all subjects of international law, including the bodies of the UN, and from which no derogation is possible'.[17] But there was nothing nearly severe enough about the sanctions regime to warrant such a conclusion being drawn in these cases; in particular to engage *jus cogens* a deprivation of property had to be arbitrary—something that was

---

[13] Ibid.

[14] *Ahmed Ali Yusuf and Al Barakaat International Foundation v Council of the European Union and others*, 21 September 2005; *Yassin Abdullah Kadi v Council of the European Union and others*, 21 September 2005.

[15] *Yusuf*, ibid. To similar effect is *Kadi*, paras [215] and [216].

[16] *Yusuf*, ibid, para [276]; *Kadi*, ibid, para [225].

[17] *Yusuf*, ibid, para [277]; *Kadi*, ibid, para [226].

clearly not the case here.[18] And the acknowledged 'lacuna in the judicial protection available to the applicants' was 'not in itself contrary to *jus cogens*'.[19] In the UK case, Mr Parker drew the same conclusion on the property point when its consistency with *jus cogens* fell to be considered in the course of his judgment in *M*.[20]

The implications of these Luxembourg rulings for Community law are stark indeed and this is why the decisions have been the subject of adverse comment.[21] Their importance for us lies in the way in which they permit a superior framework of law, rooted in the demands of the UN Security Council, to override not just human rights in general but those civil and political rights that we think of as civil liberties in particular. (I return later to consider a possible role in the national arena for the UK Human Rights Act 1998.) Matters would not be so serious if UN interventions were always specifically related to this or that particular mischief, such as (as in these cases) the Taliban or Usama Bin Laden albeit even here there is scope for abuse—by the end of 2005 the Resolution 1267 sanctions list had 466 entries: 205 individuals and 188 entities associated with Al-Qaida and 142 individuals and one entity associated with the Taliban.[22] But after 11 September 2001 the UN Security Council has begun to pronounce—and to impose international obligations relating to—the problem of 'international terrorism' in general. Resolution 1373 of 28 September 2001, adopted under Chapter VII of the Charter and so legally binding, calls on member states to create a legal framework in their national laws and institutions to prevent and suppress the financing, preparation, and commission of terrorist acts, and to co-operate with other states to this effect. The resolution established a special enforcement mechanism, the counter-terrorism committee (CTC), to monitor implementation by all states.[23] In 2004, the Council set up a counter-terrorism committee executive directorate (CTED), a body of experts charged with assisting the

---

[18] *Ahmed Ali Yusuf and Al Barakaat International Foundation v Council of the European Union and others*, 21 September 2005, paras [293] and [294].

[19] Ibid, para [341].   [20] *M v Her Majesty's Treasury*, n 1 above, para [72].

[21] See, however, the important case Case T 228/02 *Organisation des Modjahedines du Peuple d'Iran* (CFI 12 December 2006), in which the Court of First Instance annulled a decision under the counter-terrorism powers of the EU, distinguishing the *Yusuf* and *Kadi* cases on the basis that these were concerned with implementing UN dictates whereas in the case before it the restrictive laws were home-grown by the EU: see esp paras [99]–[104].

[22] Gijs de Vries, 'The Fight Against Terrorism—Five Years After 9/11', Speech at the Annual European Foreign Policy Conference, London School of Economics and King's College London, 30 June 2006. Mr de Vries is the EU Counter-Terrorism Co-ordinator.

[23] See CA Ward, 'Building Capacity to Combat International Terrorism: The Role of the United Nations Security Council' (2003) 8 *Journal of Conflict and Security Law* 289.

CTC in monitoring states' compliance with resolution 1373. The CTC does not regard itself as under any obligation to take into account human rights issues when it is doing its job: indeed, it was not until resolution 1456 on 20 January 2004 that respect for international human rights standards made it anywhere onto the counter-terrorism agenda.

The potential for civil libertarian harm here, both generally and within the UK, depends on the breadth of the definition of terrorism. By Resolution 1566 of October 2004, the following acts are said never to be justifiable:

Criminal acts, including against civilians, committed with the intent to cause death or serious bodily injury, or taking of hostages, with the purpose to provoke a state of terror in the general public or in a group of persons or particular persons, intimidate a population or compel a government or an international organization to do or to abstain from doing any act, which constitute offences within the scope of and as defined in the international conventions and protocols relating to terrorism.

This is fairly restricted and specifically refers to the already extensive UN action against particular terrorism problems.[24] In the International Convention for the Suppression of the Financing of Terrorism which entered into force on 10 April 2002, terrorism was defined more broadly as: 'Any . . . act intended to cause death or serious bodily injury to a civilian, or to any other person not taking an active part in the hostilities in a situation of armed conflict, when the purpose of such act, by its nature or context, is to intimidate a population, or to compel a government or an international organization to do or to abstain from doing any act.' The reach here is wider albeit in an agreement with a particular focus on the financing of subversive violence. States have committed to this Convention in greatly increased numbers since 2001.[25]

The most ominous item on the counter-terrorism horizon is the draft comprehensive convention on terrorism. This has proved highly controversial, having been unable (so far) to secure the support of the General Assembly. While this is largely because of a dispute about the legitimacy of political violence as a means of resistance,[26] the potential in the Convention to throw a strong chill over political freedom generally should not be underestimated.

---

[24] See B Saul, *Defining Terrorism in International Law* (Oxford: Oxford University Press, 2006).

[25] de Vries, n 22 above.

[26] See, in particular, the differences over draft Articles 12 and 18.

From this perspective draft Article 2 is the key provision, designating as a terrorist offender any person who by any means, unlawfully and intentionally, causes:

(1) Death or serious bodily injury to any person; or

(2) Serious damage to public of private property, including a place of public use, a State or government facility, a public transportation system, an infrastructure facility or the environment; or

(3) Damage to property, places, facilities, or systems referred to [paragraph 2 above], resulting or likely to result in major economic loss,

when the purpose of the conduct, by its nature or context, is to intimidate a population, or to compel a Government or an international organization to do or abstain from doing any act.

This definition displays all the usual dangers of terrorism definitions, of the type we first encountered in Chapter 3 when we analysed the deleterious effect of domestic counter-terrorism law on UK civil liberties. The breadth of the remit of the term, initially acceptably limited to serious harm to the person, gradually expands so as to embrace not only robust forms of direct action but also even (potentially at least) traditional forms of civil libertarian protest. Notions like serious damage to the environment and damage to property 'likely to result in major economic loss' are very vague and give decision-makers empowered to enforce such a definition worryingly wide grounds for the exercise of their discretion. And this is without taking into account the chill factor that would result from the mere existence of such a broad formula for what terrorism entailed. Remembering that the momentum is in the direction of the implementation of UN resolutions by both the EU and the UK governments without any intervening judgment as to the public interest, it is not fanciful to anticipate a future when inhibiting interventions in the political culture of the UK do occur under the guise of the dictates of UN counter-terrorism law, with there being little the UK authorities or the courts can do about it (short of a wholly implausible decision to leave the UN).

It is not easy to see how the need to abide by *jus cogens* can compensate for the lack of either political or legal safeguards against the erosion of political liberty: it is very much a last-gasp stop-gap against coercive extremism rather than a thought-out protection of our political liberties. Could the Human Rights Act 1998 help out, by modifying the repressive effects of UN resolutions, whether these are delivered via domestic or EU law? As we have seen the action in the *M* case was taken under the 1946 Act, a piece of legislation that, like any other, is subject to the requirements of the European Convention on Human Rights. The action of the executive under that measure, being merely discretionary rather than required, would seem to be caught squarely under s 6(1) of the Human Rights Act 1998, with its well-known demand that all public authorities act consistently with Convention rights. This might well be a route to civil liberties protection that some domestic judicial tribunal appalled by the vista of lawlessness laid out before it might feel emboldened to take. But even such a robustly civil libertarian judge would have to take EU law into account just as Mr Parker was required to do. As is well known, this code of law imposes itself on a member state even more than does the UN, not least on account of the way it can drive policy (via the Commission) and enforce its laws (via the European Court of Justice). Even the Human Rights Act 1998 must defer to its dictates.

THE EUROPEAN UNION

It is clear that the destructive spell of counter-terrorism is affecting law-making in the EU as well as the UN. The impact of the EU on public law has historically been slight: the serious terrorism problem in Europe in the 1970s and 1980s (the IRA, ETA, Red Brigade, Red Army Faction, etc) did not produce a perception of a need for common action. It might have been expected that the failure to secure passage of the EU constitution would have meant that the impact of the EU on our subject was guaranteed to continue to be marginal. If this is true then it is a marginality with ambitions to move closer to the centre-stage. As was the case with the UN, the key legal initiatives have been made possible by the galvanizing energy that spread through EU law enforcement decision-makers in the aftermath of the Al-Qaida attacks of 11 September 2001. An action plan on what was described as the 'fight against terrorism' was adopted by the European Council on 21 September 2001—this provided for the adoption of no fewer than 79 measures, only 13 of which came under the aegis of foreign affairs.[27] The key legislative intervention was the Framework Decision on Combating Terrorism, agreed on 13 June 2002.[28] The definition of terrorism adopted in that document was very broad, albeit the Decision did expressly announce its respect for 'fundamental human rights as guaranteed by the [ECHR] and as they emerge from the constitutional traditions common to the Member States'.[29] It has been under the general aegis of this

[27] See Council of the European Union, *European Union Plan of Action on Combating Terrorism* Council Doc 10010/04 (11 June 2004).
[28] [2002] OJ L164/3, 22 June. See S Peers, 'EU Responses to Terrorism' (2003) 52 *International and Comparative Law Quarterly* 227.
[29] Ibid. See also Article 2.

decision that a flow of counter-terrorism initiatives has begun to emerge from the Commission, drawing the subject in from the periphery ever closer to the core of EU activity. In December 2005 the council adopted an EU counter-terrorism strategy.

It is perfectly true that, so far, the EU's involvement in counter-terrorism has been mainly concerned with the need for greater judicial and police co-operation.[30] The main controversy has been about the risk that such efficiency might spill over into an ominous, European-wide centralization, with all the implications for a decline in individual freedom that this would entail.[31] At the international level, particularly difficult to sell have been the EU's agreements with the US on such matters as extradition, personal data, and the sharing of air-passenger information.[32] The potential impact on civil liberties can be seen, however, from the drawing up of EU terrorist lists. This initiative grew out of a council common position adopted on 27 December 2001 via a procedure which did not require the European Parliament to be consulted. Articles 2 and 3 of the Common Position direct member states to freeze 'the funds and other financial assets or economic resources' of the 'international terrorists' listed in an annex to the common position, and to prevent such funds, financial assets, or resources from being made available for their benefit. Article 4 applies to both the domestic and 'international' 'terrorists' named in the annex and instructs member states to work together to prevent and combat terrorist acts. As Marisa Leaf notes, '[t]hese lists have been drawn up without reference to any legal—let alone public—criteria' and as a result the 'risk of abuse by member states in determining those individuals and organizations to be included in the list is manifest' with the 'national political interests of individual states' having been 'from the start . . . reflected in their composition'.[33]

The making of unaccountable lists of named subversives is the stuff of authoritarian rather than democratic states. Judicial control is marginal as well, with the European Court of Justice having some jurisdiction over justice and home affairs matters but none at all over foreign and security policy—yet these positions have purportedly emanated from both heads. As we have seen, where the action emanates from the UN the Court of First Instance at least is disinclined to raise other than the vaguest of human

[30] See de Vries, n 22 above. M Leaf, 'The European Union's Twin Towers of Democracy and Human Rights Post 11 September 2001' (2004) 1 *Justice Journal* 89.
[31] For regular updates on developments in this, see the invaluable *Statewatch* magazine.
[32] See Leaf, n 30 above.   [33] Ibid, p 96.

rights-based objections. But where the legal framework can be presented as entirely EU-based, the Court of First Instance has—with a degree of courage that is as gratifying as it was unexpected—now exposed such lists as vulnerable on traditional due process grounds, in particular the denial of a fair hearing that they encompass together with the failure to supply reasons.[34] It remains to be seen whether this liberal breakthrough will work across to undo the damage done by the *Kadi* and *Yusuf* decisions.[35]

In the meantime what about Strasbourg? At first glance these terrorism lists seem exactly the kind of coercive action on which the European Court of Human Rights in Strasbourg might be able to do good, progressive work. The signs are not good, however. In *Bosphorus v Ireland*,[36] an EU regulation implementing a previous UN sanctions regime (against the then Federal Republic of Yugoslavia) was challenged as having involved a breach of Convention rights: the applicant's leased aircraft was impounded by the Irish authorities while in Dublin for maintenance. The result was that the company had lost the benefit of three of the four years for which the lease had been intended to run. Having made a tour of the law courts of Ireland and Europe, Bosphorus eventually ended up in Strasbourg, arguing a violation of its right to property under Article 1 of the First Protocol. Normally, the total absence of compensation—as was the case here—would have put an applicant like *Bosphorus* on very strong ground in Convention terms. However, the European Court did not take its normal line, with Ireland's obligation to follow EU law being a key factor in effecting the change:

[155] In the Court's view, State action taken in compliance with such legal obligations is justified as long as the relevant organization is considered to protect fundamental rights, as regards both the substantive guarantees offered and the mechanisms controlling their observance, in a manner which can be considered at least equivalent to that for which the Convention provides. By 'equivalent' the Court means 'comparable': any requirement that the organization's protection be 'identical' could run counter to the interest of international co-operation pursued. However, any such finding of equivalence could not be final and would be susceptible to review in the light of any relevant change in fundamental rights' protection.

---

[34] *Organisation des Modjahedines du Peuple d'Iran v Council of European Union*, n 21 above; see also Case 354/04 and Case 355/04, *Gestoras Pro-Amnistia v Council; Segi v Council*, 27 February 2007 (no damages for inclusion on terrorist lists).
[35] An opportunity for further development will come when Case C-229/05 *Ocalan and Vanly v Council of the European Union* comes up for decision: for a preliminary ruling clearing the way for such a hearing see the judgment of the court (first chamber) on 18 January 2007.
[36] *Bosphorus Hava Yollari Turizm Ve Ticaret Anonim Sirket v Ireland* (2005) 42 EHRR 1. For an excellent analysis see C Costello, 'The *Bosphorus* Ruling of the European Court of Human Rights: Fundamental Rights and Blurred Boundaries in Europe' (2006) 6 *Human Rights Law Review* 87.

[156] If such equivalent protection is considered to be provided by the organization, the presumption will be that a state has not departed from the requirements of the Convention when it does no more than implement legal obligations
flowing from its membership of the organization.

However, any such presumption can be rebutted if, in the circumstances of a
particular case, it is considered that the protection of Convention rights was manifestly deficient. In such cases, the interest of international co-operation would be
outweighed by the Convention's role as a 'constitutional instrument of European
public order' in the field of human rights.[37]

The court then reviewed the history of EU involvement in human rights,
and satisfied itself that there was indeed a structural commitment to their
protection sufficiently good for the system as a whole to be designated
' "equivalent" to that of the Convention system'.[38] Absolutely crucial here
was the role of the European Court of Justice as the guardian of EU fundamental human rights: everything depended on 'the mechanisms of
control in place to ensure observance of such rights'[39] and here the
Luxembourg court had pride of place. This being the case, on the facts
before it and taking all relevant circumstances into account, the European
Court of Human Rights took the view that it could not 'be said that the
protection of the applicant's Convention rights was manifestly deficient
with the consequence that the relevant presumption of Convention compliance by the Respondent State has not been rebutted'.[40] The judges were
unanimous in their ruling.

As with the Court of First Instance, we see the emergence of a two-tier
system of protection of human rights. Where the EU judges kept a residual
power to act against breaches of *jus cogens* by the UN, the Strasbourg
tribunal is on guard against manifest deficiencies in EU human rights protection. But how likely is either of these criteria to bite in any specific case?
The point is especially important in relation to the kind of political freedoms that are the subject of this book: they are diluted by the necessity for
limitations even within human rights law itself so it is hard to imagine how
even a serious attack on any of them would be struck down as arbitrary or
a breach of *jus cogens*. The conclusion is hard to resist that in both cases the
alleged fallback review of each court is little more than a camouflage for
a full withdrawal from the fray. *Bosphorus* was decided on 30 June 2005,
with the first instance decisions in the two Afghan-related cases being
handed down nearly three months later, on 21 September. Does this
chronology make possible a renewed challenge to the *Bosphorus* assumption

---

[37] Citations omitted.   [38] *Bosphorus v Ireland*, n 36 above, para [165].
[39] Ibid, para [160].   [40] Ibid, para [166].

that the EU protects human rights in an equivalent manner to the European Convention on Human Rights? Of course, there is now the important decision of the Luxembourg court subjecting EU-inspired counter-terrorism decisions to procedural review,[41] notwithstanding which the UN-mandated laws remain challengeable only on *jus cogens* grounds. It is hard to see how this criterion could be said to be equivalent to ECHR protection: *jus cogens* oversight is far from the kind of human rights protection that the European Court of Human Rights has usually required.[42] It is even harder to see how the UN itself, with its sanctions committee, its list-drawing, and the absence of any judicial (or even political) controls could be said to deliver any kind of human rights protection (in fact rather than in theory) that was 'equivalent' to Strasbourg in any way.

---

[41] *Organisation des Modjahedines du Peuple d'Iran*, n 21 above.

[42] See the Report by Professor Iain Cameron prepared for the Council of Europe, *The European Convention on Human Rights, Due Process and United Nations Security Council Counter-Terrorism Sanctions*, 6 February 2006.

Part IV

Conclusion

Protecting Political Freedom

This book has been rooted in a particular perspective on civil liberties, one that sees the subject as primarily concerned with the law and practice of political freedom. There are other ways of thinking about civil liberties, different kinds of emphases and analyses that produce a range of alternative means of identifying the topics that a proper treatment of our subject would rightly entail. I identified a number of these in Chapter 1 and explained why I was rejecting them. In summary, my main point was that the various meanings we ascribe to the term 'civil liberties' are too many and too diverse for a book of this sort to seek coherently to encompass them all. My choice to be selective in this way liberated me from the Sisyphean task of engaging in a false synthesis of conflicting propositions. Having staked out my chosen ground for the subject, I proceeded in Chapter 2 to elaborate the intellectual foundations that underpinned my approach, with Chapter 3 then supplying not only a recent history but also an assessment of the threat that political freedom faces from those concerns for national security which demand—or appear to demand—divergences from the civil libertarian ideal. With this preparatory intellectual work out of the way, the rest of the book has been about the substance of civil liberties protection in Britain, the legislation, the judicial decisions, and the executive practices that together add up to supply an answer to the question, 'What is the state of political freedom in Britain?'.

Reflecting on the way in which laws regulating civil liberties are received, as the story has been told in the central chapters of this book, it is immediately evident quite how negative the discourse has invariably been. Civil liberties is not a happy subject, or even one in which there is a mixture of good and bad news to report. The account is invariably one of erosion, of threat, of decline, of changes that are bound to be for the worse. Britain is often said to be on the way to becoming a police state or to be 'veering towards a police state' as the Archbishop of York, Dr John Sentamu reportedly put it in early 2007.[1] Around the same time, a claim

---

[1] The Conservative shadow Home Secretary David Davis has an interesting commentary on the Archbishop's remarks in the *Guardian*, 6 February 2007.

that the UK had actually become 'a police state for Muslims' was taken sufficiently seriously for the Prime Minister himself to be drawn into a robust denial.[2] Writers like Henry Porter in *The Observer* and Tony Bunyan and his team on *Statewatch* track a decline that they are sure is as inexorable as it is evident to all. It has led to the push for a new bill of rights for Britain which has attracted some support from across the parties.[3] From the perspective of these observers, freedom is something we have which government is intent on taking away, or which has already gone, or whose loss is imminent. Not even the occasional positive piece of legislation, like the Contempt of Court Act 1981, the Freedom of Information Act 2000 or (particularly) the Human Rights Act 1998 can salvage the reputation of the authorities, divert us from the repressive momentum that is all around, gathering strength with every new authoritarian initiative. The answer given by such commentators to our question about political freedom in Britain is that it is in a dire state.

How true is this account of liberty in Britain? It will have been clear from this book that it is quite right to observe that most parliamentary interventions and judicial decisions are negative in that they are invariably proposals to restrict our civil liberties. The ethical demands of our subject manifest themselves in the need to deny or at least to control the powers that are being sought—to impose a 'reasonable suspicion' here or an independent tribunal there, or to push for a 'special advocate' in this or that set of proceedings that would otherwise have remained closed to the accused. Given that the starting presumption is freedom, with all of us being at liberty to do that which no law prevents, it is inevitable that the substance of our subject should be about restriction rather than celebration. A law is not needed to guarantee what we already know we have, and the confiscation of which moreover is already stoutly protected against by old-fashioned proceedings in the criminal or civil law, actions of assault and false imprisonment if the police make a wrongful arrest, and civil actions for trespass if they barge into a property without proper legal authority. So our subject is invariably about coping with bad news: 'police respect civil liberties' is not a story and rarely makes the law reports.[4] But it is a large

---

[2] *Guardian*, 9 February 2007.

[3] Including, it would seem, the Conservatives who have established a commission to consider ways in which to improve human rights protection within the country, apart from the Human Rights Act 1998 of the effects of which the Party is critical. See C. Bryant (ed), *Towards a New Constitutional Settlement* (London: The Smith Institute, 2007).

[4] Unless somebody intervenes to try to make the police act more aggressively than they are minded to do, as was the case in *R v Chief Constable of Devon and Cornwall, ex p Central Electricity Generating Board* [1982] QB 458.

move from this observation to the sorts of claims about a police state that some supporters of civil liberties have been tempted by events into making (and to some of which I have referred above).

The challenge, and it is a real one for those who care about political freedom, is to keep a sense of proportion. How helpful is it to compare contemporary Britain's approach to freedom with that of the regime of Idi Amin in Uganda in the 1970s as Archbishop Sentamu did in early 2007?[5] When the controversy over the detention of so-called 'illegal combatants' was at its height, Amnesty International likened the regime at Guantanamo to Stalin's Gulags, and around the same time the detention of a small number of 'suspected international terrorists' (under the terms of the Anti-terrorism, Crime and Security Act 2001) in Belmarsh prison led to the prison being frequently described in the newspapers and in critical commentary as a 'mini-Guantanamo'. Valuable though such escalation of language may be in the short term, drawing public figures into the open as Amnesty did by forcing the US President into a strident denial and (as earlier noted with regard to the claim about Britain being a police state for Muslims) by provoking the Prime Minister into a response, the medium-to long-term damage to the integrity of our subject is surely so severe that such language is best avoided. The general public is not likely to be persuaded by analogies with horrific situations which few of them can credibly relate to their own lived experiences. The result is that they become desensitized to the whole civil liberties message, even when it contains something of the first importance that desperately needs to be heard.

The effect within government might also be counter-productive. Those of the civil servants, police officers, special advisers, and political leaders who have worked hard to secure some civil libertarian concession or other in this or that piece of legislation are left exposed when the resultant measure is condemned as authoritarian without any note being taken of the changes that they have secured. The precise language of the latest initiative often seems less important than its 'repressive' headline. 'Why bother?' might be the dangerous conclusion for such civil libertarian fifth columnists to draw. Most serious of all, the deployment of extreme language to describe the state of civil liberties in Britain in situations that do not warrant such terms makes its effective deployment if and when such words are really required very much more difficult. An example from the past might be the huge critical energy that was expended on the Police and Criminal Evidence Bill in 1983–4, with opponents persuading themselves and then seeking to convince others that four days detention before charge

---

[5] See 'Britain is not a police state', *The Observer*, 11 February 2007.

(albeit with magistrates' court supervision) was a scandalous invasion of liberty. Nowadays, exactly the same legislation—which finally came into force in 1986—is regarded by civil libertarians as a model of good practice, something to hold on to in the face of governmental initiatives to expand police powers. But if it was a useful and progressive codifying measure when it was proposed in 1983, why was this not said at the time, or at least when concessions had been made to opponents as it progressed through Parliament?

An historical perspective is important to the honing of that sense of proportion which the guardians of civil liberties do rather urgently need to cultivate. If we leave aside wartime, during at least two decades of the democratic era before today, the defenders of civil liberties have felt their position to be uniquely precarious: the 1930s and the 1980s. As regards the first, this was when the Council for Civil Liberties (today's Liberty) was established. Its petition against the Incitement to Disaffection Bill of 1934 as 'a grave menace to the fundamental liberties of the British people' was signed by no fewer than 63,134 people.[6] Many of the 'great and good' were drawn into the organization's campaigns, as were activist lawyers and public intellectuals—exactly the kind of people who in the 1980s would have been signatories to Charter 88. This was the movement launched in a blaze of publicity in 1988 to campaign for a written constitution to rectify the 'implausibility' of the country's commitment to the protection of civil liberties.[7] A combination of the approach to civil liberties taken by the then Prime Minister Margaret Thatcher and the fortuitous arrival of the tercentenary of England's Bill of Rights in 1688 provoked an upsurge of anxiety about political freedom during that decade. A new journal called *Samizdat* was even launched, deliberately using its title (without irony) to make a connection between Britain and the dissidents in the Soviet Bloc. Books were written with titles like *Decade of Decline: Civil Liberties in the Thatcher Years*.[8] More used to cataloguing the abuses of authoritarian regimes, the respected journal *Index on Censorship* devoted its entire September 1988 issue to Britain because, as the editorial noted, 'if freedom is diminished in the United Kingdom, where historically it has deep roots, it is potentially diminished everywhere'.[9] To the doyen of legal

---

[6] KD Ewing and CA Gearty, *The Struggle for Civil Liberties. Political Freedom and the Rule of Law in Britain, 1914–1945* (Oxford: Oxford University Press, 2000), p 248.

[7] 'Charter 88', *New Statesman and Society*, 2 December 1988.

[8] By Peter Thornton (London: NCCL, 1989). The title of KD Ewing and CA Gearty, *Freedom under Thatcher. Civil Liberties in Modern Britain* (Oxford: Oxford University Press, 1990) was more neutral.

[9] 'Britain' (1988) 17 *Index on Censorship* (September), p 1.

philosophers Professor Ronald Dworkin, liberty was considered at that time to be 'ill in Britain'.[10]

But what were these deep roots and—a question I first raised at the start of Chapter 3—when had civil liberties in Britain ever been well? The golden age of good health is something that the strongly nostalgic streak in British constitutional commentary has been searching for at least since the drafters of Magna Carta looked back fondly to the good old days under Henry II. It is often public order law that is to the fore in these discussions, so it is a good case study through which to make some general points. Viewed in the round it can perhaps be asserted that there have been three overlapping phases in the history of the freedom of public protest in the UK, with the subject having been in the hands of, successively, the military, the police, and (most recently) the law. The first corresponds to the pre-democratic era though overlapping slightly into it. This was when the executive deployed its power with confident disregard of accountability. Ministers thought nothing of taking on 'the enemy within' with what weapons they had at their disposal, and this sometimes (but not invariably) included enactment of coercive Acts of Parliament. The armed forces occasionally shot those who tried to exercise their civil liberties; more often they broke up their meetings with brutal abandon. No issue of justice arose because it was simply not thought for a moment that any kind of redress could be sought. If there were laws underpinning the military action then they were of the vaguest sort; if there were not, indemnity legislation would cure the legal difficulties retrospectively. This was the era of martial law, a subject of abiding interest to Victorian jurists and with good reason: as a tool of control it was still being deployed within the UK (albeit unruly Ireland) as late as 1920. The law played a small part in this military drama, but it was essentially a walk-on one, legitimizing an execution here or a transportation there. The idea of asserting the civil liberties of the disenfranchised through the law courts was not utterly unthinkable—*Beatty v Gillbanks*[11] was decided in 1882—but it was mainly as the overseers of state prosecutions that civil libertarians encountered the judges.

Gradual democratization and the organization of professional civil policing in the nineteenth century led to a change in the state's approach to internal security and public order. The front-line role of the magistrates and the army was slowly superseded by that of the local constabulary, its officers charged among other duties with the task of keeping the peace. In this phase, which lasted from the late Victorian period until the start of the twenty-first century, and to some extent still continues, the emphasis was

---

[10] 'Devaluing Liberty', ibid, pp 7–8.   [11] See pp 89–90 above.

on the discretionary power of the police to keep order, with the dependably flexible common law idea of a 'reasonably apprehended breach of the peace' doing duty as the promiscuous door-keeper to state power. This was the era of, among many other cases, *Thomas v Sawkins*, *Duncan v Jones*, and *Moss v Lachlan*,[12] with the authorities seemingly incapable of doing any wrong, but always ostensibly open to be called to account before an apparently independent legal process. The pressures of democratization produced a translation of many raw state powers into legislative form, a process greatly assisted by the emergency provisions that were promulgated during the First World War and which became a precedent for some at least of the illiberal enactments that followed.[13] But it was the protean common law that continued to supply the main basis for police action.

The shift to the third phase, the legalization of the control of public protest, has been underway since the turn to statutory controls in the early part of the twentieth century. But its role has gradually become more dominant as police reliance on the common law and local legislation has fallen away and the invocation of national statutes to underpin their restrictive actions has increased. Before the 1980s there were very few statutes in the field, the Public Order Act 1936 being a rare example. Since the controversial expansion of that Act in 1986,[14] the parliamentary interventions in the control of public protest have come thick and fast: the Criminal Justice and Public Order Act 1994, the Protection from Harassment Act 1997, the Terrorism Act 2000, and the Serious Organized Crime and Police Act 2005 being among the more contentious highlights. Gradually, the police have come to deploy their powers under these various statutes in preference to their previous commitment to the 'one-size-fits-all' common law. Two separate but linked developments have pushed this process along. The first has been the introduction of the European Convention on Human Rights into UK law (via the Human Rights Act 1998): the restrictions on protest that this charter permits must as a basic prerequisite be prescribed by law and while as we have seen[15] the common law just about passes muster under this head, its flexible wings have been severely cut back by the demand for foreseeability that is entailed by this new European yardstick. The second factor has been the judges themselves, increasingly impatient it would seem with police invocations of broad common law discretionary powers and more and more inclined to note the plethora of parliamentary laws that now cover the field and to

[12] See respectively pp 136–7, 136 and 137 above.
[13] The story is told in Ewing and Gearty, n 6 above, particularly ch 2.
[14] See p 140 above.   [15] See p 108 above.

counsel the authorities to rely on these. It is exactly this inclination that lies behind the important House of Lords' decision in *R (Laporte) v Gloucestershire Constabulary*:[16] their Lordships were not necessarily against the exercise of police power in the situation which arose but they were disinclined to allow the police to avail themselves of the short-cut of common law powers when parliament had laid out so many alternative routes. If *Laporte* is fully absorbed into the law, then it may be that we will have seen the last of the 'breach of the peace' power as the catch-all fallback for what is, effectively, the arbitrary control of public protest.

The same general trend can be seen in other areas of our subject, the chapters in which we dealt with the right to life, the prohibition on torture, and the guarantees of liberty, due process, and political speech. The pattern is less pronounced here, with the authorities having encountered difficulties with the independent legal process—jury trials that have gone wrong;[17] searches that have been condemned in the High Court[18]—to a much greater degree than in the field of public order. The division of the executive into the military on the one side and the police on the other is obviously also less easy to make. But all this said, the same move to legal control and away from discretionary executive action is clearly there, in the replacement of s 2 of the Official Secrets Act 1989 by its more targeted successor in 1989, in the subjection of state surveillance to legal control (in the Interception of Communication Act 1985), in the exposure of the security services to legal oversight (the Security Service Acts 1989 and 1996 and the Intelligence Services Act 1994), in the positive obligation to protect life that has been developed out of Article 2 of the European Convention on Human Rights, in the insistence on procedural fairness in the terrorism as well as mainstream criminal law, and in much else besides. It is hard to square all these changes—and those in the field of public order as well—with the idea that British freedom is in a spiral of decline.

One result of the move from discretion to law is to embed civil liberties protection more fully in the democratic process, making the erosion of freedom by the executive more likely to be spotted, and requiring those responsible to explain themselves in a way that would simply not have occurred in the past. But it is also to draw the courts further into the fray as the guardians of the legal process. In this legalized world, it is the judges who must police the front line of civil liberties protection, seeking to reconcile society's commitment to political freedom with its determination—reflected in the Acts of Parliament that we have been discussing in

[16] See pp 137–9 above. [17] See pp 147–8 above.
[18] As in *Entick v Carrington*, p 33 above.

this book—to protect the community from internal and external threat. Are they up to the task? In *Laporte*, the senior police officer on the scene had unwittingly handed the courts a stick with which to beat him by recording in a contemporaneous note that he thought no breach of the peace imminent. Supposing he had filled in the box in exactly the opposite way: would the Lords have overruled his discretion in such a situation? After *Laporte* the police now know they need to find 'imminence' before they act—how much energy will the courts deploy, not only or even mainly in the appellate tribunals but in the magistrates' courts and crown courts in particular—to ensure that this term is not abused, turned from a control into a password for irresponsible police action? To come at the point from a different angle, will the judges' oversight of the anti-terrorism control orders develop an independent critical life of its own or might it become the kind of rubber stamp that saw past generations of judges (senior and junior) agreeing whatever it was the police put before them?

As the last question suggests, any answer to these points must take into account what is, viewed in the round, the historically very bad record of the entire judiciary in protecting civil liberties in the face of executive and parliamentary action. The lesson of the past is that it is delusional to rely on judges to lead on the hard work of civil libertarian protection. In this as in other areas, there is no substitute for politics. What the judges can do— note it is 'can' not 'will'—is reflect in their case law a disposition to freedom that they see reflected in civil society as a whole. The stronger the political fuss made about freedom, the more likely it is that the judges will feel that they have room to assert themselves. This was how the detention provisions in the Anti-terrorism, Crime and Security Act 2001 went from being widely accepted to being so obviously wrong that the law lords felt able to declare them a breach of the European Convention on Human Rights just three years later.[19] It is to run entirely with the grain of our subject to say that political freedom cannot be made to depend on a supra-political band of ethical guardians. I end this book by returning to a point I first made at the end of Chapter 2. The responsibility for the political good health of this state (indeed, any democratic state) lies with those whom the civil liberties discussed in this book are designed to protect and assist; in other words, the individuals and associations that flourish in the community that a true commitment to political freedom has made possible.

---

[19] For the political background see CA Gearty, 'Human Rights in an Age of Counter-Terrorism: Injurious, Irrelevant or Indispensable? (2005) 58 *Current Legal Problems* 25.

Select Bibliography

Adjei, C, 'Human Rights Theory and the Bill of Rights Debate' (1995) 58 *Modern Law Review* 17.

Aitken, J, *Offically Secret* (London: Weidenfeld and Nicolson, 1971).

Alexander, L, *Is There a Right of Freedom of Expression?* (Cambridge: Cambridge University Press, 2005).

Allan, TRS, 'Fairness, Equality, Rationality: Constitutional Theory and Judicial Review', in Forsyth, C and Hare, I (eds), *The Golden Metwand and the Crooked Cord* (Oxford: Oxford University Press, 1998).

Allan, TRS, 'The Rule of Law as the Rule of Reason: Consent and Constitutionalism' (1999) 115 *Law Quarterly Review* 221.

Allan, TRS, *Constitutional Justice. A Liberal Theory of the Rule of Law* (Oxford: Oxford University Press, 2001).

Allan, TRS, 'Doctrine and Theory in Administrative Law: An Elusive Quest for the Limits of Jurisdiction' [2003] *Public Law* 429.

Alston, P (ed), *The EU and Human Rights* (Oxford: Oxford University Press, 1999).

Amos, M, *Human Rights Law* (Oxford: Hart Publishing, 2006).

Anderson, GW (ed), *Rights and Democracy. Essays in UK–Canadian Constitutionalism* (London: Blackstone Press, 1999).

Anderson, G, *Constitutional Rights After Globalization* (Oxford: Hart Publishing, 2007).

Anscombe, GEM, *Wittgenstein's Philosophical Investigations* (3rd edn) (Oxford: Blackwell, 2001).

Arendt, H, *The Origins of Totalitarianism* (New York, NY: Harcourt Brace Jovanovich, 1951).

Arendt, H, 'Freedom and Politics', in Hunold, A (ed), *Freedom and Serfdom. An Anthology of Western Thought* (Dordrecht: D Reidel Publishing Co., 1961).

Ashby Wilson, R (ed), *Human Rights in the 'War on Terror'* (Cambridge: Cambridge University Press, 2005).

Ashworth, A, *Human Rights, Serious Crime and Criminal Procedure* (London: Sweet and Maxwell Ltd, 2002).

Bailey, SH, Harris, DJ, and Ormerod, DC, *Bailey, Harris and Jones on Civil Liberties: Cases and Materials* (5th edn) (Oxford: Oxford University Press, 2005).

Bamforth, N and Leyland, P (eds), *Public Law in a Multi-Layered Constitution* (Oxford: Hart Publishing, 2003).

Barendt, E, *Freedom of Speech* (2nd edn) (Oxford: Oxford University Press, 2005).

Barnet, A, *This Time. Our Constitutional Revolution* (London: Vintage, 1997).

Barnum, DG, 'Indirect Incitement and Freedom of Speech in Anglo-American Law' [2006] *European Human Rights Law Review* 258.

Benn, T (ed), *Thomas Paine's The Rights of Man* (London: JM Dent, 1993).

Bennett, G, 'Legislative Responses to Terrorism: A View from Britain' (2005) 109 *Penn State Law Review* 947.

Berlin, I, 'Two Concepts of Liberty', in Miller, D (ed), *Liberty* (Oxford: Oxford University Press, 1991).

Berlin, I, *The Crooked Timber of Humanity* (Princeton, NJ: Princeton University Press, 1991), Hardy, H (ed).

Berlin, I, *Liberty* (Oxford: Oxford University Press, 2002), Hardy, H (ed).

Bingham, T, *The Business of Judging. Selected Essays and Speeches* (Oxford: Oxford University Press, 2000).

Birkinshaw, P, *Reforming the Secret State* (Milton Keynes: Open University Press, 1990).

Bock, G, Skinner, Q, and Viroli, M (eds), *Machiavelli and Republicanism* (Cambridge: Cambridge University Press, 1990).

Bonner, D, 'Responding to Crisis: Legislating Against Terrorism' (2006) 122 *Law Quarterly Review* 602.

Bonner, D, Fenwick, H, and Harris-Short, S, 'Judicial Approaches to the Human Rights Act' (2003) 52 *International and Comparative Law Quarterly* 549.

Bowes, S, *The Police and Civil Liberties* (London: Lawrence and Wishart, 1966).

Bowman, HM, 'Martial Law and the English Constitution' (1916) 15 *Michigan Law Review* 93.

Bowyer Bell, J, *The Irish Troubles. A Generation of Violence, 1967–1992* (Dublin: Gill and Macmillan, 1993).

Bradley, AW and Ewing, KD, *Constitutional and Administrative Law* (14th edn) (Harlow: Longman, 2007).

Brandon, B, 'Terrorism, Human Rights and the Rule of Law: 120 Years of the UK's Legal Responses to Terrorism' [2004] *Criminal Law Review* 635.

Brown, R, 'Kadi v Council of the European Union and Commission of the European Communities: Executive Power and Judicial Supervision at European Level' [2006] *European Human Rights Law Review* 456.

Bryant, C (ed), *Towards a New Constitutional Settlement* (London: The Smith Institute, 2007).

Bunyan, T (ed), *Statewatching the New Europe* (London: Statewatch, 1993).

Cable Street Group, *The Battle of Cable Street 4th October 1936. A People's History* (London: The Cable Street Group, 1995).

Campbell, C and Connolly, I, 'Making War on Terror? Global Lessons from Northern Ireland' (2006) 69 *Modern Law Review* 935.

Campbell, T, *The Left and Rights. A Conceptual Analysis of the Idea of Socialist Rights* (London: Routledge and Kegan Paul, 1983).

Campbell, T, 'Human Rights: A Culture of Controversy' (1999) 26 *Journal of Legal Studies* 6.

Campbell, T, Ewing, KD, and Tomkins, A (eds), *Sceptical Essays on Human Rights* (Oxford: Oxford University Press, 2001).

Charter 88, *Charter 88. New Statesman and Society* (2 December 1988).

Chrimes, SB, *English Constitutional History* (3rd edn) (London: Oxford University Press, 1965).

Clayton, R and Tomlinson, H, *The Law of Human Rights* (Oxford: Oxford University Press, 2000).

Clements, L and Thomas, PA, *The Human Rights Act: A Success Story?* (Oxford: Blackwell Publishing, 2005).

Cole, D, 'What Bush Wants to Hear' *New York Review of Books* (17 November 2005).

Cole, GDH, *Jean-Jacques Rousseau's The Social Contract and Discourses* (London: JM Dent Ltd, 1973).

Cooper, J and Marshall-Williams, A (eds), *Legislating for Human Rights The Parliamentary Debates on the Human Rights Bill* (Oxford: Hart Publishing, 2000).

Cornes, R and Le Sueur, A, *The Future of the United Kingdom's Highest Courts* (London: Constitution Unit, University College London, 2001).

Costello, C, 'The *Bosphorus* Ruling of the European Court of Human Rights: Fundamental Rights and Blurred Boundaries in Europe' (2006) 6 *Human Rights Law Review* 87.

Cowling, M, *Mill and Liberalism* (2nd edn) (Cambridge: Cambridge University Press, 1990).

Cullen, SM, 'Political Violence: The Case of the British Union of Fascists' (1993) 28 *Journal of Contemporary History* 245.

Dahl, RA, *Democracy and its Critics* (New Haven, CT: Yale University Press, 1989).

Dembour, M, *Who Believes in Human Rights? Reflections on the European Convention* (Cambridge: Cambridge University Press, 2006).

Department for Constitutional Affairs, *Review of the Implementation of the Human Rights Act* (London: Department for Constitutional Affairs, 2006).

Devins, N and Fisher, L, *The Democratic Constitution* (New York, NY: Oxford University Press, 2004).

Devlon, Lord, *Trial by Jury* (London: Methuen, 1966).

Dicey, AV, *Lectures Introductory to a Study of the Law of the Constitution* (2nd edn) (London: Macmillan, 1885).

Dickson, B, 'The House of Lords and the Northern Ireland Conflict— A Sequel' (2006) 69 *Modern Law Review* 383.

Dinwiddy, J, *Bentham* (Oxford: Oxford University Press, 1989).

Donohue, LK, *Counter-Terrorist Law and Emergency Powers in the United Kingdom, 1922–2000* (Dublin: Irish Academic Press, 2000).

Donson, F, *Legal Intimidation* (London: Free Association Books, 2000).

Doob, AN and Greenspan, EL (eds), *Perspectives in Criminal Law. Essays in Honour of J Ll J Edwards* (Aurora, Ontario: Canadian Law Books, 1985).

Duffy, H, *The 'War on Terror' and the Framework of International Law* (Cambridge: Cambridge University Press, 2005).

Dunn, J, *Setting the People Free: The Story of Democracy* (London: Atlantic Books, 2005).

Dworkin, R, 'Rights as Trumps', in Waldron, J (ed), *Theories of Rights* (Oxford: Oxford University Press, 1984).

Dworkin, R, 'Devaluing Liberty' (1988) 17 *Index on Censorship* 7.

Dyzenhaus, D, *The Constitution of Law. Legality in a Time of Emergency* (Cambridge: Cambridge University Press, 2006).

Eagleton, T, *Holy Terror* (Oxford: Oxford University Press, 2005).

Easton, S, 'Electing the Electorate: The Problem of Prisoner Disenfranchisement' (2006) 69 *Modern Law Review* 443.

Edgerton, G, 'Quelling the "Oxygen of Publicity": British Broadcasting and "The Troubles" During the Thatcher Years' (1996) 30 *Journal of Popular Culture* 115.

Elliott, M, *The Constitutional Foundations of Judicial Review* (Oxford: Hart Publishing, 2001).

Ely, JH, *Democracy and Distrust. A Theory of Judicial Review* (Cambridge, MA: Harvard University Press, 1980).

Ely Jr, JW, *The Guardian of Every Other Right. A Constitutional History of Property Rights* (2nd edn) (New York, NY: Oxford University Press, 1998).

English, R, *Irish Freedom. The History of Nationalism in Ireland* (London: Macmillan, 2006).

Epp, CR, *The Rights Revolution* (Chicago, IL: The University of Chicago Press, 1998).

Erskine May, *Treatise on the Law, Privileges, Proceedings and Usage of Parliament* (23rd edn) (London: LexisNexis, 2004).

Evans, G, 'In Search of Tolerance', in Park, A, Curtice, J, Thomson, K, Jarvis, L, and Bromley, C (eds), *British Social Attitudes: the Nineteenth Report* (London: Sage, 2002).

Ewing, KD, 'The Bill of Rights Debate: Democracy or Juristocracy in Britain', in Ewing, KD, Gearty, CA, and Hepple, B (eds), *Human Rights and Labour Law* (London: Mansell Press, 1994).

Ewing, KD, 'The Human Rights Act and Parliamentary Democracy.' (1999) 62 *Modern Law Review* 79.

Ewing, KD, 'A Theory of Democratic Adjudication: Towards a Representative, Accountable and Independent Judiciary' (2000) 38 *Alberta Law Review* 708.

Ewing, KD, 'The Unbalanced Constitution', in Campbell, T, Ewing, KD, and Tomkins, A (eds), *Sceptical Essays on Human Rights* (Oxford: Oxford University Press, 2001).

Ewing, KD, 'Transparency, Accountability and Equality: The Political Parties, Elections and Referendums Act 2000' [2001] *Public Law* 542.

Ewing, KD, *The Corruption of Democracy Party Funding in Modern British Politics* (Oxford: Hart Publishing, 2007).

Ewing, KD and Gearty, CA, *Freedom under Thatcher. Civil Liberties in Modern Britain* (Oxford: Clarendon Press, 1990).

Ewing, KD and Gearty, CA, *Democracy or a Bill of Rights* (London: Society of Labour Lawyers, 1991).

Ewing, KD and Gearty, CA, *A Law Too Far. Part III of the Police Bill* (London: Civil Liberties Research Unit, King's College London, 1997).

Ewing, KD and Gearty, CA, *The Struggle for Civil Liberties. Political Freedom and the Rule of Law in Britain, 1914–45* (Oxford: Oxford University Press, 2000).

Ewing, KD and Issacharoff, S (eds), *Party Funding and Campaign Financing in International Perspective* (Oxford: Hart Publishing, 2006).

Ewing, KD, Gearty, CA, and Hepple, BA (eds), *Human Rights and Labour Law. Essays for Paul O'Higgins* (London: Mansell, 1994).

Feldman, D, 'Human Dignity as a Legal Value' [1999] *Public Law* 682.

Feldman, D, *Civil Liberties and Human Rights in England and Wales* (2nd edn) (Oxford: Oxford University Press, 2002).

Feldman, D, 'Parliamentary Scrutiny of Legislation and Human Rights' [2002] *Public Law* 323.

Feldman, D, 'Human Rights, Terrorism and Risk: The Roles of Politicians and Judges' [2006] *Public Law* 364.

Fenwick, H, 'The Right to Protest, the Human Rights Act and the Margin of Appreciation' (1999) 62 *Modern Law Review* 491.

Fenwick, H, *Civil Rights: New Labour, Freedom and the Human Rights Act* (Harlow: Longman, 2000).

Fenwick, H, *Civil Liberties and Human Rights* (3rd edn) (London: Cavendish Publishing, 2002).

Fenwick, H, 'The Anti-Terrorism, Crime and Security Act 2001: A Proportionate Response to 11th September?' (2002) 65 *Modern Law Review* 724.

Fenwick, H and Phillipson, G, *Media Freedom under the Human Rights Act* (Oxford: Oxford University Press, 2006).

Forysth, C (ed), *Judicial Review and the Constitution* (Oxford: Hart Publishing, 2000).

Forsyth, C and Hare, I (eds), *The Golden Metwand and the Crooked Cord* (Oxford: Oxford University Press, 1998).

Foster, S, 'Prisoners' Rights, Freedom of Expression and the Human Rights Act' (2002) 7 *Journal of Civil Liberties* 53.

Foster, S, 'Prisoners and the Right to Vote—The Decision in *Hirst v United Kingdom (No 2)*' [2004] *European Human Rights Law Review* 436.

Fulford, R, *Votes for Women: The Story of a Struggle* (London: Faber, 1957).

Gallant, S and Epworth, J, *Media Law. A Practical Guide to Managing Publication Risks* (London: Sweet and Maxwell, 2001).

Gamble, A, *Hayek. The Iron Cage of Liberty* (Cambridge: The Polity Press, 1996).

Gearty, CA, 'The European Court of Human Rights and the Protection of Civil Liberties: an Overview' (1993) 52 *Cambridge Law Journal* 89.

Gearty, CA, 'Freedom of Assembly and Public Order', in McCrudden, C and Chambers, G, *Individual Rights and the Law in Britain* (Oxford: Clarendon Press, 1994).

Gearty, CA, 'Political Violence and Civil Liberties', in McCrudden, C and Chambers, G, *Individual Rights and the Law in Britain* (Oxford: Clarendon Press, 1994).

Gearty, CA (ed), *European Civil Liberties and the European Convention on Human Rights. A Comparative Study* (The Hague: Martinus Nijhoff, 1997).

Gearty, CA, 'The United Kingdom', in Gearty, CA (ed), *European Civil Liberties and the European Convention on Human Rights* (The Hague: Martinus Nijhoff Publishers, 1997).

Gearty, CA, 'Democracy and Human Rights in the European Court of Human Rights: A Critical Reappraisal' (2000) 51 *Northern Ireland Law Quarterly* 381.

Gearty, CA, 'Reflections on Human Rights and Civil Liberties in Light of the United Kingdom's Human Rights Act 1998' (2001) 35 *University of Richmond Law Review* 1.

Gearty, CA, 'Unravelling Osman' (2001) 64 *Modern Law Review* 159.

Gearty, CA, 'Reconciling Parliamentary Democracy and Human Rights' (2002) 118 *Law Quarterly Review* 248.

Gearty, CA, 'Civil Liberties and Human Rights', in Leyland, P and Bamforth, N (eds), *Public Law in a Multi-Layered Constitution* (Oxford: Hart Publishing, 2003).

Gearty, CA, 'Reflections on Civil Liberties in an Age of Counter-terrorism' (2003) 41 *Osgoode Hall Law Journal* 185.

Gearty, CA, 'Revisiting Section 3(1) of the Human Rights Act' (2003) 119 *Law Quarterly Review* 551.

Gearty, CA, *Principles of Human Rights Adjudication* (Oxford: Oxford University Press, 2004).

Gearty, CA, '11 September 2001, Counter-terrorism, and the Human Rights Act' (2005) 32 *Journal of Law and Society* 18.

Gearty, CA, 'Human Rights in an Age of Counter-Terrorism: Injurious, Irrelevant or Indispensable?' (2005) 58 *Current Legal Problems* 25.

Gearty, CA, *Can Human Rights Survive?* (Cambridge: Cambridge University Press, 2006).

Gearty, CA and Kimbell, JA, *Terrorism and the Rule of Law* (London: Civil Liberties Research Unit, King's College London, 1995).

Gearty, CA and Tomkins, A (eds), *Understanding Human Rights* (London: Mansell Publishing Ltd, 1996).

Geddis, A, 'What Future for Political Advertising on the United Kingdom's Television Screens?' [2002] *Public Law* 615.

Geddis, A, ' "If Thy Right Eye Offence Thee, Pluck It Out": *R v BBC, ex parte ProLife Alliance'* (2003) 66 *Modern Law Review* 885.

Geddis, A, 'Free Speech Martyrs or Unreasonable Threats to Social Peace?—"Insulting" Expression and section 5 of the Public Order Act 1986' [2004] *Public Law* 853.

Goldsworthy, J, *The Sovereignty of Parliament* (Oxford: Clarendon Press, 1999).

Goodin, RE, *Reflective Democracy* (Oxford: Oxford University Press, 2005).

Goold, B and Lazarus, L, *Security and Human Rights* (Oxford: Hart Publishing, Oxford, 2007).

Gray, J, *Berlin* (London: Fontana Press, 1995).

Gray, K and Gray, SF, 'Civil Rights, Civil Wrongs and Quasi-Public Space' [1999] *European Human Rights Law Review* 46.

Green, P, *The Enemy Without: Policing and Class Consciousness in the Miners' Strike* (Milton Keynes: Open University Press, 1990).

Greer, S, 'Constitutionalizing Adjudication under the European Convention on Human Rights' (2003) 23 *Oxford Journal of Legal Studies* 405.

Griffith, JAG, 'The Political Constitution' (1979) 42 *Modern Law Review* 1.

Griffith, JAG, *The Politics of the Judiciary* (5th edn) (London: Fontana Press, 1997).

Gross, O and Ni Aolain, *Law in Times of Crisis. Emergency Powers in Theory and Practice* (Cambridge: Cambridge University Press, 2006).

Hale, B, 'Equality and the Judiciary: Why Should We Want More Women Judges?' [2001] *Public Law* 489.

Halpin, A, *Rights and Law. Analysis and Theory* (Oxford: Hart Publishing, 1997).

Hampton, J, *Hobbes and the Social Contract* (Cambridge: Cambridge University Press, 1986).

Hannett, S, 'Third Party Interventions: In the Public Interest?' (2003) *Public Law* 128.

Hardy, H (ed), *Isaiah Berlin, the Power of Ideas* (London: Chatto and Windus, 2000).

Hardy, H (ed), *Isaiah Berlin on Liberty* (Oxford: Oxford University Press, 2002).

Harlow, C, 'Public Law and Popular Justice' (2002) 65 *Modern Law Review* 1.

Hart, HLA, *Law, Liberty, and Morality* (Oxford: Oxford University Press, 1963).

Hayek, F, *The Constitution of Liberty* (London: Routledge and Kegan Paul, 1960).

Hayek, F, *Law, Legislation and Liberty* (London: Routledge and Kegan Paul, 1982).

Hayek, F, *The Road to Serfdom* (London: Ash Paperbacks, 1986).

Herman, E. and O'Sullivan, G, *The 'Terrorism Industry'. The Experts and Institutions that Shape our View of Terror* (New York, NY: Pantheon Books, 1989).

Hickman, T, 'Constitutional Dialogue, Constitutional Theories and the Human Rights Act 1998' [2005] *Public Law* 306.

Hiebert, JL, 'Parliamentary Bills of Rights: An Alternative Model' (2006) 69 *Modern Law Review* 7.

Hinton, J, *Protests and Visions. Peace Politics in 20th Century Britain* (London: Hutchinson Radius, 1989).

Hogg, Q, *New Charter* (London: Conservative Political Centre, 1969).

Home Office, *Legislation against Terrorism. A Consultation Paper*, Cm 4178 (London: The Stationery Office, 1998).

Howard, E, 'The European Union Agency for Fundamental Rights' [2006] *European Human Rights Law Review* 445.

Humphries, S, *Hooligans or Rebels? An Oral History of Working-Class Childhood and Youth, 1989–1939* (Oxford: Basil Blackwell, 1981).

Hunold, A (ed), *Freedom and Serfdom. An Anthology of Western Thought* (Dordrecht: D Reidel Publishing Co, 1961).

Hunt, M, *Using Human Rights Law in English Courts* (Oxford: Hart Publishing, 1997).

Hunt, M, 'The Human Rights Act and Legal Culture: The Judiciary and the Legal Profession' (1999) 26 *Journal of Legal Studies* 86.

Hunt, M, 'Sovereignty's Blight: Why Contemporary Public Law Needs the Concept of "Due Deference" ', in Leyland, P and Bamforth, N (eds), *Public Law in a Multi-Layered Constitution* (Oxford: Hart Publishing, 2003).

Huntingdon, S, 'The Clash of Civilizations' (1993) 73 *Foreign Affairs* 22.

Hutchinson, J and Smith, AD (eds), *Nationalism. Critical Concepts in Political Science* (London: Routledge, 2000).

Hutton, Lord, *Report of the Inquiry into the Circumstances Surrounding the Death of Dr David Kelly CMG* (London: The Stationery Office, 2004).

Irvine of Lairg, Lord, 'The Impact of the Human Rights Act: Parliament, the Courts and the Executive' [2003] *Public Law* 308.

Ison, T, 'The Sovereignty of the Judiciary' (1985) 10 *Adelaide Law Review* 3.

Ivamy, ERH, 'The Right of Public Meeting' (1949) 2 *Current Legal Problems* 183.

Jacob, JM, *The Republican Crown. Lawyers and the Making of the State in 20th Century Britain* (Aldershot: Dartmouth, 1996).

Jennings, A, *Justice under Fire. The Abuse of Civil Liberties in Northern Ireland* (London: Pluto Press, 1990).

Johnson, M and Gearty, CA, 'Civil Liberties and the Challenge of Terrorism', in Park, A, Curtice, J, Thomson, K, Phillips, M, and Johnson, M, *British Social Attitudes. The 23rd Report* (London: Sage Publications, 2007).

Joseph, Sir K, *Freedom Under Law* (London: Conservative Political Centre, 1976).

Jowell, J, 'Beyond the Rule of Law: Towards Constitutional Judicial Review' [2000] *Public Law* 671.

Jowell, J, 'Judicial Deference: Servility, Civility or Institutional Capacity?' [2003] *Public Law* 592.

Jowell, J and Cooper, J (eds), *Understanding Human Rights Principles* (Oxford: Hart Publishing, 2001).

Keenan, A, *Democracy in Question. Democratic Openness in a Time of Political Closure* (Palo Alto, CA: Stanford University Press, 2003).

Kidd, R, *British Liberty in Danger: An Introduction to the Study of Civil Rights* (London: Lawrence and Wishart, 1940).

Klang, M and Murray, A, *Human Rights in the Digital Age* (London: Glasshouse Press, 2005).

Klein, N, *No Logo* (London: Flamingo, 2000).

Klug, F, 'Judicial Deference under the Human Rights Act' [2003] *European Human Rights Law Review* 125.

Klug, F, 'Human Rights: Above Politics or a Creature of Politics?' (2005) 33 *Policy & Politics* 3.

Klug, F, 'The Long Road to Human Rights Compliance' (2006) 57 *Northern Ireland Legal Quarterly* 186.

Klug, F, Starmer, K, and Weir, S, *The Three Pillars of Liberty. Political Rights and Freedoms in the United Kingdom* (London: Routledge, 1996).

Koçak, M and Örücü, E, 'Dissolution of Political Parties in the Name of Democracy: Cases from Turkey and the European Court of Human Rights' (2003) 9 *European Public Law* 399.

Koskenniemi, M, 'The Effect of Rights on Political Culture' in Alston, P (ed), *The EU and Human Rights* (Oxford: Oxford University Press, 1999).

Kramer, L, *The People Themselves. Popular Constitutionalism and Judicial Review* (New York, NY: Oxford University Press, 2004).

Lardy, H, 'Prison Disenfranchisement: Constitutional Rights and Wrongs' [2002] *Public Law* 524.

Laski, H, *Liberty in the Modern State* (London: Faber and Faber, 1930).

Laslett, P (ed), *Locke's Two Treatises of Government* (2nd edn) (Cambridge: Cambridge University Press, 1967).

Leaf, M, 'The European Union's Twin Towers of Democracy and Human Rights Post 11 September 201' (2004) 1 *Justice Journal* 89.

Leyland, P and Bamforth, N (eds), *The Contemporary Constitution* (Oxford: Hart Publishing, 2003).

Liberty, *A People's Charter* (London: National Council for Civil Liberties, 1991).

Lloyd of Berwick, Lord, *Inquiry into Legislation Against Terrorism*, Cm 3420 (London: The Stationery Office, 1996).

Lomas, OG, 'The Executive and the Anti-Terrorist Legislation of 1939' [1980] *Public Law* 16.

Loucaides, L, 'Determining the Extra-Territorial Effect of the European Convention: Facts, Jurisprudence and the Bankovic Case' [2006] *European Human Rights Law Review* 391.

Loughlin, M, 'Rights Discourse and Public Law Thought in the United Kingdom', in Anderson, GW (ed), *Rights and Democracy. Essays in UK–Canadian Constitutionalism* (London: Blackstone Press, 1999).

Loughlin, M, *Sword and Scales. An Examination of the Relationship between Law and Politics* (Oxford: Hart Publishing, 2000).

Loughlin, M, 'Rights, Democracy, and Law', in Campbell, T, Ewing, KD, and Tomkins, A (eds), *Sceptical Essays on Human Rights* (Oxford: Oxford University Press, 2001).

Loughlin, M, *The Idea of Public Law* (Oxford: Oxford University Press, 2004).

Loughlin, M, 'The Constitutional Thought of the Levellers' *Current Legal Problems Lecture*, 19 October 2006.

Loveland, I (ed), *Importing the First Amendment Freedom of Speech and Expression in Britain, Europe and the USA* (Oxford: Hart Publishing, Oxford, 1998).

Loveland, I, *Political Libels. A Comparative Study* (Oxford: Hart Publishing, 2000).

Lowe, V, ' "Clear and Present Danger": Responses to Terrorism' (2005) 54 *International and Comparative Law Quarterly* 185.

Macarthur, B (ed), *The Penguin Book of Twentieth Century Protest* (London: Viking, 1998).

Macdonald, M, 'Natural Rights', in Waldron, J (ed), *Theories of Rights* (Oxford: Oxford University Press, 1984).

Macklem, T, 'Entrenching a Bill of Rights' (2006) 26 *Oxford Journal of Legal Studies* 107.

Macpherson, CB, *The Political Theory of Possessive Individualism* (Oxford: Oxford University Press, 1962).

Macrory, R, 'Street Noise—The Problems of Control' (1984) *Journal of Planning Law* 388.

Mahoney, J, *The Challenge of Human Rights. Origin, Development, and Significance* (Oxford: Blackwell Publishing Ltd, 2007).

Malleson, K, *The New Judiciary: The Effects of Expansion and Activism* (Aldershot: Ashgate, 1999).

Marks, S and Clapham, A, *International Human Rights Lexicon* (Oxford: Oxford University Press, 2005).

Marriott, J, 'Alarmist or Relaxed? Election Expenditure and Free Speech' [2005] *Public Law* 764.

McCrudden, C and Chambers, G (eds), *Individual Rights and the Law in Britain* (Oxford: Clarendon Press, 1994).

McGoldrick, D, *From '9–11' to the 'Iraq War 2003'. International Law in an Age of Complexity* (Oxford: Hart Publishing, 2004).

Mill, JS, 'Considerations on Representative Government 1861', in Robson, J (ed), *Collected Works* (Toronto: University of Toronto Press, 1961–91), vol XIX.

Miller, D (ed), *Liberty* (Oxford: Oxford University Press, 1991).

Monk, R, *Ludwig Wittgenstein. The Duty of Genius* (London: Vintage, 1991).

Mowbray, A, 'The Role of the European Court of Human Rights in the Protection of Democracy' [1999] *Public Law* 703.

Munby, L (ed), *The Luddites and Other Essays* (Edgware: Michael Katanka (Books) Ltd, 1971).

National Council For Civil Liberties, *Southall 23 April 1979. The Report of the Unofficial Committee of Enquiry* (London: National Council for Civil Liberties, 1980).

Northam, G, *Shooting in the Dark. Riot Police in Britain* (London: Faber and Faber, 1988).

Nozick, R, *Anarchy, State and Utopia* (Oxford: Basil Blackwell, 1974).

Oakeshott, M (ed), *Hobbes's Leviathan* (Oxford: Basil Blackwell, 1946).

O'Cinneide, C, 'Democracy, Rights and the Constitution—New Directions in the Human Rights Era' (2004) 57 *Current Legal Problems* 175.

O'Connell, R, 'Towards a Stronger Conception of Democracy in the Strasbourg Convention' [2006] *European Human Rights Law Review* 281.

O'Faolain, *King of the Beggars. A Life of Daniel O'Connell* (Swords: Poolbeg Press Ltd, 1980, first published 1938).

O'Hagan, T, *Rousseau* (London: Routledge, 1999).

O'Higgins, P, *Cases and Materials on Civil Liberties* (London: Sweet and Maxwell, 1980).

Park, A, Curtice, J, Thomson, K, Jarvis, L, and Bromley, C (eds), *British Social Attitudes. The 19th Report* (London: Sage Publications, 2002).

Park, A, Curtice, J, Thomson, K, Phillips, M, and Johnson, M (eds), *British Social Attitudes. The 23rd Report* (London: Sage Publications, 2007).

Parkinson, J, *Deliberating in the Real World. Problems of Legitimacy in Deliberative Democracy* (Oxford: Oxford University Press, 2006).

Pearce, E, *Reform! The Fight for the 1832 Reform Act* (London: Jonathan Cape, 2003).

Peers, S, 'EU Responses to Terrorism' (2003) 52 *International and Comparative Law Quarterly* 227.

Pettit, P, *Republicanism: A Theory of Freedom and Government* (Oxford: Clarendon Press, 1997).

Pettit, P, 'Depoliticizing Democracy' (2004) 17 *Ratio Juris* 52.

Pocock, JGA, *The Machiavellian Moment: Florentine Political Thought and the Atlantic Republican Tradition* (Princeton, NJ: Princeton University Press, 1975).

Police Ombudsman for Northern Ireland, *Statement by the Police Ombudsman for Northern Ireland on her Investigation into the Circumstances surrounding the Death of Raymond McCord Junior and Related Matters* (Belfast: Office of the Police Ombudsman, 2007).

Poole, TM, 'Harnessing the Power of the Past? Lord Hoffmann and the *Belmarsh Detainees* Case' (2005) 32 *Journal of Law and Society* 534.

Poole, TM, 'Questioning Common Law Constitutionalism' (2005) *Legal Studies* 142.

Popper, K, *The Open Society and its Enemies* (London: Routledge, 2002).

Ramraj, VV, Hor, M, and Roach, K, *Global Anti-Terrorism Law and Policy* (Cambridge: Cambridge University Press, 2005).

Ramsay, P, 'What is Anti-Social Behaviour?' [2004] *Criminal Law Review* 908.

Richardson, L, *What Terrorists Want. Understanding the Terrorist Threat* (London: John Murray, 2006).

Rorty, R, *Contingency, Irony, and Solidarity* (Cambridge: Cambridge University Press, 1989).

Rowbottom, J, 'The Electoral Commission's Proposals on the Funding of Political Parties' [2005] *Public Law* 468.

Sands, P, 'International Rule of Law: Extraordinary Rendition, Complicity and its Consequences' [2006] *European Human Rights Law Review* 408.

Saul, B, *Defining Terrorism in International Law* (Oxford: Oxford University Press, 2006).

Saville, J, *1848. The British State and the Chartist Movement* (Cambridge, Cambridge University Press, 1987).

Scarman, L, *The Brixton Disorders 10–12 April 1981* (London: Her Majesty's Stationery Office, 1981).

Schuyler, RL and Weston, CC, *Cardinal Documents in British History* (Princeton, NJ: Princeton University Press, 1961).

Sedley, S, *Freedom, Law and Justice* (London: Sweet and Maxwell, 1999).

Sedley, S and Kaplan, LS, *A Spark in the Ashes: the Pamphlets of John Warr* (London: Verso, 1992).

Shorupski, J (ed), *The Cambridge Companion to Mill* (Cambridge: Cambridge University Press, 1998).

Sherr, A, *Freedom of Protest, Public Order and the Law* (Oxford: Basil Blackwell, 1989).

Simpson, AWB, *In the Highest Degree. Odious Detention without Trial in Wartime Britain* (Oxford: Clarendon Press, 1992).

Simpson, AWB, *Human Rights and the End of Empire Britain and the Genesis of the European Convention* (Oxford: Oxford University Press, 2001).

Singh, R, *The Future of Human Rights in the United Kingdom. Essays on Law and Practice* (Oxford: Hart Publishing, 1997).

Skinner, Q, 'The Paradoxes of Political Liberty', in Miller, D (ed), *Liberty* (Oxford: Oxford University Press, 1991).

Skinner, Q and Price, R (eds), *Machiavelli's The Prince* (Cambridge: Cambridge University Press, 1988).

Spencer, G, *Disturbing the Peace? Politics, Television News and the Northern Ireland Peace Process* (Aldershot: Ashgate Publishing Ltd, 2000).

Spencer, M, *1992 and All That. Civil Liberties in the Balance* (London: Civil Liberties Trust, 1990).

Spencer, M, *States of Injustice. A Guide to Human Rights and Civil Liberties in the European Union* (London: Pluto Press, 1995).

Stalker, J, *Stalker* (London: Harrap, 1988).

Stammers, N, *Civil Liberties in Britain during the 2nd World War: A Political Study* (London: Croom Helm, 1983).

Stevenson, J, *Popular Disturbances in England 1700–1832* (2nd edn) (Harlow: Longman, 1992).

Steyn, J, 'Deference: A Tangled Story' [2005] *Public Law* 346.

Steyn, J, 'Democracy, the Rule of Law and the Role of Judges' [2006] *European Human Rights Law Review* 243.

Street, H, *Freedom, the Individual and the Law* (5th edn) (Harmondsworth: Penguin Books, 1982).

Sunstein, CR, *Designing Democracy. What Constitutions Do* (New York, NY: Oxford University Press, 2001).

Thomas, PA, 'September 11th and Good Governance' (2002) 53 *Northern Ireland Legal Quarterly* 366.

Thomis, MI, *The Luddites. Machine-Breaking in Regency England* (Newtown Abbot: David and Charles Archon Books, 1970).

Thompson, EP, *The Making of the English Working Class* (London: Victor Gollancz, 1963).

Thompson, EP, *Whigs and Hunters. The Origin of the Black Act* (London: Allen Lane, 1975).

Thompson, WH, *Civil Liberties* (London: Gollancz, 1938).

Thornton, P, *We Protest. The Public Order Debate* (London: National Council for Civil Liberties, 1985).

Thornton, P, *Decade of Decline. Civil Liberties in the Thatcher Years* (London: National Council for Civil Liberties, 1989).

Tomkins, A, *The Constitution after Scott: Government Unwrapped* (Oxford: Oxford University Press, 1998).

Tomkins, A, 'Defining and Delimiting National Security' (2002) 118 *Law Quarterly Review* 200.

Tomkins, A, 'In Defence of the Political Constitution' (2002) 22 *Oxford Journal of Legal Studies* 157.

Tomkins, A, 'Legislating Against Terror: The Anti-Terrorism, Crime and Security Act 2001 [2002] *Public Law* 205.

Tomkins, A, *Public Law* (Oxford: Oxford University Press, 2003).

Tomkins, A, *Our Republican Constitution* (Oxford: Hart Publishing, 2005).

Tushnet, M, 'Living with a Bill of Rights', in Gearty, C and Tomkins, A (eds), *Understanding Human Rights* (London: Mansell Publishing Ltd, 1996).

Urban, M, *Big Boys' Rules. The Secret Struggle Against the IRA* (London: Faber and Faber, 1992).

Veitch, S, *Moral Conflict and Legal Reasoning* (Oxford: Hart Publishing, 1999).

Waddington, D, Jones, K, and Critcher, C, *Flashpoints. Studies in Public Disorder* (London: Routledge, 1989).

Waldron, J (ed), *Theories of Rights* (Oxford: Oxford University Press, 1984).

Warbrick, C, 'The Principle of the European Convention on Human Rights and the Response of States to Terrorism' [2002] *European Human Rights Law Review* 287.

Ward, CA, 'Building Capacity to Combat International Terrorism: The Role of the United Nations Security Council' (2003) 8 *Journal of Conflict and Security Law* 289.

Ward, I, *The English Constitution. Myths and Realities* (Oxford: Hart Publishing, 2004).

Welch, M, *Scapegoats of September 11th. Hate Crimes and State Crimes in the War on Terror* (New Brunswick: Rutgers University Press, 2006).

Whitty, N, Murphy, T, and Livingstone, S, *Civil Liberties Law: The Human Rights Act Era* (London: Butterworths, 2001).

Widgery, Lord, *Report of the Tribunal Appointed to Inquire into the Events on Sunday 30 January 1972 which led to Loss of Life in Connection with the Procession in Londonderry on that Day*, HL 101, HC 220 (London: HMSO, 1972).

Wilkinson, P, *Terrorism versus Democracy The Liberal State Response* (2nd edn) (London: Routledge, 2006).

Williams, DGT, *Not in the Public Interest* (London: Hutchinson, 1965).

Williams, DGT, *Keeping the Peace. The Police and Public Order* (London: Hutchinson, 1967).

Williams, DGT, 'Preventive Action and Public Order: The Principle of *Thomas v Sawkins*' (1985) 16 *Cambrian Law Review* 116.

Williams, DGT, 'The Principle of *Beatty v Gillbanks*: A Reappraisal', in Doob, AN and Greenspan, EL (eds), *Perspectives in Criminal Law. Essays in Honour of J Ll J Edwards* (Aurora, Ontario: Canadian Law Books, 1985).

Williams, G, 'The Case that Stopped a Coup? The Rule of Law and Constitutionalism in Fiji' (2001) 1 *Oxford University Commonwealth Law Journal* 73.

Wokler, R, *Rousseau* (Oxford: Oxford University Press, 1995).

Wokler, R (ed), *Rousseau and Liberty* (Manchester: Manchester University Press, 1995).

Young, H, *One of Us* (2nd rev edn) (London: Macmillan, 1991).

Index